Godly Ambit.

Godly Ambition

John Stott and the Evangelical Movement

ALISTER CHAPMAN

OXFORD
UNIVERSITY PRESS

OXFORD
UNIVERSITY PRESS

Oxford University Press is a department of the University of Oxford.
It furthers the University's objective of excellence in research, scholarship,
and education by publishing worldwide.

Oxford   New York
Auckland   Cape Town   Dar es Salaam   Hong Kong   Karachi
Kuala Lumpur   Madrid   Melbourne   Mexico City   Nairobi
New Delhi   Shanghai   Taipei   Toronto

With offices in
Argentina   Austria   Brazil   Chile   Czech Republic   France   Greece
Guatemala   Hungary   Italy   Japan   Poland   Portugal   Singapore
South Korea   Switzerland   Thailand   Turkey   Ukraine   Vietnam

Oxford is a registered trade mark of Oxford University Press
in the UK and certain other countries.

Published in the United States of America by
Oxford University Press
198 Madison Avenue, New York, NY 10016

Library of Congress Cataloging-in-Publication Data
Chapman, Alister.
Godly ambition : John Stott and the evangelical movement /
Alister Chapman.
p. cm.
ISBN 978-0-19-977397-8 (hardcover : alk. paper); 978-0-19-936792-4 (paperback : alk. paper)
1. Stott, John R. W.   2. Church of England—Clergy—Biography.
3. Anglican Communion—England—Clergy—Biography.
4. Evangelicalism—Church of England—Biography.   I. Title.
BX5199.S8344C43 2012
283.092—dc22
[B]
2011013983

For Margaret

Contents

Acknowledgments

FOR SOME TIME now my children have known that I have been writing a book. They find it hard to understand why it has taken quite so long to appear. These opening pages, which they will read because their names are here, may well increase their bewilderment: "How could it have taken you so long when you had so many people helping you?" The answer is a complicated one. Much easier is the task of thanking those many people who have helped along the way.

One of the most pleasant surprises of academic life has been the warm and generous community of historians with whom I have been privileged to work. Eugenio Biagini was an excellent Ph.D. supervisor who offered plenty of sound advice and encouragement. David Bebbington and Mark Noll kindly answered the letters of a would-be postgraduate student, and they have provided invaluable criticism and support ever since. Chandra Mallampalli, Richard W. Pointer, and Marianne Ruel Robins have made the history department here at Westmont a congenial place to work. Martin Brett, David Cornick, John Coffey, Ben Griffin, Matthew Grimley, Boyd Hilton, David Killingray, Graham Kings, John Maiden, Jeremy Morris, Jon Parry, Richard Rex, Mark Smith, Brian Stanley, Roger Steer, David Thompson, Todd Thompson, Grant Wacker, and John Wolffe all gave valuable help during the course of my research. I owe much to Andrew Atherstone, David Bebbington, John Coffey, Graham Kings, Mark Noll, and Stephen Tuck who read and commented on earlier drafts of this book, which is much better as a result. The responsibility for any errors that remain is, of course, mine.

Financial support for my research came from the University of Cambridge, the Lightfoot Fund at the University of Cambridge, Emmanuel College, Cambridge, Westmont College, and the Whitefield Institute. My thanks to them all, and especially to the following people at these institutions: Richard Barnes, Jeremy Caddick, David Cook, Shirley Mullen, Jon Parry, Rick Pointer, Jonathan Riley-Smith, and Warren Rogers. I also thank the many librarians and archivists who helped me, notably those at the (incomparable) Cambridge University Library, the Billy Graham Center Archives in Wheaton, Illinois, the Lambeth Palace Library, the Camden Local Studies and Archives Centre, the London Metropolitan Archives, and the British Newspaper Library at Colindale. For allowing me access to a variety of archival sources, I am grateful to Timothy Chester, Rodney Edrich, Chris Green, Graham Kings, Rusty Maclean, Jonathan Smith, Bruce Winter, and the Universities and Colleges Christian Fellowship. I am also thankful to the many people who shared their own recollections, including Michael Baughen, Michael Schluter, Frances Whitehead, and a group of delightful pensioners in the parish of All Souls.

I owe a special debt to John Stott, who died the same day I received the page proofs for this book. Stott gave me access to his personal papers, allowing me to sit in his study in London while he was traveling overseas, and giving me freedom to read everything but his most recent correspondence. He read some early parts of this work, and was generous when we disagreed. I am very grateful for his kindness. Bishop Timothy Dudley-Smith was extraordinarily helpful at the early stages of this project, despite the fact that he was at the time still completing his own biography of Stott. He and his late wife Arlette hosted me at their home in Salisbury, where he let me use the folders of Stott's work that he had painstakingly collected over the years. He also allowed me to see the transcripts of a series of twenty-one interviews he had conducted with Stott in 1992. Both these men were examples of Christian charity and of all that is good in their generation of English gentlemen.

Other friends have helped along the way. Julian Hardyman, Rick Ifland, and Art Tracewell kindly read an earlier version of the book and made many useful suggestions. I also thank the members of the history book group to which I belong here in Santa Barbara—Keric Brown, Simon Dixon, Michael Rucker, Kathleen and Jeff Sieck, and Art Tracewell—who remind me that history captivates people who don't spend their lives in academia.

I am grateful to Cynthia Read, my editor, for bringing this work to print, and to others on the staff at Oxford University Press who helped in its production. Jane Messah, Daniel Sargent, Grace Sollé, and Abigail Thorpe, all history students here at Westmont, assisted with minor details. Another student, Lauren Gaylord, worked with me on the index. I am thankful to them all for their cheerful and competent help.

This book owes much to the support of my parents, Roger and Olive Chapman. They ensured I had a good education and gently helped me make the most of it. I am deeply thankful for their love and hard work. My children, Abigail, Lucy, James, and Abraham, make me work hard so I can get home to be with them. I hope they will be people of godly ambition one day. Without my wife Margaret, this book would never have been started or finished. During my final year as an undergraduate, she gave me a vision for intellectual engagement without which I would never have embarked on a Ph.D. Since then, she has been wise counsel, strong support, unfailing inspiration, and much more. This book is dedicated to her.

Alister Chapman
Santa Barbara
January 2011

Godly Ambition

Introduction

ON APRIL 18, 2005, *Time* magazine published its annual list of the one hundred most influential people in the world. Alongside predictable names such as George W. Bush, Condoleezza Rice, Oprah Winfrey, and Bill Gates, three church leaders appeared. The first was the Roman Catholic Cardinal Joseph Ratzinger, who became pope the day after *Time* published its list. The second was Rick Warren, a popular author and pastor of Saddleback Church in southern California who later gave the invocation at Barack Obama's inauguration in 2009. The third was the English clergyman John Stott. The citation called him "a touchstone of authentic biblical scholarship that...has scarcely been paralleled since the days of the 16th century European Reformers" and said that his work had been "a significant factor in the explosive growth of Christianity in parts of the Third World."[1] However, most of the people who read *Time* that week would never have heard of him.

Six months earlier, the *New York Times* had published an article by David Brooks entitled "Who is John Stott?" Brooks, a regular columnist for the *Times*, was writing shortly after the re-election of George W. Bush to the White House, an election in which the influence of evangelical Christians had been discussed endlessly. Brooks suggested that the representatives of that tradition whom the media usually presented as normative, such as Jerry Falwell and Pat Robertson, were in fact caricatures. It would be much better, he went on, if more people knew about John Stott. Stott "believe[d] in evangelizing among non-believers," was "pro-life and pro-death penalty," and did not believe "that all faiths [were] independently valid," yet he spoke with a voice that was "friendly, courteous and natural....confident, joyful and optimistic." He was the person whom "if evangelicals could elect a pope...they would likely choose," and an "authentic representative" of evangelicalism in a way that Falwell and Robertson were not. Yet Brooks assumed that most of his readers had no idea who Stott was.[2]

This book is an answer to Brooks's question, who is John Stott? The story starts in London, where Stott was born in 1921 and grew up in a privileged and cultured family. It follows him to boarding school and Cambridge, where he received the best formal education England had to offer. Stott was ordained on leaving Cambridge in 1945 and went to work at the church of All Souls Langham Place in the center of London. Five years later, he took charge of the church and instituted a comprehensive plan to convert people who lived in the surrounding area. This book relates his evangelistic efforts in central London and his work preaching the gospel to university students. It also examines his attempts to increase evangelical influence in English society and politics and in the Church of England. A final chapter looks at Stott's ministry worldwide and how he became one of the best-known religious leaders in the world.

The book also explains Stott's significance, why it was that he made it into *Time*'s list and the *New York Times*. A large part of the answer lies in Stott's prominence in evangelicalism, which was one of the world's fastest growing religious movements during Stott's career. The number of evangelicals in the world grew from 71,800,000 in 1900 to 210,500,000 by 2000. If one includes Pentecostals, the number in 2000 was 733,300,000.[3] In the United States, evangelicalism has often been associated with conservative politics. The bedrock of the Religious Right was evangelical, and the two were often synonymous in public discourse. But evangelicalism is a much older and much more diverse stream of Christianity. Evangelicals span the political spectrum and the whole range of Protestant denominations. Historically, they trace their roots to the Reformation, the Puritans, and the evangelical revivals of the eighteenth century.[4] Doctrinally, they adhere to the ecumenical councils of the early church and the teachings of the Protestant reformers. What distinguishes evangelicals from other Protestants is that they are especially committed to certain aspects of Christian truth and practice. David Bebbington has identified four such emphases in what has become a standard definition of evangelicalism, namely, (1) their strong devotion to the Bible; (2) the importance of a personal conversion to Christ; (3) preaching and piety that centers on the redeeming sacrifice of Jesus Christ on the cross; and (4) a belief that faith must be constantly expressed in word and deed.[5] Stott's ministry took place in an era when evangelical churches were flourishing on every continent. These churches often became important for the political life of their nations, as well as the personal lives of their members. The extraordinary growth of evangelical Christianity in Africa and Latin America in particular has changed the political landscape of many countries.[6] Philip Jenkins has gone further and argued that the growth of conservative Christianity outside the West is changing the shape of international affairs, especially in Africa, where the contest between Muslims and Christians is sometimes fierce.[7]

Stott was one of the most influential figures in this growing movement. He first made his mark as an evangelist to students, preaching at major universities worldwide. His growing reputation ensured many invitations to preach, as well as ready buyers for his many books. In the United States alone, he sold more than a million books and several million booklets.[8] His 1958 *Basic Christianity* has been translated into fifty-four languages, and another fifteen of his books have appeared in more than a dozen languages.[9] Stott became one of the best-known Christians in the world, traveling more widely than all the popes during his career except John Paul II. Just as important as his travels was Stott's ability to exploit a new global organization for evangelicals, namely the Lausanne movement. Lausanne was made possible by the American evangelist Billy Graham, who in 1974 used his organization's finances and fundraising abilities to bring together thousands of evangelical leaders from 150 countries at a conference in Lausanne, Switzerland. Stott was a central figure at the conference and in the organization it spawned. Both gave him a platform to mold churches worldwide. In particular, he encouraged evangelicals to use their minds and to get involved with social issues. These had often been weak points for evangelicals in the twentieth century, and they earned a reputation of anti-intellectualism and social conservatism. But Stott's strong advocacy of intellectual endeavor and social action did a great deal to legitimize them both. Evangelicalism became more intellectually robust and more politically active on both right and left. Stott was a standard bearer for changes that made the evangelicalism of 2000 look very different from that of 1940. Placed alongside the influence of his thousands of sermons and four dozen books, this made Stott a giant in one of the world's most vibrant religious movements. He became a pattern for Christian leaders on every continent. To use David Brooks's words: "Tom Wolfe once noticed that at a certain moment all airline pilots came to speak like Chuck Yeager. The parallel is inexact, but over the years I've heard hundreds of evangelicals who sound like Stott."[10]

This book, however, starts with Stott in England. In the early years of his ministry, Stott's principal desire was to see a Christian revival in England. It is well known that Christianity has hardly been a success story in England since 1945, but the standard tale of secularization, of declining church attendance and the attenuation of religion in political and social life, is not the whole story. Many evangelical churches proved resilient to the general pattern of decline, and Stott's experience in London in the 1950s and 1960s helps explain why. It shows that the rise and fall of churches was as much about the decisions and beliefs of individual people as it was about long-term social processes. In the political realm, Christianity continued to mold politicians and their policies, and here again Stott played an important role. In short, the secularization narrative can mislead, as well as illuminate. This book also looks at Stott's leadership of evangelicals in the Church of England and their growing strength, which is important background to the contemporary arguments about homosexuality in the global Anglican Communion.

Yet first and foremost this is a book about Stott himself. It aims to explain why Stott did what he did and thought as he did—for example, why he decided to become a minister in the Church of England rather than a missionary, why social and political engagement became a major priority for him in his late forties, why he devoted so much of his time and energy to churches overseas. This is a key difference between this book and the two-volume authorized biography by Stott's friend, Bishop Timothy Dudley-Smith. These volumes provide an excellent chronicle of Stott's life and will remain an indispensable source for all future studies of Stott. However, Dudley-Smith said that his aim was "to supply information rather than to make judgments."[11] This is not entirely true: Dudley-Smith does discuss the reasons for some of Stott's decisions. But this book aims to analyze and assess Stott's career more fully and with more distance.

While the questions about Stott's career and thought may be obvious, how to answer them is less so. Stott kept diaries on his overseas travels, but he never recorded his inmost thoughts in a journal. He gave a number of interviews, including a series of twenty-one with Dudley-Smith, but retrospective distortions are hard to avoid. So how can we answer sticky questions about motivation and desires? An analogy helps explain the approach taken here. The comments of Oliver Cromwell to Sir Peter Lely, when he asked the portrait painter to "remark all these roughnesses, pimples, warts, and everything as you see me," have passed into folklore. They were used by Stott in a letter to Dudley-Smith, in which Stott asked his biographer to portray his life with "warts and all." Dudley-Smith said that he found it hard to see any "warts," but this is only half the story.[12] There are other important questions that have to be asked. With reference to Lely's portrait of Cromwell, for example, why is the sitter dressed in armor, and why does he have long hair? The answers to those questions may simply be that Cromwell liked wearing armor and had a preference for long hair, but it is more likely that he was reflecting or reacting against social conventions in ways that would have communicated something to contemporaries who saw the finished work. For example, it was significant that Cromwell was wearing prestigious cuirassier armor, an important sign of status for a new ruler seeking legitimacy.[13] The answers to this second set of questions are arguably more interesting than the question of likeness, for they promise to uncover the aspirations, assumptions, and commitments of the subject. The only way to obtain answers to such questions is by attention to the conventions of the day.

The same is true for studying Stott. When he grew out his sideburns in the 1970s that tells us about more than just his shaving habits. It spoke of his desire to move with a changing culture even if that meant moving from some of the mores of the English upper classes. The fact that he continued to wear ties more often than jeans pointed to the limits of this shift. What was true of Stott's grooming and couture was even truer of his thinking, speaking, and writing, which were all shaped by his intellectual and cultural contexts. Stott was a leading figure in helping evangelicals to see the formative power of culture, and understanding his own contexts helps explain the shape of his life and thought. Thus, the Second World War, the winding up of the British Empire, the Swinging Sixties, the Vietnam War, and the politics of Margaret Thatcher are not just background for a study of Stott: they help us understand him. Born and educated in an era when many Britons saw their country as strong, proud, and Christian, Stott lived to see all three claims lose their plausibility by the time he reached mid-career. At the same time, global evangelicalism boomed. These two shifts defined Stott's career, which illumines them both. Indeed, Stott's life is so fascinating in part because he was caught in the midst of these conflicting trajectories. He had to deal with revival and marginalization.

The raw materials on which this book depends are therefore Stott's writings and a wealth of other material on the religious, political, social, and cultural worlds in which he lived, thought, and expressed his views. Stott's published work amounts to more than forty books and dozens of articles. In addition, Stott generously granted me access to his personal papers, including travel diaries, sermon notes, and vast quantities of personal correspondence.[14] Context has come from newspapers, novels, films, committee minute books, local archives, House of Commons proceedings, and the writings of other church leaders. Timothy Dudley-Smith and Timothy Chester kindly allowed me to use the transcripts of interviews that they conducted with Stott and I have interviewed a number of other significant figures.[15]

The result is an interpretation of Stott's life that emphasizes that he was both a Christian seeking to honor God and a very talented man who believed he had key roles to play in God's work in the world and wanted to play them. In short, he combined two things that might seem incongruous: godliness and ambition. Stott believed that Christians could and should be "ambitious for the spread of [God's] kingdom," and that once that fundamental ambition was in place they were then free to have "secondary ambitions," to "develop their gifts, widen their opportunities, extend their influence and be given promotion in their work—not to boost their own ego or build their own empire, but rather through everything they do to bring glory to God."[16] This is how Stott lived. Stott longed to see the church grow in numbers and depth. At the same time, he was determined to use his abilities to the full and believed that would mean leadership and prominence. The difficulty in practice, of course, was that godly ambition and selfish ambition were sometimes hard to tell apart. As Stott preached and taught, God was not the only one who got glory. Stott enjoined humility, but pride remained a struggle.[17] Being ambitious for Christ's sake was a heady mix.

Some readers may be troubled by this way of looking at Stott's life. Those more skeptical of religious belief and motivation may doubt Stott's claims to be working for the glory of God and see them as a mask for self-promotion. But it is important to take others' self-understanding seriously. As Cambridge intellectual historian Quentin Skinner has put it, "the historical task... [should] be conceived as that of trying so far as possible to think as our ancestors thought and to see things their way."[18] In Stott's case, this means seeing the world as a place where God has revealed himself through Jesus Christ and through the Bible, and where people need to come to Christ for salvation. We will never understand Stott unless we start with his beliefs, which he held thoughtfully and tenaciously. That does not mean we must always accept a person's account of their actions—at times it may be necessary to go beyond their own self-perception. But we must start by making the attempt to see things their way. On the other hand, there are those who may prefer their heroes to be without blemish. But as Stott would have said, we are all fallen people, and therefore it is appropriate to ask the critical questions. This book therefore departs from the practice of at least one evangelical chronicler, who believed that the difficult parts of the story are sometimes better left out.[19]

This book does not say everything to be said about Stott. As a historical study, it does not cover the finer points of Stott's theology, and there is more to be done on Stott's sermons and books. Any definitive assessment of his career and importance will have to wait for the distance and full access to the archives that future decades will allow. What follows is an interpretation of Stott's thought and career that emphasizes their English roots, roots that are fundamental for making sense of how this very English clergyman became one of the most influential Christians in the world. It is a critical yet sympathetic account of a gifted and determined man who wanted to do all he could to further God's kingdom and became a Christian star in the process. It is a story of godly ambition that tells us much about religion in England and the world in the twentieth century.

I

Conversion

Home and School

IN 1921, JOHN Stott was born in London to Arnold and Lily Stott. Arnold Stott was an accomplished young doctor with consulting rooms on Harley Street, an address that had long been associated with the finest and grandest of the English medical profession. The new baby was named after Arnold's father, John Robert Stott, who had been a cotton magnate in Manchester. The family John joined in 1921 was thus wealthy and successful. He grew up in London's West End in a household that included his mother, father, and two older sisters, a nanny, and several servants. As a small child, John enjoyed the use of a private garden for subscribing residents and regular trips to the countryside. As he grew up, the delights of this comfortable home included family music making (John played the cello) and formal dinners for five with dancing in the dining room afterwards. It was a different world from the interwar Britain that most people knew, especially once economic depression began to bite in the 1930s.[1]

John Stott's family was also upright and caring. Lily Stott helped new domestic servants to settle in to life in London. She and Arnold taught their children to be moral, cultured, and curious. Arnold introduced John to the joys of butterflies and birds (the latter became a lifelong interest for John), while Lily took the children to the nearby Anglican church of All Souls Langham Place, and taught them to read the Bible and say their prayers. Music had a central place in family life, as did French, and John studied both from an early age. The family supported the Conservative Party. Arnold Stott was severe, but Lily was a warm, affectionate mother, the one to whom John ran when upset.[2] This was a classic upper-middle class family: comfortable, cultured, content, and part of a self-contained world that offered much to its offspring.

Arnold and Lily Stott had high hopes for their only son. They therefore decided to send him away to boarding school, which had long been the training grounds for England's elites.[3] When John turned eight, his parents dropped him off at Oakley Hall in Gloucestershire, a school run by a former army man that was a far cry from the warmth of home. After five years at Oakley, Arnold and Lily took John to Rugby School, which was one of the most prestigious private boarding schools in the country. The boarding environment allowed Rugby and schools like it (known in England as public schools) to control almost every aspect of these boys' lives, which they did without apology in order to socialize their charges in the values of the English upper and upper-middle classes.[4] Respect and discipline were instilled by masters and senior boys, sometimes with cane in hand.[5] Hierarchy was taken for granted in schools where it existed not only between teachers and boys but also among the boys themselves, with elaborate systems of head boys and prefects. Boys were taught to be gentlemen, with the appropriate dress codes and an emphasis on the right manners and accent. They were kept away from their working-class peers and encouraged to see them as inferior and irresponsible. Male superiority was also a logical assumption at these entirely male and highly prestigious institutions. Teamwork and heroism were bred on the sports fields, imperial patriotism on the parade grounds of the all but obligatory army cadet forces. Christianity of a strongly Anglican sort was central to the life of schools like Rugby, where in Stott's day there were thirteen compulsory religious services every week—six in the school chapel and daily evening prayers in every boarding house. Taken together, these were the values that defined the English elites, or what was becoming known as the establishment.[6] Arnold Stott's father had sent Arnold to Rugby and it had helped him to secure his place in this class; Arnold sent John there with the hope that he would do the same.

Life at school was hard at times. John was homesick. He was caned ("I got very very sore this morning"). His relationship with his distant parents was sometimes awkward.[7] But John flourished at Oakley Hall and then at Rugby, and it is difficult to imagine how Arnold and Lily Stott could have been more proud. John excelled academically, winning scholarships first to Rugby and then to Trinity College at the University of Cambridge.[8] He sang solos at carol services and played the cello in the Rugby orchestra. He played the title role in *Richard II*. Sport was not his strong suit, but he competed ably in cricket, soccer, rugby, and cross country.[9] He also made it to the top of the hierarchy of boys by becoming head of school at both Oakley and Rugby. This was a position of remarkable importance at Rugby, the ultimate in leadership training for any young man: according to one contemporary writer, it was unlikely that a head boy would ever be as important again.[10] One of Stott's responsibilities as head of the school was to chair a group of senior boys, and the minutes for their meetings reflect a keen attention to the levels of the school hierarchy as reflected in pupils' clothing (notably their ties) and a desire that the school be better organized so that the senior boys should have the appropriate "dignity" and even increased authority.[11] As the head boy at Rugby, John was well on his way to a position in the English establishment that would give him a great deal of dignity and authority. But eighteen months before John Stott became head of the school, he had made a decision that would complicate his progress enormously. He had decided to devote his life to Jesus Christ.

Becoming an Evangelical

One Sunday afternoon in February 1938, an Anglican clergyman named Eric Nash visited Rugby to speak to a small group of boys. Nash was forty years old and single. He was an unassuming yet eccentric figure who avoided tomato pips, took a bewildering array of medications, and enjoyed juvenile humor.[12] He was on the staff of the Scripture Union, a firmly evangelical organization founded in England in the nineteenth century to convert children. Nash's brief was to spread the gospel among boys at England's top public schools, which explains his visit to Rugby. Stott was at the meeting that day, where Nash encouraged his listeners to make a personal decision to follow Christ. After a drive with Nash later in the afternoon Stott decided to take that step. He knelt beside his bed and invited Jesus Christ into his life.

This was a classic evangelical conversion. Christianity was certainly not new to John Stott. He had learned it at his mother's and nanny's knees, at Sunday school at All Souls, in classroom and chapel at Oakley Hall and Rugby, and in classes for his confirmation in the Church of England in 1936. He not only knew the faith, he also practiced it devoutly, reading his Bible and saying his prayers, attending additional, voluntary services at Rugby, and spending time alone in one of the school's chapels.[13] He was unusually religious at a school where singing in chapel had degenerated into "polite moo-ing," according to one correspondent in the school magazine.[14] But this was the moment when Jesus Christ came alive for Stott. It was a dramatic experience that justified talk of being born again. He would always see it as the defining moment of his life. Yet even at the time he was able to understand it in terms of continuity and change: on the day after he knelt beside his bed and committed his life to God, he wrote in his diary, "Up until now, Christ had been on the circumference and I have but asked Him to guide me instead of giving Him complete control."[15]

The devout schoolboy was attracted by Nash's earnestness. Nash had an explanation for the spiritual helplessness that Stott seems to have felt at the time—namely, that he had never taken the all-important step of personally accepting Christ. In the days after his conversion, Stott experienced relief and fresh vigor. "I really have felt an immense and new joy throughout today," he wrote on February 15. "It is the joy of being at peace with the world—of being in touch with God."[16] The change was decisive and enduring.

Nash's influence on Stott was immense: strongly committed to the nurture of new converts, he took Stott under his wing and introduced him to the beliefs and practices of conservative evangelicalism.[17] Nash wrote to Stott weekly for over five years, his letters often filled with detailed instruction.[18] Nash was the primary influence on Stott's spiritual development for the next several years, and much of Stott's own life, thought, and ministry would be traced from the outline provided by Nash.

Yet although Nash was an Anglican clergyman visiting an Anglican institution, his visit to Rugby in the winter of 1938 was furtive. The truth was that his message was unwelcome at Rugby and the other leading public schools.[19] Headmasters and housemasters at these boarding schools were understood to be standing in for the children's parents, and many of these parents would have been horrified if their children had embraced evangelical religion at school. In this respect, the otherwise puzzling remark by Stott that the Sunday afternoon gathering had no name becomes telling: the meeting was strictly off the record and conducted with a good deal of "secrecy" (to borrow the word used in this connection by Stott's authorized biographer, Timothy Dudley-Smith, who was himself influenced by Nash).[20]

Why exactly was Nash's Christianity so unwelcome? It was not just that it was evangelical, for evangelicalism had long come in a variety of shades and temperatures. There was a significant range in England in the 1930s. There were moderates whose evangelicalism was irenic and who had honorable positions in the English establishment, people like Christopher Chavasse, an Olympic athlete who became Bishop of Rochester in 1940, and Max Warren, who went on to become general secretary of the Church Missionary Society.

Stott would later say that evangelicals were scorned and sidelined during this period, but this view obscures the significance of people like Chavasse and Warren.[21] There was also a group of liberal evangelicals who soft-pedaled or jettisoned beliefs that they saw as unacceptable in the modern world, including a literal, six-day creation, the infallibility of the Bible, and an understanding of the Cross that emphasized Christ's suffering of God's judgment for others' sins.[22] Evangelicalism's conservative wing was made up of people whose commitment to these beliefs became more determined in the first three decades of the century. A few were thoroughgoing fundamentalists, committed to highly literal readings of the Bible, suspicious of social reform and the life of the mind, and eager to fight for their beliefs.[23] Others were conservative evangelicals who wanted to stand for the old truths but did so with less belligerence. At the universities, they joined groups associated with the Inter-Varsity Fellowship of Evangelical Unions (of which the Cambridge Inter-Collegiate Christian Union was the epicenter). On the mission field, conservative evangelical Anglicans formed their own break-off from the Church Missionary Society, known as the Bible Churchmen's Missionary Society. And each summer, many conservatives traveled to the Lake District in Northern England to worship and learn together at the large Christian convention in Keswick. Sitting on the shores of Derwentwater, they could by and large ignore the social trauma of industrial England and talk about their favorite topics, personal holiness and foreign missions.

Nash was on this more conservative end. His converts found a natural home in the Inter-Varsity Fellowship groups when they went off to university. At times, Nash looked like a fundamentalist, with his lack of interest in social issues and a large dose of self-denying otherworldliness. He was influenced by the American fundamentalist preacher Reuben Torrey. Torrey had started out as a lieutenant to the famous evangelist D. L. Moody and went on to become an international preacher in his own right. He was a leader in the fundamentalist movement, believing that Christians had to "attack error," as well as teach the truth.[24] One of Nash's booklets, *How to Succeed in the Christian Life*, borrowed its title from one of Torrey's works, and Nash lent out copies of Torrey's books to his converts, including Stott, covering them in brown paper to keep them from the eyes of parents and schoolmasters.[25] And like many in the Scripture Union, Nash's practice was shaped by methods common in fundamentalist circles in North America, including preaching for definite decisions and diligently enquiring into people's spiritual status. John Stott's conversion was a textbook case.[26]

This heritage explains why Nash was unwelcome at Rugby and schools like it. The link to America was awkward. The United States was increasingly seen as a rival to Britain's world power, something that would make anti-American sentiment common among Britain's elites after the Second World War.[27] But the big problem was that Nash's emphasis on the need for personal conversion upset one of the ruling assumptions of places like Rugby—that Christianity was the cultural birthright of any Englishman baptized and confirmed in the Church of England. Convinced evangelicals had long been disliked for their belief that such cultural Christianity was inadequate and needed to be consummated in conversion and a warm, personal relationship with Jesus. Most Rugby parents were quite content with more conventional forms of the faith and were unlikely to be sympathetic to a revivalist at the school. Like many in the eighteenth and nineteenth centuries, they were suspicious of evangelical religion and its "enthusiasm." From a teacher's perspective, little good could come from a divisive approach to one of the school's foundations.[28] In the nineteenth century, Thomas Arnold, Rugby's most famous headmaster, had articulated a vision of church and nation in which the Church of England was a comprehensive, inclusive institution that made talk of a moral and spiritual society possible. It remained a popular idea in the mid-twentieth century.[29] But Nash wanted conversions. Earlier in his career, Nash had been asked to leave Wrekin College, a public school where he had served as chaplain, despite the fact that Wrekin was a school with strong evangelical roots. Even there, it seems, his desire for thoroughgoing conversions was not appreciated.[30]

Nash's Christianity was also countercultural in its otherworldliness. Nash had drunk deeply from a world-denying stream of Christianity prevalent among fundamentalists and other conservative evangelicals on both sides of the Atlantic since the end of the nineteenth century.[31] Nash's careful avoidance of alcohol, tobacco, and the theater mirrored a general strictness on such matters among Anglican conservative evangelicals striving for personal holiness.[32] However, Nash was more radical. He was a pacifist, a view that was rooted in a commitment not to be distracted by earthly concerns from the principal task of evangelism—he saw the Second World War as an inconvenience as much as a tragedy.[33] He shared with many evangelicals the belief that Christ could return at any moment and concluded that rescuing people from God's judgment had to take priority over concern for the future of a civilization that might not last long even were the Germans and the Japanese defeated.[34] He was irritated when one of his boys decided to fight in Asia in 1945 rather than stay in England to help him in his ministry.[35] There was some truth to the observation of one conscientious objector who, when sent to work on the land during the war, remarked that some of the Christians he worked with were not so much pacifists as "complacent spectators at what they took to be Armageddon."[36] It is difficult to overstate how abhorrent such views were in the public schools of the 1930s, where social duty and patriotic sacrifice were almost unquestionable virtues. Rugby was particularly unlikely to prove hospitable to such a creed: one of its famous old boys was the First World War poet Rupert Brooke, and the school chapel contained a memorial to him inscribed with his most famous words: "If I should die, think only this of me; / That there's some corner of a foreign field / That is for ever England." In the world of the public schools, Nash's Christianity was offensive, as well as unwelcome.

Why did Nash make the effort to visit these schools, given their antipathy to his message? Why, given that there were plenty of other children in England who needed to hear the gospel, did he focus his attention almost exclusively on the tiny minority at the public schools? The answer is that Nash shared the belief that these schools were the source of the country's leadership. For all the ways in which Nash's message clashed with the culture of Rugby, the two were in perfect harmony on this point. Nash wanted to see public schoolboys converted because of the disproportionate influence he believed they could have on English society. He focused his life's work on the English public schools, and the top thirty at that, because he believed that converts from these places would be "multiplication tables," whose influence could spur a more widespread revival of Christianity in England.[37] Stott became a leader in Nash's work, and he embraced his mentor's strategy. "Aim to get the cream of the school," Stott wrote to boys leading school groups that were part of Nash's network, "so that it may be won for Jesus. Boys of influence who will occupy positions later from which they can be of great service to Him."[38] Nash's vision was very different from the prevailing norms in the public schools, but it was an evangelical reflection of attitudes common in that world: schoolmasters and Nash alike shrugged off criticism that their work was socially divisive and elitist by stressing that their overriding interest was the production of leaders.[39] It was a different world from that of American evangelicalism, where evangelists like Billy Sunday and Billy Graham had imbibed a more republican spirit and wanted to win the ears of all.[40]

Nash's demeanor was carefully tuned to the culture of the public schools. He knew the bombast and bluster that characterized some conservative evangelicals were not going to win him a hearing in the upper echelons of English society. Rather than rocking the boat unnecessarily, Nash wanted to keep it as still as possible so he could get on with fishing. So while his message raised hackles, his approach was profoundly conservative: for example, at the camps that he ran for public schoolboys he respected parents' wishes that their boys not associate with boys from the working classes.[41] He was winsome and self-effacing, gentlemanly in all but content. He did not want anything to get in the way of these boys' conversion. So although many of Nash's roots were in the revival meetings of North America, he was still a recognizably English and Anglican figure.

Such was the Christian culture to which Nash introduced Stott. Stott took to it with enthusiasm: he became a leader at the Sunday afternoon meeting at Rugby and at Nash's camps for public schoolboys. He was soon giving evangelistic talks of his own. But these were a delicate couple of years for Stott, as he sought both to evangelize his peers and to continue his rise to the top of the school.[42] As head of school, he had to edit the school magazine, which he did with considerable levity and discussion of gas masks, rugby matches, influenza, and bird-watching—not religion.[43] As he finished Rugby and headed off to Cambridge, John Stott had been initiated into the ways of the establishment and the ways of the evangelicals and had proved himself adept in both. Both Arnold Stott and Nash were proud of him, and both had high hopes for their golden boy. Both accepted the hierarchical and snobbish assumptions embedded in John's editorial comments on the behavior of working-class boys who wandered onto the boarding school's playing fields and refused to get off (even when spoken to "civilly"), saying "A plenty o' time; oi'll git out o' the way when 'er cooms, mister."[44] But keeping the two parts of his life together was to become increasingly difficult for John Stott. It became impossible when toward the end of his time at Rugby he decided to avoid service in the Second World War on the basis of a desire to pursue ordination to the ministry of the Church of England. Arnold Stott, who had gleamed with pride as his son carried off two major school prizes at the end of his final year, was devastated.[45]

The Pacifist

John Stott left Rugby in the summer of 1940 and began his studies at Trinity College, Cambridge, the following autumn. University life in wartime was very different. The streets went unlit and all windows blacked out at night to make life more difficult for German bombers. A few raids hit their targets, with Stott's building at Trinity grazed by one bomb. Evacuated students and lecturers from London's universities took up residence in the city. Students debated free speech (although there were no complaints when a fascist publication was closed down). Soft collars were the order of the day because of a shortage of starch.[46] For Stott, however, the greatest shadow over his first year was caused by the looming date of his twentieth birthday in April 1941, when he would be called up to serve in His Majesty's Armed Forces. Stott had applied for exemption, but it was unclear whether he would get it. As his case unfolded, his family was torn apart. It would be the hardest year of his life.

Stott requested exemption on the basis of his decision to pursue ordination in the Church of England. Stott had started contemplating the ministry in 1939.[47] Ordination was no longer the promising route to riches and prestige for people in Stott's class that it had been in the nineteenth century. But for a public schoolboy serious about his faith, Anglican ordination was a logical step: Stott's experience was probably similar to that of someone who later worked with him at All Souls Langham Place, who only a week after his conversion at boarding school had prayed, "Lord, do you wish me to become a clergyman in the Church of England?"[48] Stott wanted to use his life this way so he could share the evangelical good news that he had recently come to understand and that he was already busy proclaiming.[49] It was a holy calling, and Stott borrowed language from the apostle Paul to tell his parents that he had been "separated unto the gospel of God."[50] Nash would have been encouraging Stott in this direction. He sat down with the leaders on his camps to discuss their futures, and in many cases he urged them to be ordained: his vision for the spread of the gospel in England demanded lots of gospel-preaching clergymen.[51] Getting the head boy of Rugby involved would have been a source of particular satisfaction. Indeed, Nash was so committed to the work in England that he discouraged his boys from reading missionary biographies, fearing he would lose them overseas.[52] Of course, Stott could have served in the war and then gone on for ordination: an esteemed former teacher told Stott that "a man who has lived some years a soldier will make a far better parson afterwards."[53] But Stott found it impossible to agree with this reasoning for the simple reason that he had become a pacifist.

His pacifism was a product of his conservative evangelical faith. Stott came to it as his personal Bible reading (long the centerpiece of evangelical devotion) took him to the Sermon on the Mount and Jesus' injunction to turn the other cheek. Nurtured in a Christian culture where the Bible spoke in a straightforward, literal manner, he latched on to Jesus' words and held them tight.[54] Historically, pacifism had been uncommon for Christians in Europe. Ever since Christianity ceased to be a minority religion in Europe in the fourth century, a refusal to fight was most characteristic of churches that had defected from the mainstream of Christendom, and during the Second World War a significant proportion of pacifists in Britain came from groups on the sectarian and often fundamentalist end of the Protestant spectrum.[55] These were people who interpreted the Bible as literally as possible, whether Genesis 1 or the Sermon on the Mount. Stott was not in a sectarian church, but Nash's work had many of the marks of a sectarian organization. Nash was a pacifist and surely the major influence on Stott at this point—even if he did not encourage Stott to become a pacifist his approach to Scripture and the Christian life created a framework in which it was hard for Stott to read the Sermon on the Mount any other way.[56]

The normal way to get an exemption from military service was to make one's case as a conscientious objector. The difficulty for Stott was that in October 1939 (eighteen months after his conversion) he had been taken by his school to a military post in Birmingham where he had declared his willingness to fight. Applying for exemption now on the basis that he was a pacifist was unlikely to persuade anyone, let alone a skeptical tribunal. However, there were other categories of people who did not have to fight, including people planning on ordination. So it was on the grounds of a desire to become a clergyman that Stott tried to avoid the war.

At first, it looked as though only people who had already begun their theological education would be exempted.[57] Gradually, however, it became clear that if someone had expressed a desire to be ordained before the war broke out, they could apply. The lack of clarity in the early months of the war is unsurprising, and Stott was likely helped by the fact that the tribunals were not able to cope with the numbers coming forward as conscientious objectors.[58] What is remarkable is how many people were prepared to help this earnest teenager. The Bishop of Coventry made the journey to Rugby to see him, and involved in the correspondence were another bishop, the principal of a theological college, and two Cambridge academics.[59] John Stott's position at Rugby and then at Cambridge gave him access to people with power to influence decisions, access that most pacifists did not have. Ironically, it was Stott's proximity to the establishment that allowed him to challenge its ideals as boldly as he did.

John Stott's father was appalled. A major general in the Royal Army Medical Corps with a daughter in uniform, Arnold Stott was mystified and angered by his son's refusal to serve.[60] Duty was calling, Rugby and the family had trained John to answer, and he was defiant. To make matters worse, the church was hardly the sort of prestigious profession Arnold desired for his only son. Serve now, train later, was the argument Arnold and Lily Stott put forward, but it made no impression on John:

> Daddy I want you to realise that I *must* follow my call. Men down the ages have had to face similar problems, and those who've yielded to the will of the majority have often gone under and never come to the surface again. And I know enough history to know that it's the men who have stood up for their ideals and championed their cause, come weal come woe, that have left the world a better place. I would not presume to claim equality with the mighty, but I am seeking to follow their example in my own sincere and humble way. I can do no more and I ask to be respected.
>
> Think not that I am going to live a normal, peaceful, comfortable, secluded life. I'm going to throw myself body and soul into the struggle for right.[61]

The divine call had been sensed, and nothing could be allowed to stand in its way. Or to put it another way, John Stott still believed in duty, but it was now unmediated duty to Christ, not to family, school, or country. This was not simply a question of Christian attitudes to warfare—it was John Stott telling his father that he had a higher call that justified and even required the rejection of some of the core values of the English establishment. Stott was determined to please God above anything else and scrutinized his behavior accordingly.[62] God's call was "irresistible."[63] Questions of national security did not enter into it.

Assurance of salvation, the idea that one can be certain of one's right standing before God, had long been a central feature of evangelical religion, and for many evangelicals certainty in one sphere fostered certainty in others.[64] In one letter to his sister, Joy, Stott spoke of his decision in terms of "what I *know* is right."[65] Stott's resolution might be regarded as admirable, pig-headed, or somehow both. It is certainly hard to believe his later defense that no one told him that Christians had long argued that wars could sometimes be just—surely the non-pacifist clergy to whom he spoke had some explanation for their own position.[66] One of his old teachers told him frankly: "I declare to you that you are wrong."[67] But Stott's determination and his state of mind made him unable to hear what others had to say.

From his perspective, he did not have much of a choice if he was to be faithful to his God. There was surely an element of the adolescent urge to assert one's independence at work here: in a surviving draft of a letter to his father he wrote, "I'm 19 + H of S [head of school] + am not the ignor unexp [inexperienced?] public schoolboy that you take me for."[68] Here was a test of commitment—Christ or parents?—and Stott's uncompromising, world-denying faith ensured that his assertion of independence at this point was total. Had not Jesus himself said that those who did not hate their families could not be his disciples?[69]

Stott's twentieth birthday in April 1941 was the key date. If he did not have an exemption by then, he had to report for military service. The early months of 1941 were tumultuous in the extreme. John received a letter from his mother saying that she was "horribly anxious." No one in the family could understand his position, she said, which seemed to her "soft and swollen headed." One letter from John "lay on the dining room table for hours" before Lily Stott could "pull [herself] together" and open it. When she did, "it felt as tho' my inside dropped down to my shoes."[70] Later in life, John Stott recounted that when he tried to embrace his father "he would turn away from me."[71] And John's spirits would not have been lifted by allegations that conscientious objectors detained in Cambridge had been "treated in a brutal manner, being kicked, beaten with rifle butts and placed on bread and water in solitary confinement."[72] There was the question of whether he would be granted an exemption, and the question of whether his infuriated father would continue to support him financially. Eventually, both were resolved in his favor, but his father made it clear that he continued to support his son only "with great reluctance and unhappiness."[73] John Stott therefore continued his studies at Cambridge for the duration of World War II.

John Stott's pacifism, the way he justified it, and the response of his family had far-reaching consequences. Most obviously, his decision hardened and required a commitment to ordination. His pacifism and desire to be ordained were intimately linked as the latter became the only way in which he could give expression to the former without the risk of imprisonment.[74] Stott had to make an irrevocable decision for Anglican ordination much more quickly than would otherwise have been the case. In addition, the falling out with his family pushed him even more firmly into Nash's orbit. At a time when his father would barely speak to him, it was not surprising that Stott gravitated toward this fellow pacifist who provided an understanding ear. Stott wrote later that Nash was "almost a surrogate father" during these years, and his desire to please his adoptive parent was entirely natural.[75]

In the long run, however, the conflict drew Stott away from Nash's highly focused, almost sectarian approach and toward the religious mainstream. One of Stott's key points in correspondence with his parents was that becoming a clergyman was a form of national service.[76] "You are fighting a physical war against 'flesh & blood,'" Stott wrote to his father in February 1941, "in order that Man may have peace with man. I am fighting a spiritual war against 'principalities and powers' in order that man may have peace with God. I have been called to one war; you no doubt to the other. Both are service to our country. I respect you for your's [*sic*]. Will you respect me for mine?"[77] For Nash, Christian ministry was about heaven and getting people there, but in the context of his desire to avoid military service Stott began to conceive of ministry more in terms of its usefulness for society. In 1941, Nash expressed a desire that should anything happen to him Stott should take over his work at the public schools (a remarkable statement on the closeness of their relationship and on the abilities of a twenty-year-old student), but the terms in which Stott framed his desire to be ordained called for something more socially acceptable—such as the local church ministry for which he eventually opted. John Stott had lost his father's respect, and the intense drive that characterized the rest of his life likely came not only from his desire for the glory of God but also from a desire to prove himself. Yes, he had decided to become a clergyman, but he was going to be a great one.[78]

Nevertheless, the damage had been done. Arnold Stott's pride had turned to shame, and his hopes that his son would become a leading figure in the English establishment had been dashed by what he saw as a cowardly decision to watch the war go by and a nonsensical determination to enter a second-rate profession.[79] John continued his studies at Cambridge, but for his father it brought little cause for joy or hope.

Cambridge

Stott was a student at Trinity College, Cambridge. Founded by Henry VIII, it had long been the grandest and richest of the Cambridge colleges and during Stott's time its academic stars included philosopher Bertrand Russell and the historian George Macaulay Trevelyan. But wartime Trinity was not its usual self. Mushrooms grew on the hallowed ground of Trinity's Great Court. A shortage of domestic servants meant that students had to wash their own clothes in the bathrooms. The bird-watching that Stott enjoyed so much was disrupted by bomber squadrons on their way to Germany, noise that was at times unbroken day and night.[80] Some changes in university life would have gratified him, such as the apparent increase in sobriety and chastity.[81] Most importantly, however, the war had an adverse effect on Stott's education: less than 40 percent of the university's teaching staff remained by the end of 1942, with the humanities hit especially severely.[82]

As significant as anything, however, was the fact that Stott was at Cambridge in the first place. In the United States, keen conservative Protestants were more likely to go to evangelical and fundamentalist institutions for both undergraduate education and ministerial training. The fissures that had taken place in numerous American denominations in the wake of controversies between fundamentalists and their opponents in the early twentieth century were replicated in higher education, and there was a growth in colleges providing a conservative evangelical education.[83] Billy Graham, for example, went to the decidedly evangelical Wheaton College in Illinois. Similarly in continental Europe, Roman Catholics had been setting up universities they could call their own since the beginning of the nineteenth century. For a public-school educated Anglican evangelical like Stott, however, the route to ordination lay through a place like Cambridge. Two things followed. The first was that intellectual isolation was impossible: no matter how conservative the evangelical, he or she would be exposed to alternative views. The second was that social isolation was also impossible: Stott and those like him continued to live in the religiously cool atmosphere of the English elites. Of those who arrived with Stott at Trinity College in 1940, for example, fully half had been to one of only eleven top public schools.[84] Establishing an effective subculture, where deeply conservative views could be held with little need for reflection, was thus a tall order: evangelicals like Stott were continually reminded that their religion was countercultural, and the temptation to moderate their views to accommodate the broader culture was always there. This dynamic was one of the major reasons why fundamentalism was unpopular with Anglican evangelicals in England. The irony was that the very social structure that Nash and his like sought to exploit militated against the maintaining of a rigorously conservative stance.[85] Stott's years at Cambridge were to be marked by a modest but significant moderation in his views.

Over in Oxford, C. S. Lewis was encouraging students to take their studies seriously in wartime because the world was always in crisis and the life of the mind was a legitimate Christian vocation.[86] Stott, however, had a more narrow vision for his education. He began with French and German, subjects he had excelled in at school and part of his parents' dream of seeing him in the diplomatic corps one day. But Stott no longer had much interest in diplomacy, and little vision for the mission field, where French and German could have been useful. He wanted to be a minister as soon as possible and so he switched to theology for his third and fourth years at Trinity. He then moved across town to Ridley Hall, an evangelical training college for Anglican clergy, for another fifteen months of theology before his ordination.

Stott was a diligent student. He often worked for eight hours a day and was known to lock himself in his rooms for twelve hours at a stretch.[87] Such dedication was unremarkable for a top boy from Rugby, but it was rather surprising for one of Nash's protégés. Nash was a product of a stream of conservative evangelicalism that distrusted academic endeavor. It was, after all, scholars who had come up with the most powerful recent objections to scriptural teachings such as the divine creation of the world and the divine inspiration of the Bible. Many evangelicals engaged in spirited controversy on these and other issues, but Nash belonged to the camp of those who avoided these debates wherever possible.[88] When visiting his acolytes at university, he sometimes encouraged them to cut lectures.[89] Conservative evangelicals like Nash were gripped by the urgency of reaching the lost: talking theology was not going to help.[90] It was certainly common for conservative evangelicals studying theology at Cambridge to neglect lectures and libraries in favor of pastoral and evangelistic endeavors among their fellow students.[91] It is therefore a little surprising that Stott applied himself to his studies as much as he did, and with evident success: he gained first-class marks in French and then in theology, was elected a senior scholar by Trinity, and earned distinctions in two of his ordination exams.

Stott studied hard because that is what he had always done. An old friend called him compulsive.[92] But also hanging over him was the fear that his father would stop paying the Cambridge bills, and John did not want to give him any reason to reconsider his grudging acquiescence in his son's continuing studies. In one letter to his father, John made a point to report that he was "managing to put in 7–8 hours' work a day."[93] Even with all his son's academic success, Arnold Stott came very close to cutting him off in 1943.[94] John also wanted to continue with his demanding role of organizing Nash's camps, something his father disapproved of and which Stott would have found it difficult to justify if his academic work had suffered.[95] John Stott may also have felt some broader cultural pressure to prove that he was not a shirker: it was easy for Cambridge residents to be suspicious of the young students they saw wandering around town while their own sons were off fighting the war.[96]

Things became trickier when Stott gave up French and German for theology. The Faculty of Divinity of his day was hardly a bastion of liberal theology: one of its leading lights was the Congregationalist C. H. Dodd who would become widely respected for his intelligent defense of Christian orthodoxy. But for someone reared on the works of American fundamentalist Reuben Torrey, the faculty produced a lot of anxiety. One of Stott's tutors, John Burnaby, wrote of the "ordeal" suffered by theology students whose settled beliefs were brought into question in their Cambridge courses.[97]

There was one lecturer whom Stott appreciated, and he gave Stott a vision for how to combine faithfulness and success in the world of Cambridge theology. J. S. Whale was a Congregationalist whose doctrine was typically conservative but who presented it with a winsomeness that was very different from the combative or dismissive approaches favored by some conservative evangelicals. For example, Whale's understanding of what Christ accomplished on the cross was very close to that common among conservative evangelicals, but he presented his view in as measured and palatable a way as possible.[98] Stott also recalled the influence of the New Testament scholar C. F. D. Moule during his time at Ridley Hall, although in the story that has come down Stott and others would gently tease Moule when he failed to hew to the doctrinal positions of his more conservative uncle, Bishop Handley Moule.[99] C. F. D. Moule was a recognizably evangelical theologian but he was too liberal for Stott's liking. Stott's beliefs were still similar to those he had learned from Nash.

For the most part, Stott was wary of his lecturers, and he did not develop close relationships with any of them.[100] Yet he still excelled. The hours he spent at his desk in the university library paid off, and the additional hours poring over the Bible helped too. But it is still a little puzzling that Stott the conservative evangelical achieved a first-class degree. Whale's example surely helped, although it is unlikely that examiners would have rewarded answers that were rigorously conservative. Stott may have adopted a strategy of laying out what the faculty wanted to hear without committing himself either way. Or perhaps Stott began to agree with his teachers. Oliver Barclay, a fellow pacifist and close friend of Stott's at Cambridge who went on to become the general secretary of the Inter-Varsity Fellowship, recalled that during his theological studies Stott "struggled quite acutely at times."[101] And there are hints in the records of the conservative evangelical Cambridge Inter-Collegiate Christian

Union (CICCU), that some may have worried that Stott's convictions had become a little shaky. As early as his second year at Cambridge, Stott was being asked by the executive committee of the CICCU to teach a series of special Bible studies for first-year students, the first of several similar invitations over the next few years.[102] In 1944, however, as Stott approached the end of his theological studies at Trinity, the committee seems to have been reluctant to invite Stott to speak at evangelistic meetings for new students. At the meeting on June 7, his name was proposed as one of the possible speakers, but two weeks later the list was amended and Stott's name excluded.[103] The following week, his name was reinstated, raising the possibility that his omission in the minutes for June 21 was merely an oversight, but when the committee met again after the summer vacation and was looking for more speakers, Stott's name was missing from the list again.[104] Stott spoke at a CICCU conference that October, so he had not been blacklisted. But the evidence leaves open the possibility that people other than Barclay were aware of Stott's theological struggles, and that they were worried about his doctrinal soundness. This may have been the time when Nash's letters to Stott were (on his own account) so full of rebuke that he needed to "pray and prepare ... for half an hour" before he could open them.[105] It is certainly possible that Stott temporarily modified some of his beliefs in the face of the acumen of the Cambridge Divinity faculty.

Regardless of the reasons for Stott's success, his desire to do well in theology in a doctrinally diverse institution was significant. He moved away from the militancy characteristic of some in his circle, the suspicion of academics characteristic of others, and the intellectual disinterest of yet more.

Stott's involvement with the Cambridge Inter-Collegiate Christian Union contributed to these changes. Founded in 1877, the CICCU traced its origin to the ministry of Charles Simeon, the evangelical vicar of Holy Trinity Church in Cambridge from 1782 to 1836, but the decisive influence on its early development was the highly successful visit to Cambridge of the American revivalist D. L. Moody in 1882. The CICCU was committed to overseas missions, and it played a key role in the international Student Volunteer Missionary Union (SVMU) that at the end of the nineteenth century had called for the evangelization of the world in their generation. In an attempt to secure more workers for this daunting task, the British arm of the SVMU, the Student Christian Movement (SCM), moved away from some of its conservative evangelical positions, and in 1910 the leaders of CICCU decided to part ways with the SCM.[106] Visits from conservative evangelical stalwarts such as Reuben Torrey shored up their position in the following years, as the CICCU became known in the university for its uncompromising and at times offensive approach to truth and evangelism. An infamous episode was the CICCU's evangelistic mission to the university in 1926, when Willy Nicholson, a preacher from Ulster, caused great offence in the university community. Among other things, he loudly assured one man who walked out of a service that he would be damned.[107] More moderate influences were also at work, however, including the Scottish preacher Graham Scroggie and others associated with the Keswick Convention, who showed that conservative evangelicalism and fundamentalism were not necessarily the same thing.[108] By the time Stott arrived at Cambridge, it was those who agreed with Scroggie who were exerting the greater influence, as was evident in the waning of the star of Basil Atkinson. Atkinson, who held a senior position at the Cambridge University Library, had written several fundamentalist titles in the interwar period, and for many years he had used his informal role as mentor to CICCU leaders to encourage them to stick to a more fundamentalist line. There was no change in CICCU's doctrinal position, but the group was making conscious efforts to sand down some of its rough edges.[109]

Douglas Johnson, the first General Secretary of the Inter-Varsity Fellowship (IVF), was critical in the moderates' ascendancy, and in Stott's development. The IVF had been formed in 1928 to provide a national umbrella organization for conservative evangelical student groups like CICCU, and Johnson was determined that it would be resolutely conservative yet not mired in the mud and mud-slinging of fundamentalism.[110] In 1943, Johnson and other IVF leaders told their counterparts in the SCM that on the deity of Christ, the purpose of his death, the rebellion of humanity, and the need for the Holy Spirit's work in regeneration there could be no compromise, but in correspondence Johnson was at pains to present the IVF as a rational and respectable movement.[111] It was not as obscurantist and unscholarly as their critics maintained, he urged, and their beliefs were founded on scholarship and science, not "angularity of character."[112] To make this even clearer, Johnson worked to strengthen the intellectual and particularly the biblical and theological foundations of conservative evangelicalism (although it is important not to overstate interwar weakness in this area).[113] A Biblical Research Committee was established in 1938 and in 1945 the IVF opened Tyndale House as a center for evangelical biblical research in Cambridge.[114] Stott met Douglas Johnson while he was at Cambridge, and Stott was doubtless heartened and inspired by a senior conservative who took the academic study of the Bible so seriously.

Arnold Stott had encountered the CICCU when he was a student at Cambridge and advised his son not to get involved with those "anemic wets." John made and kept a promise that he would not join, but he was very involved in the organization throughout his time at Cambridge.[115] He attended Bible studies, invited friends to evangelistic services, and served as a reader and an usher at the main CICCU services. By his final year, he was composing position papers for the organization.[116] In many ways, the CICCU was a perfect bridge between the narrowness of Nash and a slightly more open style of evangelicalism.[117]

The decision of CICCU's leaders to move away from their organization's fundamentalist roots made sense in Britain during the Second World War. People saw the war against Hitler as a struggle between good and evil in which God was unquestionably on Britain's side, and the churches were enjoying a new lease of life after years of decline. Extra church services were put on, and millions listened to religious broadcasts on the BBC (most famously those by C. S. Lewis that were later published as *Mere Christianity*).[118] Ideas of atonement, which had lost favor among the upper-middle classes toward the end of the nineteenth century, gained renewed currency at a time when death and evil were near the top of people's minds (John Stott's mother referred to the Nazi threat as "truly devilish").[119] Christians were thinking about how to win back people alienated from organized religion, and were dreaming of a postwar world in which people would again make Christianity the center of their lives. The best known of these visions was Archbishop of Canterbury William Temple's *Christianity and Social Order*, a captivating and influential picture of a just and generous society that became part of the intellectual foundations of the welfare state set up in Britain after the war.[120] But Temple's program was one of many. Evangelicals in the Church of England were excited about Bishop Christopher Chavasse's commission on evangelism, which in 1945 produced *Towards the Conversion of England*, a report that urged the church to renew its efforts to reach those outside.[121] People in the IVF were also looking forward to a new day for Christianity once hostilities were over.[122] As early as 1941, Stott was justifying his desire to press on toward ordination with reference to "post-war reconstruction": in a letter to his father, he quoted a comment in *The Times* about the necessity of "definitely Christian" education in any "scheme of national reconstruction."[123] Christians in the IVF and elsewhere were feeling optimistic about the future of Christianity, and in such an environment simply talking about the old paths sounded stale. The storms that had shaken conservative evangelicals in Britain in the earlier part of the century had subsided. It was time to leave the cultural backwaters of fundamentalism and contest the cultural mainstream.

For Stott, this shift in the IVF helped to clarify his vision for ordained ministry as national service. The model he had received from Nash may have been sound and strategic, but it was too clandestine and otherworldly to qualify as serving England, at least in most people's eyes. But perhaps there was a way to be conservative evangelical and other than marginal. Perhaps all those social talents he had honed at Rugby did not need to be buried after all. Certainly, Nash's appointment of Stott as his right-hand man suggested that success in the world of the public schools could transfer into success in Christian leadership. And as an Anglican clergyman, he would still be a part of the establishment, even if not a very prestigious one. Dudley-Smith quotes a recollection of an incident that took place in 1945 at the last Nash camp Stott attended. Unusually, Stott joined a group of less conformist leaders staying up late one night and began throwing eggs around and saying that he would not go to bed just because Nash told him so.[124] Stott was growing up, and under the influence of Whale, Johnson, and others he was growing away from Nash, his father in the faith, and toward a type of Christianity that was interested in this world, as well as the next.

Stott was ordained in St. Paul's Cathedral in December 1945. The cathedral had survived the war owing to the efforts of volunteers who ran around its roof during the blitz putting out fires caused by incendiary bombs. Pictures of its intact dome rising through the smoky devastation of London became symbolic of British resistance to Hitler.[125] It was an auspicious place for Stott to make his ordination vows, and it surely confirmed his vision of the Anglican ministry as a way of serving his country. In some ways, the timing was also auspicious: the war had recently ended, and the work of national reconstruction was under way. However, it was under way with a Labour government, which had defeated Churchill and the Conservative Party in the general election of July 1945. Almost half the population and most of the working classes had voted for the left-wing Labour Party, in large measure because they did not believe Churchill understood their concerns. Stott faced a similar problem. He was almost entirely unfamiliar with the 98 percent of the population who had not been to public school and university.[126] But these were the people he would have to reach if Christianity was to be a central part of the reconstructed nation.

In the long run, the struggles Stott faced as he sought to reach the English people help explain his rise to global prominence. In 1945, however, optimism was the order of the day: perhaps evangelical religion could once again reign in the hearts and minds of the English people. This was what Stott worked for as he left St. Paul's and headed across London to the parish of All Souls Langham Place. But he remained a product of Harley Street, Rugby, and Nash, and retained a vision for the importance of reaching the top 2 percent. He preached to students in London and elsewhere. Stott's university ministry distils many of the opportunities and difficulties Stott faced in the changing culture of postwar Britain.

2

Students

JOHN STOTT'S MINISTRY to university students did not come to an end with his graduation. University College London was very close to his new base at All Souls, and he traveled regularly to Cambridge and Oxford to preach to students. In 1952, he returned to Cambridge to lead a week-long series of evangelistic events organized by the CICCU. The aim was to present the gospel to students and win converts for Christ. The CICCU students called this week their "mission" to the university. Stott was the preacher at the eight evening services, giving sermons with titles such as "Why did Christ die," "What must I do," and "What lies beyond?"[1] He had a staff of thirty assistants who spoke at smaller gatherings and counseled interested students. Hundreds attended the evening services in Great St. Mary's Church. On the final night, people sat in the choir stalls, on extra chairs lining the aisles, and stood on the gallery staircases, but there was still not enough room. The *Cambridge Daily News* took note, commenting on the size of the congregations. The student newspaper, *Varsity*, called Stott an "extremely clear and lucid preacher" and congratulated him on a "highly successful" mission. As many as three hundred committed their lives to Christ.[2] It was the most successful CICCU mission in living memory.

Stott was overjoyed. He was soon in demand for similar events, and over the next twenty-five years led university missions all over the world. It was a major commitment that took him away from London for weeks at a time. His congregation at All Souls, where he was now rector, or senior minister, had predictably mixed feelings: they were glad to have a famous preacher but frustrated by his absence.[3] Yet for Stott these missions were as important as anything he did. He believed that countries followed their leaders. For Christianity to spread, it was vital that those leaders followed Christ.

When Stott reported to his congregation on the 1952 Cambridge mission, he told them that "scores of leaders of the future were born again that week."[4] Two years later, he asked them to pray for the mission he was to lead in Oxford, where "many of our nation's future leaders" would "come under the influence of the Gospel."[5] His hopes for Durham University students were less lofty, but still the focus was on the potential influence of the future teachers and clergy training there.[6] It was the same when he went overseas. When he was preaching at Makerere College in Uganda in 1959, he wrote of "the strategic importance of this college in which are 900 of East Africa's future leaders from the three territories of Uganda, Kenya and Tanganyika."[7] Before his visits to universities in India, Malaya, and the Philippines four years later, he spoke of his longing that God would "raise up more Christian leaders in the countries of the East."[8]

Stott's clearest statement about the strategic importance of university work came in an address to supporters of the evangelical Inter-Varsity Fellowship in 1958. Having stressed that "all evangelistic activity is important," he went on to argue "that special importance attaches to student evangelism." "The majority of the world's leaders in politics, education, medicine, the law and the church," he explained, "are university graduates. Today's leaders were yesterday's students; today's students will be tomorrow's leaders."[9] Stott did not tell his listeners why it was important to have Christians in such positions: he assumed that they too would believe that an ideal way of spreading Christian faith and values in society was through a trickle-down from Christian leaders. The idea had a long history in England: William Wilberforce had held similar convictions in the late eighteenth century.

So the influence of Nash and the idea of converts who would be "multiplication tables" lived on. Stott held traditional upper- and upper-middle-class attitudes about the culture-shaping importance of the higher levels of society's hierarchy. Stott wanted to reach all sorts of students—he forged links between All Souls and the Regent Street Polytechnic and led missions at places like Leeds University and the Royal Agricultural College at Cirencester—but he focused on the universities of Cambridge and Oxford, the places where the cream rose.[10]

In postwar Britain, this approach could appear progressive, as well as elitist, for the ancient universities were slowly becoming more socially diverse. For Anglicans like Stott this made university evangelism look even more strategic. The Church of England had often struggled to reach the lower classes, but as representatives of these classes started to arrive at Oxford and Cambridge it raised hopes that were they converted they might help the church reach those classes more effectively. This was the hope of another evangelical Anglican, Maurice Wood. Wood was the vicar of St. Mary Islington in north

London, a church that hosted the most important annual gathering for evangelical Anglican clergy. The church was very close to the Arsenal football club stadium at Highbury, and the Church of England's struggles to grab the attention of the working classes were glaringly obvious for Wood as he watched tens of thousands walk through his parish to Highbury but not to his church. He became a strong supporter of Billy Graham's evangelistic work in Britain and was enthusiastic when he heard that Graham would be leading the 1955 CICCU mission. Writing shortly before the mission, Wood commented on the fact that Cambridge now drew students from every level of society, before suggesting that "If Christ is received into the hearts of men and women in Cambridge in this coming week, an immense impact will eventually be made upon whole areas of the country which are not easily accessible to the Gospel, because of the difficulty the church experiences in reaching to every class."[11] For Stott and others, then, evangelism at Oxford and Cambridge had more to do with strategy than snobbery.

Stott was elated as he sat in his study after the 1952 Cambridge mission and wrote the editorial for the All Souls parish magazine. He told his readers that his nine days in Cambridge had been "inspiring and exhilarating."[12] After another visit to Cambridge a few years later he was similarly enthusiastic. "It must surely be almost without precedent," he wrote, "that 450 undergraduates should assemble in church on a Saturday evening for the solid study of the Bible." He then commented on the marvelous bass singing (the CICCU was still all male) at the evangelistic service the following evening, when nine hundred turned up. "The contemporary movement of the Spirit of God in the student world," Stott said, "is one of the most encouraging signs of our generation."[13] There were scores of converts again when Stott led the 1958 Cambridge mission, and although he found the atmosphere at Oxford "both cramping and oppressive," one hundred young men invited Christ into their lives during his 1954 mission there.[14] Stott was effective elsewhere—for example, scores were converted on his 1956–57 tour of universities in North America—but the evidence suggests that he was especially fruitful at England's two ancient universities.[15] Stott was an insider there: he understood the world of Oxford and Cambridge, which continued to be dominated by boarding school boys like himself. And what had attracted him to a fervent, evangelical faith attracted others who, like him, had learned about Christianity in their homes and schools but who wanted a deeper experience of Christ.

His sermons were tightly reasoned expositions of the Christian gospel. Basil Atkinson called Stott's addresses "masterful": he "clarif[ied] the Gospel, so that no mind could escape its meaning." Another commented on the way that Stott's meaty sermons were "almost unrelieved by illustrations."[16] The published version of his mission sermons, *Basic Christianity*, quoted professors and other authorities, anticipated counterarguments, and provided suggestions for further reading. One sympathetic reviewer said that while "it would not be true to call the book dull; it would not be honest to avoid the word 'solid'."[17] In the introduction, Stott said that many people had "a sneaking suspicion" that Christianity was not "intellectually respectable," and set himself the task of showing that it was.[18] In chapter two, Stott declared that his purpose was "to marshal evidence to prove that Jesus was the only begotten Son of God."[19] When he turned to the resurrection of Christ in chapter four, he stated that "certainly many impartial students have judged the evidence to be extremely good."[20]

Stott preached this way because he believed that the path to students' wills was through a rational appeal to their minds.[21] Some may have been surprised to hear a conservative evangelical preaching this way given the reputation for anti-intellectualism that they had gained in the earlier part of the twentieth century, but Stott's approach was not an aberration. The evangelical tradition had deep roots in the Enlightenment, when John Wesley, Jonathan Edwards, and others were convinced that religion and reason went together. Stott agreed, and believed that evangelicalism would never return to the heart of English society unless many were similarly persuaded. Douglas Johnson and the Inter-Varsity Fellowship had helped Stott see that Christianity and the life of the mind were not antithetical, but it was Stott who demonstrated it for literally thousands of students through his sermons. When Stott preached, "intellectual conquest" was the goal.[22]

Stott borrowed techniques that came from the American revivalist tradition, including the use of smaller gatherings after his talks to help inquirers toward a decision. But his method and manner were very different from others in that school. Some of CICCU's previous speakers had been decidedly confrontational. Ulsterman Willy Nicholson asked hypocrites to stand up and leave his services in 1926, while at the 1949 mission the American Donald Grey Barnhouse raised "the fury of the theologians" with preaching that included illustrations of lost sinners dropping into hell.[23] When the CICCU's Executive Committee looked back on the 1949 mission, they acknowledged the harm that had been done and concluded that "the next Mission and especially the Missioner must be very respectable."[24] Stott was their final if not unanimous choice, and this desire for a less inflammatory speaker may have been decisive. The Cambridge student newspaper said that Stott was "gracious and courteous." There were no "fireworks." Maurice Wood spoke of his "quiet presentation of the gospel."[25] Not for him the histrionics of Nicholson or the feistiness of Barnhouse: the urgency of the gospel was communicated by content, not tone. This was hardly surprising for a product of Rugby and Cambridge, but this was precisely its significance. As he preached at places like Oxford and Cambridge, he was preaching to people like himself, and many listened. Stott's urbane manner was largely subconscious, but there was also a strategic decision here. Like moderate evangelical Anglicans in the nineteenth century, Stott aimed for broad social influence and eschewed "enthusiasm" in order to disarm critics from the genteel classes who equated conservative evangelicalism with extremism.[26] Stott would have been encouraged when, at the end of the 1952 CICCU mission, he received a letter that noted "the very favourable attitude of the university authorities and dons" to the event. "Many of them," the letter went on, "were very much impressed."[27]

However, Stott did not think that the only reasons for his success were his gifts and the approach that he took. It was obvious that what was going on at Oxford and Cambridge was part of a more widespread return to Christianity in Britain during the fifteen years after the Second World War. As an Anglican, an evangelical, and a university evangelist, Stott was at the heart of three of the brightest spots of British Christianity in this period. The Church of England was in very good spirits. Easter communicants increased by a fifth in the eight years after 1947 and confirmations rose from a little over 140,000 in 1950 to over 190,000 ten years later.[28] The clergy were oozing confidence: the Bishop of Lichfield spoke of the tide turning as people returned to God; the editor of *The Churchman* spoke of Christianity "taking the offensive in Britain"; and Maurice Wood, speaking in the wake of Billy Graham's 1954 Greater London Crusade, expressed his belief that God was granting England "a measure of revival."[29] Within the Church of England, it was the evangelicals who were doing particularly well. Hugh Gough, the evangelical Bishop of Barking, said in 1955 that "quite clearly" they were experiencing the beginning of another evangelical revival.[30] Non-evangelicals also commented on the remarkable response to the evangelical message during these years.[31] And the renewed interest in Christianity was particularly evident among students. It was a golden age for Christianity at Cambridge, where it was not only Stott and CICCU members who were encouraged: the more liberal college chaplains were too. The vicar of the University church said that student religion

had fresh vigor and was "a force...in contemporary Cambridge."[32] For one
writer in the Oxford University magazine, Christianity at Oxford was "very
evidently more lively than...almost anywhere else in the country."[33]

Changes in the intellectual climate were part of the reason for the
evangelicals' success at England's universities. The work of T. S. Eliot, C. S.
Lewis, and others had done a good deal to repair Christianity's reputation
among the middle and upper classes. Lewis's famous wartime radio broadcasts, later published as *Mere Christianity*, bore similarities to the sermons
that became Stott's *Basic Christianity*. Both were carefully reasoned, lucid
arguments for an orthodox, supernatural Christianity.[34] In theology, the tow-
ering figure was Karl Barth, who like the evangelicals was conservative and
dogmatic.[35] In philosophy, the rise of logical positivism, with its rigorous standards for verifiable truth and frequently antireligious conclusions, may ironically have helped preachers like Stott who argued that Christianity was rooted
in "verifiable history."[36]

British culture was also congenial to conservative evangelical beliefs during these years. The Second World War had fostered a climate of moral seriousness in Britain. The language of good and evil was needed and used and
evangelical preaching about sin and atonement thus made a good deal of
sense.[37] It continued to make sense after the war had ended, as the Cold War
encouraged people to keep thinking of the world in terms of a struggle between good and evil.[38] There was much talk in the West about atheistic
Communism, which made Christianity more central to national identity in
many countries.[39]

The Second World War also gave a tremendous boost to the British elites.
On the eve of the war, Britain was the only European country where the traditional social elites retained most of their influence, and the fact that Britain
won (under the very patrician Churchill) helped them hang on to it.[40] The
war fed the image of Britain as a finely ordered society. Putting vast numbers
of men into uniform created a "common culture of reference" that encouraged a sense of hierarchy, and the continuation of obligatory military service
for young men after the war ensured that that culture continued.[41] So although
there was an awareness of a more classless society in postwar Britain, as José
Harris has argued, there were still many who clung to an older vision of society
as a well-ordered, hierarchical family.[42]

That such sentiments were as strong in the mid-1950s as they had been in
the 1940s owed much to the accession and coronation of Elizabeth II in 1952–53.
On coronation day, Britain's princes and princesses, dukes and duchesses,

lords and ladies, archbishops and bishops put on a display that dazzled despite the pouring rain. Golden coaches and ermine robes, coronets and crowns, orb and scepter were all there to see for the millions who gathered to watch on their tiny television sets. It warmed the cockles of the hearts of those who still saw society as a benign pyramid. In retrospect, it is easy to see the pomp as a reflection of the need to support a creaking Empire, but at the time many saw it in a much more positive light.[43] An editor at *The Times* hoped for a new Elizabethan age, with "Christian values re-established, morals reasserted, conscientiousness revived, energy renewed, and national unity restored."[44]

For Anglicans in particular, this was a wonderful moment. Although the majority of people in England no longer attended the Church of England, the national church had a virtual monopoly on such royal occasions, and the televised coronation gave it an unparalleled opportunity to display its glories to the people.[45] The coronation was, after all, a religious ceremony, and the Archbishop of Canterbury, Geoffrey Fisher, had a part in the proceedings second only to the new Queen herself. He understood the significance of the event. To a loud chorus of approval, he said that "the Country and Commonwealth last Tuesday were not far from the Kingdom of Heaven."[46] The sentiment was echoed by the Bishop of Lichfield, who wrote that the coronation "became a deep spiritual experience for countless thousands of people."[47] Another leading Anglican was heartened by the way the coronation had made the Christian nature of the state so visible to so many.[48] Fisher spoke of how proud he had been of his church.[49] The early 1950s was a good time indeed to be a priest in the Church of England, as their place in the establishment allowed them to bask in the reflected glory of the new Sovereign.

Stott and his fellow-evangelicals were affected by the same mood. "One ventures to hope," Stott wrote enthusiastically in the parish magazine, "that the whole nation will go to Church on Coronation Sunday, and that throughout these sacred days we may find new inspiration for service through the example of this most courageous of ladies."[50] Maurice Wood came to All Souls to speak at the Empire Youth Service in 1952.[51] The monarch's name held significance for some evangelicals, who hoped for a return to the religion of the Reformation in a new Elizabethan era.[52] Max Warren, an evangelical who was general secretary of the Church Missionary Society, said that the coronation had contributed to the religious revival of the mid-1950s because by it the nation had been "touched to higher things."[53] For English evangelicals, the early 1950s felt very Victorian. It was possible to believe again that life revolved with a "moral dynamic" around the sacred symbols of "nation, monarch, established church, social hierarchy, sabbath, bible, marriage, family, [and] work."[54]

It is therefore not surprising that Christianity was on the rise in Britain after the Second World War. And it is not surprising that earnest students were attracted to a form of Christianity that demanded the sort of moral seriousness needed of aspiring leaders. This was, after all, the era when social pressure had led Princess Margaret not to marry Peter Townsend because he was a divorcé and a royal servant. The BBC, the Church of England, the Arts Council, and other establishment organs were confidently seeking to transmit upper-middle-class tastes and values down the social scale. "'Ordinary people'…were persistently spoken for and over the top of, their views often ignored, their voices shouted down. Knowing what was good for people, controlling what they could and could not consume, was taken for granted as the prerogative of the activator class."[55] The strategies of Nash and of the IVF made sense. English evangelicals were not as weak in the interwar period as some have maintained, but they were bruised.[56] Now younger leaders like Stott dreamed of renewed cultural influence, of an age where church and society might be united again in a Christian moral order.

Historians have called the postwar years an Indian summer for the Church of England and British Protestantism more generally.[57] The metaphor is potentially misleading, for unlike an Indian summer there was no reason for those who were enjoying it to think that the sunshine they were enjoying would fade. For Anglican evangelicals, however, sun also meant heat. If they wanted to capitalize on the opportunities afforded by the religious renaissance, so did others in the Church of England. In the mid-1950s the buoyant conservative evangelicals came under fire. Significantly, for Stott, the controversy centered on the growing strength of conservative evangelicalism at England's top universities.

The Fundamentalism Controversy

In between Stott's Cambridge missions of 1952 and 1958 was Billy Graham's in 1955. Three months before Graham arrived, H. K. Luce wrote a letter to The Times to complain. Luce was an Anglican clergyman and a teacher at a boarding school in Durham. He was as opposed to conservative evangelical religion as Stott's teachers at Rugby had been. For him, religion was the glue that held schools and society together, not a zealous adventure for a few. "The recent increase of fundamentalism among university students," his letter began, "cannot but cause concern to those whose work lies in religious educa-tion." Religion was to be reasonable, and Luce was sure that Graham's was not. "The proposal that Dr. Graham should conduct a mission to Cambridge University raises an issue which does not seem to have been squarely faced by Christians in this country. Universities exist for the advancement of learning; on what basis, therefore, can fundamentalism claim a hearing at Cambridge?" "Is it not time," Luce concluded, "that our religious leaders made it plain that while they respect, or even admire, Dr. Graham's sincerity and personal power, they cannot regard fundamentalism as likely to issue in anything but disillu-sionment and disaster for educated men and women in this twentieth-century world?"[58]

Graham was one of the most important figures in postwar British reli-gious life. Tall and American, dressed like a movie star with a smile to match, Graham was exotic and enticing for the many British people who were enthralled by the life they saw in American films. Graham came to Britain as a speaker for Youth for Christ in 1946 in what was to be the first in a string of visits that included major crusades in London in 1954 and London and Glasgow in 1955. In 1954, Graham preached for three months in the boxing arena at Harringay, North London. Thirty-six thousand dedicated their lives to Christ.[59] One hundred and twenty thousand gathered at Wembley stadium for the final rally. When he led the CICCU mission in 1955, despite the com-plaints of Luce and others, hundreds were converted.[60]

After the dust had settled, debate centered on whether Graham's converts remained converted. More recently, however, historians have been asking other questions about Graham's significance. Ian Randall has argued that the real importance of Graham's visits lay not so much in the numbers converted but in relationships developed between British Christian leaders, in fresh recruits for pastoral ministry, and in the overall "recharging" of evangelical batteries.[61] Alana Harris and Martin Spence studied Graham alongside the American Catholic Patrick Peyton, who also led large crusades in Britain at the same time, and have emphasized the preachers' common message of hope and action in the context of social dislocation and Cold War apocalyptic fear.[62]

For evangelical leaders like Stott, however, much of Graham's significance lay in the encouragement he gave them to keep moving away from the mar-gins of society. Graham did this in part by his very success: his crusades made the gospel a conversation topic and the crowds fed dreams of revival. A London funfair even made a waxwork of him.[63] But just as important was

Graham's determination to win as wide a hearing as possible for his message. Graham was the latest in a long line of American preachers who had shaped English evangelicalism, a line that included D. L. Moody and Reuben Torrey. But whilst Torrey had moved Nash and others in a more dogmatic direction, Graham helped lead the postwar generation to a more moderate stance. Graham still spoke of truth and falsehood, life and death, heaven and hell, but he did so without the abrasiveness of many of his predecessors. He had decided, to quote Mark Noll, to "trade...angularity for access."[64] So when shortly before his arrival in England in 1954 it emerged that a calendar for Graham's supporters told them that the Labour Party's socialism and "its accompanying evils" had destroyed England's historic faith, Graham simply smiled and apologized.[65] This made it all the more galling, of course, when some people in England insisted on calling him a fundamentalist.

Ever since some American evangelicals started styling themselves as fundamentalists in the early twentieth century, it has been difficult to distinguish between the two groups. George Marsden has suggested that as a rule of thumb "a fundamentalist is an evangelical who is angry about something."[66] Fundamentalism was never as large a movement in Britain as it was in the United States, but it certainly shaped not only Nash but thousands of British evangelicals. This made it easy for critics of evangelicals to paint them as fundamentalists in an attempt to spoil their image, and this is what Luce was doing in the mid-1950s. He was not alone. Every edition of the *Crockford's* directory of Anglican clergy contained a famously anonymous preface whose author was therefore free to speak candidly about the state of the church, and in 1953–54 the author lamented that "a considerable number of actual and potential ordination candidates are biblical 'Fundamentalists' or so close to being so that no ordinary magnifying glass can detect any significant difference."[67] But it was Luce's letter that made fundamentalism a matter of public debate because it started a lengthy correspondence in *The Times* on the subject. The controversy rumbled on after *The Times* had moved on to other things, with a trenchant article entitled "The Menace of Fundamentalism" coming from the pen of the Bishop of Durham and later Archbishop of Canterbury Michael Ramsey in 1956.[68] It was obvious that the critics were aiming not just at Graham but at British evangelicals too: Luce's letter said as much when he referred to "the recent increase of fundamentalism among university students." Stott was the rising star in this movement and clearly implicated. For Stott and others like him who longed to see evangelicalism regain its prominence, the attacks in *The Times* were a cruel irony.

Three points of disagreement arose as evangelicals and their critics argued about fundamentalism. The first was the nature of the atonement: were Graham and others like him right to talk bluntly about Christ dying in place of others to suffer God's wrath for their sins? This was seen in a contribution to the Cambridge student newspaper at the time of Graham's 1955 CICCU mission by John Burnaby, the Regius Professor of Divinity and one of Stott's former teachers. "The 'substitutionary' doctrine of the Atonement can be read into the New Testament," argued Burnaby; "it cannot be read out of it."[69] More prominent still were questions concerning the doctrine and use of Scripture. Everyone in the debate agreed that the Bible was the Word of God, but Luce and others became anxious when people like Graham and Stott started claiming that the Bible was infallible or inerrant. This claim that the Bible was free from error and the associated position that, where possible, it should be taken literally, seemed naive or worse to people reared on a more skeptical theological diet.[70] Did seemingly intelligent people like Stott really still believe that Jonah was swallowed by a fish? For the critics, listening to Graham preach, with his formulaic phrase "the Bible says," was like hearing fingernails run down a blackboard. Finally, there were the methods used by Graham and his English counterparts, especially their calls for people to make a decisive commitment to Christ. This was the key point in the critique of Michael Ramsey. Ramsey was an accomplished theologian, the stereotypical absent-minded academic who as a bishop made people worry that he would go astray in church processions. Willy Nicholson's blistering CICCU mission during his student days at Cambridge had repulsed him, and he developed a lifelong suspicion of revivalism of any sort.[71] In 1956, Ramsey caricatured the approach of conservative evangelical preachers as follows: "Hither, young man: drown your worries in the rapture of conversion: stifle your doubts by abdicating the use of your mind. A rousing sermon, a hurricane of emotion, a will to leap in the dark—and peace at once and for ever."[72]

Stott was irritated by these attacks. They targeted evangelism at the universities at a time when it was bearing more fruit than it had for generations. Luce was trying to save Cambridge from Graham. R. C. Marsh, writing to *The Times* from Trinity College, Cambridge, agreed: he could not bear fundamentalist intolerance in a university town.[73] Michael Ramsey said in his letter that, "The successes of this preaching are won, particularly within the universities, at a cost both of moral casualties and of an alienation of thoughtful men and women from the Christian faith."[74] Ramsey's article on "The Menace of

Fundamentalism" was published in Durham just before Stott's mission to the university there.

The primary concern here was the spiritual health of the students, but there was something else at work. The success of Graham and Stott frightened Ramsey, Luce, and others like them. These men entered the debate with such vigor because they feared for the future of the Church of England if conservative evangelical growth at Oxford and Cambridge continued. England's ancient universities continued to be the training grounds for many Anglican clergy and the source of most of its bishops, and the success of conservative evangelicalism in these institutions was already being transferred into an increasing proportion of ordination candidates from that wing of the church.[75] That fewer and fewer of these evangelicals were disappearing to the mission field made the situation in England even worse. For decades, conservative evangelicals had had pariah status in the Church of England, solidified when their efforts helped secure the rejection of a revised prayer book in 1927–28, and the sight of their number increasing filled other churchmen with horror.[76] The editor of the weekly *Church Times* saw it as nothing less than "a great danger…to Christianity in this country."[77] The author of the *Crockford's Clerical Directory* preface of 1953–54 put it bluntly: "That no small proportion of the inadequate number of candidates now admitted into the Church's ministry should be committed to this erroneous dogmatism diminishes hope for the future appeal of the Church's message among normally minded and educated people."[78] In an era when religion was gaining fresh prominence in England, it mattered a great deal who was seen as representative of the Church of England. Ramsey and others who thought like him held the traditional positions of influence, but it was the evangelicals who were stealing the show through their association with Billy Graham and threatening to steal the future through their ordination candidates.[79] The controversy was about power, as well as ideas.

English evangelicals were rattled. It was bad enough to be called fundamentalists, worse yet for Anglican evangelicals when Ramsey, just appointed the Archbishop of York, called their views a "menace" and "*heretical*."[80] For an archbishop to call one's views heretical was serious indeed for clergymen whose first promise in their ordination services was to "respect and be guided by the pastoral direction and leadership" of their bishop.[81] The conservative evangelicals were in an unenviable position.

Evangelical Anglicans responded in a number of ways. CICCU stalwart Basil Atkinson tried bravura. He wrote a letter to *The Times* saying that

Graham's gospel did not need defending for it would endure long after "the modernistic conceptions of to-day" had been thrown away.[82] Philip E. Hughes demanded that Archbishop Ramsey either establish his charge of heresy in detail or withdraw it.[83] In time, the fullest response to the accusations came from the pen of J. I. Packer. Packer was emerging as an astute theological and political thinker on the evangelical wing of the church, and he went on to become one of the most well-respected evangelical thinkers on both sides of the Atlantic. It was the Fundamentalism crisis that led in 1958 to his first book, *"Fundamentalism" and the Word of God*, which became a classic evangelical defense of the truthfulness of the Bible.[84]

Stott moved more quickly than Packer. He feared that these public slurs would make it more difficult to win students and others to Christ. So he tried to defuse the tension. Stott did this by writing a cool letter to *The Times* that aimed to define the word "fundamentalism," whose meaning he felt had been too widely assumed and too widely applied. He began by noting the term's association in the *Oxford English Dictionary* with a conservative, orthodox understanding of the Christian faith and its origin among North American Baptists, although it is doubtful whether his readers would have agreed with his statement that this constituted a "noble origin" for the word. He then remarked that the term had subsequently become one of "opprobrium," used to describe "the bigoted rejection of all Biblical criticism, a mechanical view of inspiration and an excessively literalist interpretation of Scripture." He went on: "It is doubtless in this sense that your correspondents have employed the term, and in this sense that Dr. Billy Graham and others associated with him have repudiated it." The difficulty, of course, was that it was not "doubtless" that this was the definition that Ramsey, Luce, and others would have used. For one, it only focused on the doctrine of Scripture and ignored the other two points of controversy, namely the doctrine of the atonement and the question of methods. And even on the doctrine of Scripture, the critics granted the term "fundamentalism" a much wider semantic range and one that included Stott's own position of the inerrancy of the Bible.[85] In the rest of the letter, Stott argued that the central issue in the controversy was "the place of the mind in the perception of divine truth," arguing that what was needed was childlike submission to divine revelation. But Ramsey would have had no difficulty in continuing to see Stott as a fundamentalist.[86]

Someone who was not convinced by Stott's arguments was one of his old theology tutors from Cambridge, John Burnaby. Burnaby did not think it was possible to believe in the infallibility of Scripture without "doing violence to intellectual honesty."[87] He wrote to Stott and asked him to clarify the difference between a traditional, conservative view of Scripture and fundamentalism, closing with the quip, "The 'little child' is receptive, but he is also very inquisitive and likes to 'understand' things!"[88] Stott wrote a detailed response in which he sought to put clear water between his own position and the one he had attributed to fundamentalists in *The Times*: advocating a place for higher criticism as long as its conclusions did not depend on "subjective criteria and philosophical presuppositions"; stressing that the conservative evangelical did not see the Bible as a textbook; and affirming his belief that God used the personalities of the biblical authors, not dictation.[89]

There were differences between Stott's position and more conservative ones, but that did not necessarily mean he was off the hook of fundamentalism.[90] Burnaby did not think so: in his reply he said, "I find it difficult to distinguish what you say, if I have understood it rightly, from "fundamentalism" as commonly understood."[91] This was the rub: the lack of definition meant the term functioned in different ways for different people, and although Stott wanted to pin it on those to the theological right of himself, for more liberal spirits like Burnaby Stott was about as conservative as one could get.

Perturbed, Stott forwarded the correspondence to his old friend and Inter-Varsity Fellowship leader, Douglas Johnson, hoping for some clarification and perhaps some fresh arguments from this senior conservative. But Johnson was not surprised that Burnaby had found it difficult to tell the difference: "'Traditionalism' + ordinary 'fundamentalism,'" he wrote to Stott, "are of course almost synonyms."[92] In the privacy of personal correspondence, Johnson acknowledged just how close he and the Inter-Varsity Fellowship were to old-style fundamentalism. He agreed with most of what the theological warriors of the early twentieth century had been arguing for, and so did Stott. Some of the details were different, and the presentation too, but their doctrine was very similar. Johnson did not want to put too much space between Inter-Varsity evangelicals like himself and fundamentalism. The fundamentalist legacy was a constant and helpful warning against the dangers of sliding from orthodoxy.[93]

Even though Burnaby was not convinced, it was important that Stott wrote the irenic letter to *The Times* that he did. Stott did believe in the inerrancy of the Bible, a highly conservative commitment to biblical truthfulness that had become common among American fundamentalists and that made him a fundamentalist on many definitions.[94] But his willingness to reason calmly with his detractors meant that he did not fit another part of the description, namely belligerence.[95] That was not surprising for someone raised to be unfailingly polite, but it was also strategic. He did not want to alienate the very people he was trying to reach. He longed to see the spread of the gospel among university students continue, and believed that that required a measure of social acceptability. In addition, his didactic tone showed that evangelicals like him did think, thus counteracting the charge of anti-intellectualism. He may not have won over Burnaby, but his approach helped to ensure a continued hearing for conservative evangelicalism among the sorts of people who read *The Times*. On the sort of hierarchical view of society that Stott had learned from Rugby and Nash, that was the kind of access that mattered.

There was more work to do, however. Stott had been ruffled and knew he had to help other troubled evangelicals to stand firm. He therefore wrote an article for the November 1955 edition of the evangelical *Crusade* magazine in which he expanded on some of the points he had made in his letters to *The Times* and to John Burnaby. Having outlined three "extravagances" of fundamentalism (which were found "particularly in the United States"), he emphasized the importance of holding "the more traditional and conservative" approach to Scripture and went on to define and defend divine revelation and inspiration.[96] The following year Stott wrote another piece for *Crusade* justifying the practice of calling people to make a decisive commitment to Christ.[97] Again, the purpose was to encourage conservative evangelicals to stand firm for their beliefs and practices, and the calm and careful way in which he did so helped provide reassurance to English evangelicals. It mattered little that his views were still so conservative that an American Lutheran reviewing the book version of the articles could say that he had done a distinct service to "the Church Militant."[98] And in one respect he had no desire to put space between himself and those who owned the opprobrious term. In the first of these articles he wrote that fundamentalists were people who held on to the fundamentals of the faith, and said he hoped that in this sense at least all his readers were fundamentalists.

Stott could have taken a more combative approach, or encouraged his fellow evangelical Anglicans to break away from their church in order to pursue a more populist strategy. But Stott was very different from those American conservatives who had taken the routes of populism and secession: he was determined to use his status as an insider for the furtherance of Christianity in England. And maintaining and taking advantage of his establishment connections made especially good sense in the 1950s, when proximity to the establishment seemed a boon.

The controversy lingered, but it was soon apparent that it would not pose a grave problem for conservative evangelicals in the Church of England or the universities. Stott's aim throughout was to secure a continued hearing for the evangelical gospel, particularly in the universities. The results of his 1958 Cambridge mission suggest that he was successful.

Turning Against the Establishment

There was therefore little immediate change in Stott's message in the wake of this controversy. Perhaps his comments about intellectual respectability would not have been so front and center in the introduction to *Basic Christianity* in 1958 without it, but there was no fundamental change on this or any other point. A principal reason for this was confidence: in the 1950s, Stott was seeing lots of people converted under his ministry. Stott's message and his methods worked, and there was no need to fix them. Greater influence in church and nation seemed assured.

But for all the excitement about Christianity's return to the national consciousness, it never really captured the cultural limelight. The fundamentalism controversy included more than two dozen letters and even a leading article in *The Times*, but it never became a matter of national debate. Evangelicalism did not make the headlines or the airwaves; it never captured the conversation in parliament or pubs. Contrary to evangelical folklore, even Billy Graham attracted only modest attention in the press: one of the very few articles published on his crusades in the London *Evening Standard* made the editorial cut because it told the humorous tale of a rain-soaked service on Streatham Common where Graham's music director, Cliff Barrows, had to give up trying to play his trombone and heavier members of the platform party had to move to the center as the stage sank in the mud.[99] And although Michael Ramsey may have intended his article in the Durham diocesan magazine as bad advance press for Stott's 1956 mission at the university, both the student newspaper and the local press were much more interested in the visit to Durham of famous "crooner" Dickie Valentine.[100]

Things got worse after 1960. After a mission at Oxford in 1964, Stott noted the growth of anti-Christian influence in the university and concluded that "the tide of post-war Oxbridge [Oxford and Cambridge] 'religiousness' has turned."[101] In 1970 he led a university mission in Liverpool, the home of the Beatles and much of the popular culture of the era, but his report had little cheer: "We certainly cannot claim to have made any significant impact—or even dent—on the university as a whole."[102] It was not that British culture had changed overnight: evangelical churches continued to thrive. But popular culture was moving in more liberal directions and student culture was moving with it, away from the conservatism that had been a remarkable feature of university life in the 1950s.[103] Overseas, things looked even less conservative. As Marxism became more popular, Stott studied the ideas of Malcolm X, Mao Zedong, and Jomo Kenyatta.[104] In time he became convinced by some of what they said. In a sermon in 1968, Stott reflected on the student unrest that was affecting universities in many parts of the world:

> But we should have some sympathy with the spirit of revolt. We need to realise that students are (at least in part) protesting against the adult world which they have inherited, against the mess which they feel we have made, against the bastions of privilege and every entrenched establishment, against injustice, inequality and inefficiency.
>
> I ask myself: should not the Church be protesting, rather than being among the chief objects of protest? Must the Church be regarded as always reactionary and never radical, as bent on defending the last ditches of status and privilege?[105]

Stott was gingerly starting to criticize the establishment that had once looked such an asset for him. In the 1971 revised edition of *Basic Christianity*, he acknowledged that large numbers now "detest[ed] the establishment and its entrenched privileges," and added a paragraph that called "the church as an organization.... archaic, inward-looking and reactionary."[106] However, the core of his message continued to be human sin and divine redemption, not left-wing politics.

But the glory years did not return. In 1977, Stott went back to Cambridge for his final student mission. The university was now a very different place, with pictures of topless women in the student newspaper, Black Sabbath at a college event, open discussion of pot usage, and a stripper at the debating society ball.[107] Hundreds still attended the mission each evening, but there were many fewer commitments to Christ.[108] The student press was suspicious, accusing Stott of brainwashing and divisiveness.[109] Stott handled the press but he looked awkward in the student world of the late 1970s. Earnestness was still his modus operandi, but humor and irony now seemed to be the way to win skeptical students' attention. The younger generation of university evangelists in England, for example, David Watson, were warmer characters from evangelicalism's charismatic wing. Stott was also, of course, getting older, making it even harder to win a hearing with many young people.

Nevertheless, Stott's university missions were crucial in his ascent to evangelical leadership. His successes at Cambridge and Oxford established his reputation among evangelicals in England and the trips to lead missions overseas made him an internationally known figure. In addition, speaking at universities consolidated Stott's deliberate, rational approach to the faith and preaching it, which became his hallmark and a major way he shaped global evangelicalism. Stott's growing friendship with Billy Graham was also important for his career. Stott stayed with Graham and his family for Christmas in 1956 (in the middle of a string of missions at North American universities), and over the years the two became good friends. Stott benefited from his relationship with the best known evangelical in the world, who was also the head of his own well-funded organization. Graham brought him to New York to address ministers as part of his crusade there, and then to Berlin and Lausanne to give keynote addresses at major global conferences on evangelism. Graham was not exactly a patron, but as in the geopolitical special relationship between American and Britain it was clear who was the senior partner.

For evangelicals interested in converting students, some of the high hopes had gone by the late 1960s. But conservative evangelicalism remained strong in the universities, even if the scale of conversions was not as great.[110] Indeed, although the number of converts dropped off after the mid-1950s, the tact and tenacity of Stott and others in the midst of the fundamentalism controversy helped to legitimize the conservative evangelical Inter-Varsity movement at Britain's universities. There were not hundreds of converts at Stott's Cambridge mission of 1977, but hundreds did come, many of them members of CICCU. And over the years many Inter-Varsity converts did become Anglican clergy, leading to a stronger evangelical presence in the Church of England that fulfilled the fears of Ramsey and Luce.

The two things that stand out in this story are the extraordinary nature of the 1950s, which gave Stott and others hope that the religious tide could be turned through the conversion of large numbers of the country's future leaders, and the frightening nature of the 1960s, when the future looked a good deal more grim than it eventually turned out to be. It made sense for

Stott to embrace radical ideas in the 1960s, for the situation seemed grave indeed. It also pushed him to focus more on the church beyond Britain. The hopes of the 1950s left an enduring mark, however, and the dream of shaping the culture and the question of how to do so remained. Stott had already been trying other strategies for quite some time, in his parish in the West End of London.

3

Parishioners

ALL SOULS LANGHAM Place stands at the top of Regent Street in central London, a few hundred yards north of the Oxford Circus underground station. Its parish was and is remarkably diverse. It has long been home to many of London's grandest stores and some of its most expensive properties. In the 1940s, the All Souls parish magazine contained adverts for many of the finer local establishments, including Jaeger, John Bell & Croyden ("An Aristocrat Among Merchants"), and the Wellbeck Hotel ("An hotel sought after by people of discrimination").[1] But the parish also had a historically working-class district known as Fitzrovia, large numbers of immigrants, and a Bohemian side (with a couple of fashionable pubs for local literati including Dylan Thomas). All Souls church was built in the 1820s as part of a government-sponsored plan to build new, large churches in the growing cities of industrial England. Designed by Buckingham Palace architect John Nash, the building is essentially a box, without the sort of symbolic floor plan common in many older churches. Nash focused his talents on the spire and classical portico that jut out into Langham Place and peer down Regent Street. He wanted this grand, curved entrance to help smooth the awkward kink at Langham Place between the top of Regent Street and the southern end of Portland Place. This was the church Stott attended as a boy, and he returned there in 1945 to begin his work as a parish clergyman. All Souls had suffered extensive bomb damage during the war and so the congregation was meeting in nearby St. Peter's, Vere Street, another church in the parish. But this did not bother Stott. He was excited to start his ordained ministry in London's West End, which seemed the perfect place to dream of influencing England for Christ.

Harold Earnshaw Smith, the rector, or senior minister, of the church, had invited Stott to serve as one of his curates, or assistant ministers. Earnshaw Smith had offered Stott the post earlier that year when he had visited Cambridge to preach for the Cambridge Inter-Collegiate Christian Union (CICCU). Earnshaw Smith was a true blue evangelical who had worked for the Inter-Varsity Fellowship, served as a missionary in Nigeria, spoken at the Keswick Convention, and supported the CICCU while a chaplain at Gonville and Caius College. Earnshaw Smith's ministry at All Souls was a textbook case of evangelical Anglican parish life. Evangelism was a major priority, as were foreign missions. Pastor and congregation cherished the liturgy of the Church of England and believed that the national church had a special role to play in God's purpose for their nation. There were special, civil services at the church attended by local dignitaries. Earnshaw Smith believed that the British Empire had "a spiritual destiny in the world," and that in the difficult postwar years God was "disciplining" the nation that they might fulfill it.[2] Yet as much as he saw himself as part of the English establishment, Earnshaw Smith was also experiencing the decline in income and prestige common for Anglican clergy during these years. In March 1950 he told his congregation that he had just bought a car from a doctor heading off to the mission field. "Hitherto I have generally hidden our battered old car behind the Church or at the side," he wrote in the parish magazine, "but in future you will see our smart green one at the front among the Rolls Royces!"[3]

Stott settled quickly into a range of duties in the parish. He led youth clubs, organized evangelistic events, preached sermons, and made pastoral visits to homes in the parish. He was eager to learn the ropes from his experienced rector, but seven months after his arrival Earnshaw Smith was laid up in bed with what turned out to be the first in a series of debilitating illnesses. This meant more responsibility for Stott, who started editing the parish magazine, preaching more often, and launching initiatives of his own, such as the Active Service Fellowship for lay evangelism. What he lost in apprenticeship he gained in experience. It is clear from Stott's comments in the parish magazine that he assumed his new responsibilities with relish.

Earnshaw Smith died in March 1950 after an attack of cardiac asthma. The choice of successor was a complicated process. The All Souls church council had a say, as did the Bishop of London, but there was another layer of complexity because All Souls was what was known as a Crown living. This meant that the appointment of the rector was finally the monarch's prerogative, and conversations about Earnshaw Smith's successor therefore included the Prime Minister, his patronage secretary, and the king. The church council worried that a non-evangelical might be foisted on them, and asked that Stott be considered for the post. Stott agreed to put his name forward, and three months later King George VI approved his appointment. "I never dared even to pray that I might be given the privilege of being your new Rector," Stott wrote in the parish magazine, but he did not seem to have been particularly surprised.[4] He knew he had the gifts and the energy needed to run a large London church, and everyone could see the congregation had already been growing under his leadership. His work at All Souls was the heart of his ministry for the next twenty years.

Toward the Conversion of the Parish and England

One week after Stott heard of his appointment, he preached a sermon in All Souls telling the congregation his vision for the church. He called it his "Five-Point Manifesto." Based on the description of the early church in Acts 2, Stott said that the church should come together in study, fellowship, worship, prayer, and evangelism. But Stott's language and later his efforts gave pride of place to the last of these. Under the parochial system of the national Church of England, each church was responsible for the Christian instruction of the population that fell within its parish boundaries, and this was a responsibility the new rector took very seriously. "May our Church be a *Centre of Evangelism,*" he said in his manifesto sermon. "All Souls with St. Peter's is a Parish Church. Our first duty is local, and yet our impact on the neighbourhood is small and the percentage of Christians in the population negligible. The multitudes are outside."[5] Later that summer, Stott returned to the same theme in the church magazine. "The question which rests most heavily on my heart at present," he wrote, "is how to reach the hungry multitudes who are without Christ. We are not unmindful of the fact that many come to St. Peter's who do not live in the parish. Nevertheless, God has entrusted to us the care of some 10,000 souls living within the parochial boundaries."[6] In October, he told his congregation that "the thronging multitudes who live between Baker Street and Tottenham Court Road, New Cavendish Street and Oxford Street may never have a chance of hearing the glad tidings of a Saviour who died to redeem them and lives to empower them, unless we tell them."[7]

The major influence on Stott's longing for the conversion of his parish was Richard Baxter. Baxter was an English Puritan whose 1656 *The Reformed Pastor* had long provided inspiration for earnest Protestant clergy in the English-speaking world. Stott read the book while still at Cambridge, and it had given him a thrilling picture of tireless ministry.[8] Baxter wrote:

> The ministerial work must be carried on diligently and laboriously, as being of such unspeakable consequence to ourselves and others. We are

seeking to uphold the world, to save it from the curse of God, to perfect the creation, to attain the ends of Christ's death, to save ourselves and others from damnation, to overcome the devil, and demolish his kingdom, to set up the kingdom of Christ, and to attain and help others to the kingdom of glory. And are these works to be done with a careless mind, or a lazy hand? O see, then, that this work be done with all your might![9]

In the seventeenth-century English debates over church government, Baxter sided with those who had little time for an elaborate church hierarchy. It was practical, gospel ministry that really mattered, and he wanted the national church to be little more than a federation of parish churches where the clergy taught the gospel to those under their care. Baxter stressed that "the work of conversion is the first and great thing we must drive at," and Stott concurred.[10] The dream of seeing hundreds of his parishioners converted was what fired him. He was a faithful representative of the evangelical Anglican tradition, where parish work had long been the top priority.[11]

But Stott's dreams were bigger than his parish. His longings for the parish of All Souls were the basis for a vision for reaching the whole of England. Addressing clergy at a conference for the Anglican diocese of London in 1952, Stott said that if all the churches of England diligently shared the gospel in their local communities, it might "turn the tide" for Christianity in the country.[12] He told his listeners what he was doing at All Souls and urged them to go and do likewise. The following year he brought a similar message to the Islington Clerical Conference, the big annual gathering for Anglican evangelicals.[13] In his parish magazine, Stott told his congregation that if every parish church adopted a strategy like theirs, "it should be possible within a number of years to bring the Gospel to every man's door in England."[14]

What was striking here was not the idea. Parish evangelism was not novel for evangelical Anglicans, and nor was talk of winning the country for Christ. What was striking was Stott's drive and confidence. Stott had become rector of a prominent church before the age of thirty and now just a couple of years later he was speaking at major church meetings and urging people to follow his example. When he started to travel overseas, he took a filmstrip of his All Souls evangelistic program to show to pastors. Stott was not afraid of leadership: he desired, expected, and sought it. In 1950, he had asked Earnshaw Smith to give him the title of Assistant Rector, and he had had the courage to write to a newspaper magnate offering articles for his papers. In both cases, Stott emphasized that he was seeking God's glory, not his own ("I have no desire to be 'Assistant Rector' for the glory of the thing," Stott told Earnshaw Smith, and he assured the newspaperman that he was "seeking neither money nor publicity for myself"), and there is no good reason to doubt his honesty.[15] But here was a young clergyman trying to balance Christian humility with a desire to use his talents and make his mark.

The location of All Souls made it easy for Stott to hope that others would follow his example. London had long been the hub for much of English life, and Stott would not have expected any raised eyebrows when he said that every English road "will ultimately lead you to London."[16] Moreover, All Souls stood at the top of Regent Street in the heart of the city. The church had gained even greater prominence in the 1930s when the BBC built Broadcasting House across the street. Stott was excited by the church's strategic location. This was palpable as the congregation prepared to move back to the restored church of All Souls in 1951. "It is difficult to exaggerate the privilege which has been given us," he wrote in the parish magazine. "Here in the heart of London's West End…we are opening our most beautifully decorated and thoroughly equipped Church of All Souls."[17] There was a sense in which Stott saw All Souls as merely a local parish church, one of thousands of others in England, and this was what he stressed when encouraging others to take up his strategy of parochial evangelism.[18] Yet its visibility, and its location at the center of London's commercial and social life meant that Stott saw the church as "a strategic point with unrivalled opportunities."[19] The hope was that where London led the rest of the country would follow, a geographical expression of the hierarchical vision of English society. When Stott introduced his successor Michael Baughen to All Souls in 1970, he was clear that central London was a step up from Baughen's former parish in Manchester.[20]

Yet closer inspection would have revealed that there were problems, as well as possibilities, inherent in the church's location. All Souls had been built as part of John Nash's plan for Regent Street, which he designed as a new thoroughfare in central London. The church was to serve a socially diverse parish that included both the wealthy residents of Portland Place and the working classes congregating in the streets east of the church; but it was orientated toward the former. This was partly owing to the church's traditional design: with an altar at the eastern end, it had to open up westwards onto

Langham Place and therefore toward the more expensive streets of the parish. But this orientation was also a reflection of the place of the church as part of Nash's Regent Street project, for which he had a definite social rationale. "My purpose," Nash told a government select committee in 1828, "was, that the new street should cross the Eastern entrance to all the streets occupied by the higher classes, and to leave out to the East all the bad streets, and, as a sailor would express himself, to hug all the avenues that went to the good streets."[21] In his proposal for the project in 1812, he said he wanted the street to serve as a dividing line between "the inhabitants of the first classes of society, and those of the inferior classes," "a boundary and complete separation between the Streets and Squares occupied by the Nobility and Gentry, and the narrow Streets and meaner Houses occupied by mechanics and the trading part of the community."[22] One only has to walk down Regent Street and compare the number of streets entering it from the prosperous west with the much smaller number entering from the east to see what he meant.

In this context, the date of the construction of All Souls becomes important. After the French Revolution of 1789 the English propertied classes were worried about revolt and enlisted the church in support of the status quo. The situation remained volatile even after Napoleon's final defeat at Waterloo in 1815, with Luddite machine-breaking and the bloody Peterloo demonstration in Manchester in 1819. Anglican clergy threw in their lot with the authorities, often doubling as magistrates. As they became more closely linked with the governing classes, their church lost the allegiance of the bulk of the English people.[23] All Souls did serve the inhabitants of those narrow streets, but its construction as part of a deliberate program of social division and even social control presented it with a tangible expression of the problems faced by many Anglican churches in their attempts to reach the working classes.[24]

As Stott thought about how to reach his parish, he thought first about the church's services. For Stott, salvation came through hearing God's Word, and that typically happened in church. So he set about designing services for the unconvinced and unconverted. Known as guest services, these were held on the second Sunday evening of each month, and from 1955 a guest service was also held once a quarter in the morning.[25] The idea was to have regular, well-publicized, specifically evangelistic services so that "keen members of the congregation" could "bring to them their non-churchgoing and uncommitted friends" to hear the gospel.[26] In form, they were an amalgam of Anglicanism and revivalism, with a slightly abbreviated form of the traditional service of morning or evening prayer, an evangelistic sermon, a follow-on meeting for people who wanted to learn more, a special prayer that those who wanted to commit their lives to Christ could recite, and an invitation for people to come forward and testify to their new faith.[27] In the follow-on service, those who stayed were presented with the ABC of how to become a Christian, the same outline that Nash had used with Stott on the day he was converted—people were encouraged to *admit* their sin, *believe* in Jesus' death as the sole means by which their sins could be forgiven, and then ask Christ to *come* into their lives.[28] It was a revival meeting with liturgy and robes.

Stott kept using the Book of Common Prayer despite the recognition that the services, which required more than one service book to be used intelligently, were confusing for non-Anglicans.[29] This is what evangelical Anglicans did in these years. Before the revisions of the church's liturgy in the 1960s and 1970s they stuck to their service books, with a special fondness for the Book of Common Prayer. People unfamiliar with the liturgy received "some explanatory comments" but not much else.[30] Stott, who had been an accomplished singer and cellist at Rugby and a member of the chapel choir at Trinity College, Cambridge, was steeped in the liturgy and musical culture of the Church of England. His commitment to it was very clear in the parish magazine. Worship was to be "dignified," and care was taken to ensure that the congregation was instructed in the proper conduct of the liturgy. "Good enunciation" was important.[31] The church had an instrument to encourage musical refinement: the new organ at All Souls had been designed and built by the firm that had built the instruments at St Paul's Cathedral, Westminster Abbey, and Salisbury Cathedral, and the British Arts Council used it for recitals.[32] The church choir also put on concerts, singing works such as Bach's *St John's Passion* and Stainer's *Crucifixion*.[33] Psalters and clerical robes were still the order of the day when Stott stepped down in 1970.[34]

But before his parishioners would come to the guest services Stott had to make contact with them, for the great majority of them did not attend the church. He therefore decided to train lay people to visit every home in the parish, sharing the gospel and inviting people to services as they went. The idea of training the laity for evangelism was certainly not new in the Church of England. Stott seems to have borrowed many of his ideas from the Church Army, an Anglican evangelistic organization that specialized in parish evangelism and evangelism training. The organization had close links to All Souls in the 1940s: Stott spoke at a Church Army campaign in a parish near

Wembley during his first year at the church, and All Souls had a Church Army worker on its staff, Phoebe Jordan.[35] Stott worked closely with Jordan—for a while they were the only two on the church staff—and it is likely that much of the inspiration for the church's evangelistic initiatives came from her and the Church Army. For example, Stott's training scheme for evangelistic workers bore similarities to a Church Army course that All Souls people attended.[36] Maurice Wood, a leading evangelical Anglican who acknowledged his debt to the Church Army, was implementing a similar program at St. Ebbe's, Oxford in the late 1940s and early 1950s.[37] There was little new in Stott's scheme for parish evangelism.[38]

However, Stott was not too worried about originality. He just wanted the work of evangelism to get done and knew that there was no way he could do it on his own. As he put it in his manifesto sermon in 1950: "The task is beyond the power of the clergy. A staff of 10 … could not do it. There are only two alternatives. Either the task will not be done, or we must do it together, a task force of Ministers and people thoroughly trained and harnessed as a team for evangelism."[39] Equipping his congregants for evangelism was therefore a top priority. Before the end of 1950 the first training school was announced, a course designed to produce a "well-trained task force" to reach the parish for Christ. Stott gave lectures on "The Theology of the Evangel," "The Life of the Evangelist," and "The Technique of Evangelism," and there was an exam at the end. Those who completed the course were commissioned by the Bishop of Willesden in an annual service, becoming official "Commissioned Workers" of the church. The principal task awaiting them was house-to-house visitation, knocking on all the doors of the parish and sitting down with everyone from wealthy doctors to immigrant seamstresses to tell them about Jesus. Over time there was some diversification, so that visiting the sick, nurturing new Christians, and youth club leadership were also options. But door-to-door evangelism was the priority. By 1957, 316 people had been commissioned. Stott regularly appealed for more to join the ranks (especially men), for they were the hands and feet of his plan to reach his parish. How they were received on the doorsteps of Portland Place and Grafton Way would prove decisive for Stott's plan of evangelism.[40]

There were other evangelistic ventures. The church ran open air services at the Oxford Circus underground station. People went "fishing" with evangelistic tracts on the busy streets around the parish. There were lunchtime services during the week, advertised by loudspeakers. Youth clubs met in the evenings, and there were gatherings for international students.[41] There were also many ministries devoted to nurturing Christians: at one church meeting in 1952 Stott used the language of the postwar welfare state, saying that the church "cater[ed] for all ages from the cradle to the grave."[42] But Stott's strategy to reach his parish with the gospel was at the heart of his work at All Souls. His longing was that All Souls would be a model for local evangelism that was successful and imitated, toward the conversion of England.

Fruit and Frustrations

As he looked down from the pulpit Sunday by Sunday, the new rector saw lots to encourage him. The numbers at St. Peter's were growing steadily as Stott took over, and it was not long after the move to the significantly larger All Souls that its 900 seats were filled morning and evening.[43] By 1955, Stott announced that they were going to have to relay services to St. Peter's church because "there are days . . . when it is hard for some to secure a seat."[44] Numbers on the electoral roll (roughly equivalent to the church's membership) had never topped 300 in the 1930s and 1940s, but averaged over 760 between 1955 and 1970.[45] Confirmation candidates averaged twenty-eight in the first three years of Stott's time at All Souls and forty-one thereafter.[46] Some of the growth was doubtless owing to Christians moving from other congregations, but many of the new faces were new converts. Looking back on ten years of guest services, Stott wrote: "Not once as far as I can remember, has there failed to be a response from some who have come forward seeking Christ or professing faith in Him."[47] In 1958, the chair of the church's evangelistic committee reckoned that the number of such commitments was about 200 each year.[48]

All Souls was one of many evangelical churches thriving during these years. The electoral roll at Maurice Wood's church, St. Mary Islington, grew steadily in the 1950s and held its own in the 1960s, despite a major purge of the roll in 1965. At Emmanuel Parish Church, Northwood, Middlesex, the trend was similar. At St. Helen's Bishopsgate in the City of London, Dick Lucas's congregations grew from fewer than twenty communicants when he was instituted as rector in 1961, to 400 at the weekday lunchtime services and 100 on Sundays by the early 1970s. Christ Church, Chadderton, flourished in the 1950s and 1960s. All this happened at a time when the total numbers on Anglican electoral rolls were declining. Numbers more than halved between the early 1950s and the mid-1970s at two of the most famous Anglo-Catholic churches in central London, All Saints Margaret Street and St. Alban the Martyr, Holborn. The membership of other non-evangelical churches in the center of London also declined during these years.[49]

Evangelical churches flourished for many of the same reasons that Stott's university ministry did. The postwar era, with its deference and moral earnestness, was excellent soil for evangelical Anglicans who were conservative socially, as well as theologically. And as Dominic Sandbrook has argued, this cultural conservatism continued into the 1960s for many, when a lot more people grew their own vegetables than bought Beatles records.[50] One index of people's concerns in Stott's parish was the local newspaper, the *Marylebone Mercury*. In the 1950s, it was filled with indignant reports on local crime. On June 1, 1951, the front page alone carried articles on "Systematic thieving," "Overcharged for nylons—two fined," "She stole again," "French girls from convent school admit shoplifting," "Mother guilty of murder," "Widow's 'low-down' theft," "Admitted theft on first day," "Grave injury to public," and several other crimes.[51] People wanted righteousness, and Stott's preaching attracted them. He too worried that "the morals of the country" were "at a low ebb" and that most people had "no conscience about it."[52]

Michael Ramsey said that conservative evangelicalism flourished after the war because of "the craving for authoritarian security" but the reality was more complex.[53] Yes, people did want security, but if they had wanted authoritarianism there were churches that offered that much more convincingly than All Souls. Stott's message and manner were always more authoritative than authoritarian, and they were combined with an openness to the broader culture and a commitment to many of the values of the English establishment. All Souls flourished because it combined a definitive message with a degree of openness: the well-educated people who came to the church did not have to deny the rest of their social world to come to All Souls.[54] In this context, the Bach concerts and emphasis on enunciation take on added significance. All Souls was a comfortable and appealing place for many of those who agreed with the sort of conservative values being broadcast by the BBC next door during the 1940s and 1950s.

When one looks at the type of people who came to All Souls, several groups stand out. Many non-Anglicans, or nonconformists, attended. This sort of move to the established church was becoming increasingly common among Baptists, Congregationalists, and others. It reflected the weakening of nonconformist identity as the political clout its churches had exercised in the nineteenth and early-twentieth centuries diminished and as the IVF spread interdenominational bonhomie among students. Social aspirations had long attracted many university-educated nonconformists toward the established church, with all the useful connections it provided.[55] All Souls was especially welcoming, with Stott in the vanguard of those who insisted that Anglican Communion tables should be open to people from other denominations.

Many of London's Christian students made All Souls their church home, and Stott's high profile in the IVF ensured that the church was a logical choice for evangelical graduates new to London.[56] There were plenty of professionals: the church had a system of lights for on-call doctors, and there was a separate congregation at St. Peter's where the All Souls clergy ran shorter services aimed at professionals and their children. By the mid-1960s, there were approximately seventy children from this congregation away at boarding school.[57] Over time, more and more people from overseas made their home at All Souls, but these were typically students and not the Caribbean immigrants who found many English churches so unwelcoming.

All Souls attracted lots of women. They regularly made up two-thirds of those confirmed and the bulk of the commissioned workers, and in a list indicative of the most common professions of All Souls members—"shop assistants, typists, secretaries, nurses and teachers"—it is the female bias of these jobs that stands out.[58] The church was predictably conservative on gender: the Church of England required its clergy to be male, and an insert in the parish magazine encouraged women to submit to their husbands and raise their children.[59] This fits with Callum Brown's characterization of the English churches as transmitters of conservative values. But to picture All Souls as a bastion of conservative gender roles and values would be wrong: the church allowed women to have meaningful (although still subordinate) roles in the evangelistic work that was the center of the church's life, and mini skirts were permissible.[60]

Stott was thus surrounded by young women. Yet unusually for an Anglican minister, he decided to remain single. Of course, a romantic relationship between a senior pastor and a member of the congregation would have been awkward, and Stott became rector of All Souls when he was only twenty-nine. Even before that time, however, he had shown little interest. Rugby and Trinity College were all male, and Nash was a bachelor who challenged his charges to be single and therefore undistracted for the work of the gospel. Stott did not seek out female company, and he had few opportunities for regular, normal interaction with women other than his secretary, his house-keeper, his cook, and his co-worker, Phoebe Jordan. On his account, he did consider pursuing a relationship twice, but pulled back on both occasions.[61] As a teenager, Stott had had the expected crushes. He was not averse to warm relationships. It does seem, then, that Nash was the key figure here. And it seemed to work for Stott. He found Nash's vision of singleness for ministry more attractive than any of the women he met, and as he moved through his twenties he saw the freedom it gave him to work extraordinarily long hours. Once he started doing university missions and traveling overseas, a family could have really cramped his calling and his career. After the trauma of his rift with his parents, Stott knew how demanding and difficult close relation-ships could be, and his itinerant ministry was too important. Born from his relationship with Nash, Stott's singleness made his extraordinary commit-ment to ministry overseas possible.

Over time, Stott did develop a close friendship with one woman, his sec-retary Frances Whitehead. Approximately five years Stott's junior, Stott hand-picked her for the role, and she served him for over fifty years. Her duties included everything from typing, to bookkeeping, to driving with him down to his writing retreat in Wales. One of his study assistants, who was able to watch their relationship closely, said that Whitehead gave Stott "the personal developmental advantages of being married without being married."[62] She worked almost as hard as he did, giving up her private life to work for Stott.[63] Her mother called Stott a slave-driver.[64] Initially, Whitehead received little public recognition but after a couple of decades Stott started to express warm thanks in the prefaces to his publications.[65] In 2001, he cheered for her in a book preface on the occasion of her receiving an honorary masters degree from the Archbishop of Canterbury for her work as his secretary—almost certainly at his suggestion.[66] She was also starting to appear in photos with Stott, including the one celebrating his honorary doctorate from London Bible College in 1998. The final photograph in a published collection of trib-utes to Stott pictured Stott and Whitehead together in his study; the book's dedication was "to Frances Whitehead, without whom this portrait would have been very different."[67] Stott was no longer the severe professional he had been in the 1960s; he had mellowed, and he valued Whitehead's faithful com-panionship more and more as he aged. It was an affectionate, devoted rela-tionship of two people who had both sacrificed any hope of family for the sake of Stott's ministry. It would be surprising if neither of them had ever thought of marriage to the other. Stott talked about Whitehead in terms usually reserved for spouses, expressing his hope that he would pre-decease her.[68] She became Aunty Frances to go with Uncle John. But Stott remained single, while Whitehead, still working in her eighties, basked in a little reflected glory from a famous man she respected.[69]

By the late 1950s, however, Stott was getting frustrated. Simply put, there were not enough converts. "The masses are not in the least impressed by us," he said in a sermon in 1958. "They see nothing in us to arouse their interest or concern. They consider our Christianity irrelevant. They shrug their shoulders and steer clear of us if they possibly can. A thousand horses would not drag many of them to church."[70] In a sermon the following year, Stott raised the question of the effectiveness of the church's witness. "Oh," said an imaginary interlocutor, "don't you know? We have our annual training school, and our commissioned workers, our house-to-house visitors and our regular guest services." "Yes," Stott replied, "but are we content with this, when only a trickle of people are finding Christ? Have we no concern for the thousands who live in our parish, who are strangers to the love of God in Christ?"[71] Five years later, he was worried that the guest services might "degenerate into a fruitless exercise in 'preaching to the converted.'"[72] The church was still full, but as congregations and confirmation candidates fell from the peaks that had sparked hope of revival, this was not enough.[73] Stott's parish evangelism was running into difficulties in similar ways to his university ministry.

Stott was especially disappointed that his parish had not responded in the way he had hoped. Back in 1951, as he contemplated the reopening of All Souls, Stott had hoped that people from the parish would start coming to church. He encouraged his congregation to "extend them a warm, unselfish welcome as they begin to come back."[74] But they had not come to the church before it was bombed and did not come in the 1950s. In his 1967 book *Our Guilty Silence* Stott outlined his strategy for the training of lay evangelists and door-to-door visiting in the parish in terms very similar to those used in his 1952 address to the London Diocesan Conference. The plan had been in operation for more than fifteen years, but it was plain from Stott's comments in the book that the response had been meager. What the dedicated visitors saw was not scores of conversions, but rather "the size of the gulf in contemporary England which separates the masses from the Church."[75]

The use of the word "masses" suggests that it was the working classes of the east end of his parish that Stott had in mind here. After all, All Souls had plenty of educated and professional people, to such an extent that in one sermon Stott could refer to his congregation simply as "a middleclass [*sic*] bourgeoisie."[76] Another of his sermons made the class composition of All Souls very clear:

> Let us examine ourselves. If we have domestic servants, do we treat them as human beings to be considered, or as underlings to be bossed around? Are we on friendly terms with our neighbours, or do we perhaps not even know them? How do we run our business and care for our employees? If we are landlords, what do our tenants think of our Christianity? If we are shareholders, do we take an interest in the enterprise in which we have invested our money, or are we only bothered about fat dividends? How do we treat the tradesmen who come to our door? Are they living people, or mere appurtenances of the vehicles in which they deliver our goods? Are we considerate and courteous to the assistants from whom we buy in the shops? Have we any loving concern for our friends, relatives or neighbours, who may be poor, lonely, sick, depressed and need our friendship and love?[77]

From the beginning, Stott had wanted to see the diversity of the local population represented in the congregation, but despite his efforts and the efforts of the commissioned workers, such diversity was elusive.[78]

Why did the working classes not come to All Souls? The people of Fitzrovia, as the area east of the church was known, were a very diverse group—socially, ethnically, and religiously—but few of them would have felt at home in a pew at All Souls. There was a strong Jewish presence in Fitzrovia, especially on Hanson Street and Cleveland Street.[79] There were Catholic immigrant communities from Ireland, Cyprus, and Spain, who went to the Catholic church of St. Charles Borromeo on Ogle Street.[80] Even for many of those whose family had been in England for generations, All Souls would have been a very foreign place. This was largely owing to the growing estrangement of much of the English working classes from the Church of England since the end of the eighteenth century.[81] For many, Christianity and especially the Church of England were associated with the powerful and the wealthy, and people from the lower classes were frequently put off by the accent and lifestyle of the clergy.[82] Many would have seen themselves as Christians but did not see regular churchgoing as necessary.[83] And Stott's practice of not baptizing children unless he was sure that their parents had a solid grasp of the Christian faith surely alienated many working-class people in the parish, for whom infant baptism would still have been important.[84]

To make matters worse, the rise of the welfare state had severed many of the traditional charitable links between the churches and the working classes.[85] In 1957, All Souls formed a Social Action Committee to discuss the church's responsibilities to its neighbors, but it found that "in the Welfare State, provision is made to cover practically every aspect of economic and material distress."[86] One woman who lived in the parish during this time recalled that she took no notice of the wealthier classes and what they were doing—they lived in an entirely separate world.[87] The cultural differences were huge. All Souls was a church of Bach not beat groups, received pronunciation not regional accents. Stott may have seen the "multitudes" of his parish as "hungry," but few were interested in what All Souls had to offer.[88]

Over time, Stott became more and more aware of just how great was the cultural gap between people like him and those who lived in Fitzrovia. By the mid-1950s, he was admitting that they would not be crowding into All Souls any time soon. He decided to plant a mission hall, a center for services, youth clubs, and other forms of community work in the parish's east end. This was not entirely new at All Souls: the church had run a variety of services in Fitzrovia for years.[89] But what became the Clubhouse was a substantial and costly initiative. Announcing the venture in 1956, Stott made the obvious point: "Our services in All Souls are not altogether suitable for the members of the parish who are resident between Euston Road, Tottenham Court Road, Mortimer Street and Great Portland Street. We need simple, non-liturgical services for them."[90]

Stott's language here was significant. There were hints of condescension toward these people who needed "simple" services, or "homely mission services" as he also called them.[91] Other members of the church's clergy had similar attitudes. "I wonder," wrote one of Stott's assistants in the parish magazine, "whether you have ever strolled away from the stately precincts of Portland Place and the lovely Georgian streets which grace the west-end of our parish into that crowded area bounded by Euston Road, Tottenham Court Road and Goodge Street. The bustle of business (especially the dress trade!), the variety of nationalities and the large number of everyday folk are some of the facts which strike you." He went on to describe a new initiative to try to reach these folk, a parish paper, whose style was to be "similar to that of the cheaper daily papers—'chummy, punchy and gossipy!'" "We especially hope," he continued, "it will be 'readable' to the man in the street."[92] Another assistant minister quoted one Clubhouse regular who, when visiting the toilets at a motorway rest stop on a trip to Coventry Cathedral, was overheard saying,

"It's gotta thing wot dries yer 'ands autimatic."[93] These patronizing attitudes vitiated the church's attempts to reach the people of Fitzrovia.

Such condescension was unsurprising in the 1950s. The cultural gap that existed between the church's private boarding school-educated ministers and the English working classes was immense and serviced by very few bridges. The sort of people who lived in Fitzrovia might have listened to the American Billy Graham but life was much harder for an upper-class Englishman like Stott.[94] The English elites showed little interest in working-class culture. In the early years, Stott displayed little sense that clergy from different backgrounds might be better able to relate to the people of Fitzrovia: his first handful of assistant ministers were all men from the elite boarding schools and Oxford and Cambridge. This was the time when Jim Packer wrote to Stott asking to join the church staff as one his assistants. Packer went on to become one of the leading figures in Anglican evangelicalism, but there was no post available at All Souls. Even if there had been, however, Packer would have been an unlikely fit: he had never been to one of the top private schools.[95] Stott was a compassionate pastor, giving up his bed on occasion to the homeless, but it was not obvious to him in 1950 that his poorer neighbors might find the Queen's English a turn-off.[96] When it did become obvious, the result was separate services for separate classes and the acknowledgment that All Souls was a church for the well educated, who listened gladly to Stott's learned preaching, his impeccable accent, and the refined music.

The Clubhouse opened in November 1958, funded largely by the members of All Souls. It soon became a popular recreation spot for local young people. "They are a very cosmopolitan lot," the Clubhouse leader wrote in the parish magazine, "Greek and Turkish Cypriots, with a mixture of Chinese, Indian, Italian and Spanish. You will find Church of England, Greek Orthodox, Roman Catholic, Muslim and Jew."[97] Mods, members of a popular working-class subculture of the time, also started coming. But the work of evangelism was hard. People did make decisions to invite Christ into their lives, but it often seemed as though there was little enduring difference.[98] For Stott, the response was still disappointing. And the problem was not just that these people seemed distant from Christ. It was also that their lack of response undermined a fundamental assumption that Stott had learned from Rugby, Cambridge, and Nash: that where society's leaders went, the rest would eventually follow. The conservative, hierarchical vision of society sounded good in theory, but when Stott tested it in his parish he found that reality did not match. This helps explain why Stott moved away from his instinctive conservatism as the 1960s progressed.

Stott was also disappointed that fewer middle- and upper-class people were making their way to All Souls and to Christ. The church was still a great success on almost every measure, but Stott wanted revival and ultimately the conversion of England, not just success. By the late 1950s it was plain to Stott and other English evangelicals that the revival they had thought might be coming in the heady days of the Graham crusades had not occurred. As the editor of the evangelical magazine *Crusade* put it in 1959, Graham's Harringay campaign "was not the beginning, as some hoped, of imminent revival in the land."[99] When Graham failed to fill stadiums in Manchester and Glasgow during his 1961 visit to Britain, the situation looked bleak indeed.[100] For Stott, the story at All Souls was the same as the one at the universities: fewer outsiders seemed to be interested in listening to what he had to say.

As Stott looked at England in the 1960s he saw rapid changes in the society he had grown up in, a society that had seemed so permanent and so right. The conservative England of the 1950s, still proud of its defeat of Nazi Germany and with a beautiful queen and patrician Churchill at the helm, had given way to a less self-assured version. This was obvious to all when Britain got rid of most of its remaining colonies in the 1960s, which made life especially difficult for the country's traditional elites. The journalist Peregrine Worsthorne had recognized as early as 1959 that the changes in Britain's world role presented a challenge to the upper echelons of a hierarchy that looked increasingly unstable as its imperial base crumbled.[101] During the 1960s, British leadership came to be symbolized by the chic of Carnaby Street, not Whitehall, by the Beatles, not Churchill, and this was a problem for Stott and others who had profited from the moral seriousness and sense of national destiny that the empire had encouraged. The upper-middle classes no longer saw their future in the civilizing service of empire, and therefore saw less need for the Christianity that had long helped to justify it. When it became clear that Britain was not ruling the waves, or anywhere else for that matter, as it had, "perceptions of British society as a divinely ordained and successfully functioning hierarchy were much diminished."[102]

As the 1950s gave way to the 1960s, deference and earnestness were out and satire was in.[103] The establishment came in for more and more criticism. This was especially hard for Anglican clergymen, who were the target of one of the most famous set pieces of the satire boom, a farcical sermon by Alan Bennett that caricatured the upper-class accent of many clergy (including

Stott), made fun of their mawkish homiletical ploys, and questioned their intelligence and integrity. Declining prestige now followed hard on the heels of declining income. One sign of how much things had changed was that the most famous of the satirical television programs, *That Was the Week That Was*, was shown on the BBC—that long-time bastion of establishment values. To make matters worse for All Souls, it was the middle and upper classes, the sort of people who might have been drawn to All Souls, who were tuning in to these programs. As the 1960s went on and as newspapers and television became increasingly daring, more and more stories came out that made the comic seem tragicomic. The most famous was a sex scandal in 1963 in which John Profumo, the Conservative government's Minister for War, was forced to admit to having sex with a prostitute who was also sleeping with an attaché from the Soviet embassy. The establishment looked outdated, unprincipled, and effete.[104] For Stott, this was very disorientating. His English heroes tended to be upper-class and socially secure Christians such as Charles Simeon and William Wilberforce, but they gave little help on how to live in an era when those at the top of the pile were publicly scorned.

Callum Brown has argued that the crucial factor in church decline in Britain during this period was the rise of a new feminist movement that took women away from the churches. Women had long been the backbone of most churches, including All Souls, and once they felt free not to be religious the results were catastrophic. Brown attributes this shift to the replacement of the old version of pious, sacrificial, nurturing femininity by a vision of freedom and enjoyment found in women's magazines and other media.[105] Hugh McLeod has challenged this view, and explained the decline in church-going in terms of other social trends. People's incomes were rising, and as they bought televisions and cars they had more options for what to do on Sundays. The rise in home ownership led to an increase in "do-it-yourself" projects that kept people busy refitting their kitchens and bathrooms at the weekends. Joining anything was going out of fashion, with political parties, dance halls, and sports clubs all seeing memberships decline during the decade.[106] A gardening boom was symbolic of this growing shift in British life from the public to the private sphere.[107] Some evangelicals recognized that they were not the only ones suffering from a drop in interest—the editor of *Crusade*, for example, noted after Graham's 1961 visit to Britain that the-aters, ice rinks, and even prominent politicians were finding it as difficult as the churches to get people out.[108] But this was scant consolation. Especially hard hit, McLeod points out, were gender-specific activities, such as attending soccer matches and church. A new picture of marriage that emphasized friendship led more couples to do more together. And McLeod suggests that it was this, more than feminist ideas, that meant there were fewer women in church in 1970 than there had been ten years earlier.[109] The permissive society did not help, however. In a subsequent article, Brown presented strong evidence that the growing number of people in favor of premarital sex were less likely to go to church regularly.[110]

The tide was now firmly against Stott. The *Marylebone Mercury* carried adverts for a school of strip tease and suggestive pictures of dancing girls. Some Harley Street doctors advertised their abortion services in foreign newspapers and paid commissions to taxi drivers who brought women to their consulting rooms. And a clinic round the corner from All Souls saw a stream of women from stores and offices in the West End who wanted to take the new birth control pill. Stott was certainly not prepared to follow the lead of another local vicar who put pictures of local "dolly birds" into his parish magazine, nor the one who held a beauty pageant at the church fête.[111] Now the sermons at All Souls were more at odds with the contents of the local newspaper. This was bound to make it harder to get people in and get them converted. And it made it harder for Stott to dream about the conversion of England.

Stott addressed the cultural changes going on around him in a sermon at All Souls in May 1968. He provided a depressing picture of contemporary Britain.

What would Amos [the biblical prophet] say if he were to visit England today? He would surely pronounce the same message of judgment. Why? Because our streets are filled with lewdness, our shops with shameless pornography and our statute books with permissive legislation, condoning homosexual practices between consenting adults in private and granting abortion on easy terms; because our community life is marred by social and racial prejudice and we have not learned to care for the good of all; because one bride in six is pregnant on her wedding day and one birth in twenty is illegitimate; because throughout the entire United Kingdom all crime figures have increased every year for the last twenty years; because New Scotland Yard have three-and-a-half million criminal records and register more than one thousand new convictions every day; because of the increase of drug addiction, sexual promiscuity, venereal disease, robbery with violence, black magic and spiritism; because our nation has turned from the righteousness and the religion inherited from our fathers; because many many [*sic*] church leaders have rejected the word of God, preferring and propagating lies instead.

Indeed, has not the judgment of God already begun to fall? Since World War II England has declined from greatness to mediocrity. It is not just that former colonies have been granted political independence (for this was right and necessary), but that economically and politically, in international and domestic affairs, the stature of our country has steadily shrunk. Any observer can see both our loss of prestige overseas and our religious and moral decline at home. Are these two trends not connected? The Roman Empire fell to internal moral corruption before it fell to the armies of marauding barbarians.[112]

As Stott looked at England in the late 1960s, he saw little reason for hope. The country was under the judgment of God for its sin. For Stott, however, this sin included not just drug abuse, illicit sex, pornography, racism, and crime, but also sins of the soul—magic, spiritism, and the abandoning of Christianity. Britain's decline was "religious and moral." Stott saw God's hand in Britain's international and economic decline, and although he made it clear that he approved of the dismantling of the British Empire there is a wistfulness here for the days when Britain was great. And for Stott, it had been great because it was Christian and upright. In the 1940s and 1950s, Stott saw his country as a Christian one that needed to be revived. By the late 1960s, he was lamenting the demise of Christian England.

However, cultural changes are not enough to account for the declining response at All Souls. Some of the evangelical Anglican churches mentioned earlier in the chapter were holding their own or even growing during this period—resilience that was remarkable as the Church of England hemorrhaged members in the 1960s (confirmations dropped 40 percent).[113] All Souls, by contrast, was shrinking—there were empty seats when Stott gave up the day-to-day responsibility for the church in 1970.[114] To understand the full picture, we must go back to the late 1950s and look further at how Stott responded to the disappointments he was facing in his parish.

Response and Retirement

Initially, Stott placed his hopes in a revival. What the church needed was a supernatural visitation of the Spirit of God. "We need 'revival,' " he told the congregation in late 1959. "There is an awakening desire throughout the Church that God will intervene in mighty power and manifest His glory and holiness among us," he wrote in the parish magazine in March 1960. "We are becoming increasingly dissatisfied with the life of the Church as it is. So much of our worship is perfunctory, our fellowship is superficial and our witness ineffective. The multitudes of our country go on their way untouched by the gospel. It seems that nothing can alter this situation but a manifestation of the Holy Spirit's presence in power." Three months later he returned to the subject: "Some of us can thank God that He has led us in recent months to see that what the Church needs above all today is . . . *the power of the Holy Spirit.* This is why we speak about 'revival.' " Three years later he was still on the same theme. "We need 'revival,' a mighty supernatural visitation of the Holy Spirit in the community. Nothing else will save our Church from its spiritual torpor or our country from lapsing into complete paganism." Further examples could be multiplied almost at will.[115] Stott's desire for revival was fuelled by reports in 1960 that some of the miraculous gifts associated with Pentecostalism had emerged in an Anglican church in southern California. Before long several of the clergy at All Souls, including Michael Harper, had experienced a similar awakening. Stott was hungry for revival and wondered whether this was the answer to his prayers.[116]

This was not comfortable ground for Stott. When he addressed his congregation's fears about revival in a sermon in November 1959, he was also preaching to himself:

> Perhaps the very word "revival" conjures up for us scenes of emotional exuberance, to which there is a deep-seated aversion in the British character. We are reserved and shy. Most of us are timid Timothys. We abhor fanaticism. We are lovers of decorum and the golden mean. Extremes and enthusiasms embarrass us. But there is no need to be anxious! The God who bids us "stir up" the gift that is within us has also given us the spirit of power, love and self-control.[117]

Stott had reservations about the idea of revival. But once the religious interest of the mid-1950s began to fade, revival seemed to be the only hope for the re-Christianization of England. And for the sake of the gospel, Stott was willing to lose face with all those other upstanding Englishmen who would have been horrified and full of scorn if a supernatural revival had come to All Souls.

Stott watched the All Souls clergy who claimed a fresh infusion of the Spirit, hopeful that it would lead to extra fruit in their ministry and in particular a stream of conversions. When this did not happen, Stott came to the conclusion that this was not the revival for which he had hoped. In the end, Stott decided in late 1963 that the Pentecostal doctrines of what became known as the charismatic movement were unbiblical.[118]

Stott had been praying for revival since the late 1950s and there had been no sign of it. He was now twice-shy about revival.[119] The word had been co-opted by the charismatics and it suddenly and almost totally dropped from his vocabulary. He had contemplated the possibility of social ostracism and considered trading access for angularity if the latter would bring conversions, but when the conversions did not come Stott looked for other options.

The question was how could he win a hearing for the gospel in an increasingly apathetic climate. Stott had always been concerned to craft his presentation of Christian truth to make it relevant to his hearers, but the new situation called for heightened efforts.[120] A turning point came in 1967 with the arrival from New Zealand of a new assistant minister at All Souls, Ted Schroder. Schroder believed that the fresh cultural mood demanded a fresh apologetic approach. "We fail to adjust our approach to the contemporary scene at our peril," he wrote in the parish magazine. "If we don't bother to relate our faith in Christ to the problems of our day we are irrelevant."[121] Schroder was responsible for a series of creative evangelistic initiatives, including a gospel folk group, visiting underground clubs in the seedy streets of Soho, and handing out tracts with Che Guevara quotations at demonstrations.[122] He drew some attention from the *Marylebone Mercury* with a series of talks for unmarried young people on sex.[123]

Schroder helped Stott to be bolder in his attempts to contextualize the gospel. Stott began to talk about "relevance" a good deal more. He tried to introduce services that used modern English rather than the antiquated English of the Book of Common Prayer. He also started to address contemporary issues in his sermons, although it was obvious that, unlike Schroder, he found this awkward.[124] In one sermon he raised the subject of sex: "I would prefer not to," he complained, "because everybody seems to be most unhealthily preoccupied with sex today. Nevertheless, because of this it seems necessary to say something Christian about it."[125] More will be said in chapter 5 on the reasons for Stott's growing preoccupation with social issues, but part of the explanation was his desire to win a hearing for the gospel in late-1960s London. As fewer people showed interest in listening to what he was talking about, Stott determined to spend more time talking about what they were talking about. He was not willing to sacrifice the dream of pervasive, Christian cultural influence and focus on those who still shared his view of the world.

Yet a few years later, Stott left his parish ministry in central London to devote his time to writing, church politics, and a global preaching ministry.[126] Stott had, of course, always been involved in ministry outside his parish, conducting student missions, writing books, speaking at conferences for clergy, and playing a role in wider church affairs. But as the 1960s went on these endeavors took up more and more of his time, with a predictable impact on his involvement at All Souls. The 1950s and early 1960s had been full of fresh initiatives at the church, but there were far fewer in the second half of the decade. By contrast, every year seemed to bring a new major commitment beyond the parish. Stott also wrote much more in the 1960s, producing twice as many books as in the 1950s.[127] Stott's attention was drifting away from his church. His editorials in the parish magazine were increasingly consumed with matters of wider church politics rather than parochial affairs.[128] Simply put, Stott was not as devoted to the work at All Souls after 1963. In one staff meeting Ted Schroder accused him of not paying attention, and Stott later admitted that the conversation had not interested him and that he had "switched off."[129] Eventually, all this produced obvious discontent in the staff and the congregation, and in one sermon one of his assistant ministers gave a parable of the church as a garden that was prevented from flourishing because of the shadow cast by a great statue in the middle.[130]

On September 20, 1969 Stott told the church council that he wanted to stand down. "The need for better pastoral oversight of both congregation and staff has become increasingly apparent in recent years," he said. "The present inadequacies are due largely to my growing extra-parochial commitments." Far from wanting to rein in those commitments, Stott felt that he "should be more free" to devote himself to "wider responsibilities." He believed this was God's will for him.[131] The council accepted his proposal unanimously that very day. Fifteen months later, Michael Baughen took the helm and within a few years All Souls was bursting again.[132]

Some of the explanation for the declining response at All Souls, therefore, lies in the changing priorities of its increasingly busy rector. This becomes even more apparent when we set it against other evangelical Anglican churches that held their own during this period. Indeed, the real congregation at All Souls dwindled even more than the head count on Sundays, given that growing numbers of those who attended were evangelical pilgrims who had heard Stott overseas and wanted to visit his home church. The explanation for the declining congregations at All Souls, then, is much more complex than any simple story of secularization or the death of Christian Britain.

Speaking of his retirement many years later, Stott said, "I felt I had given the Church all I had to give."[133] He was tired of parish ministry after twenty-four years and running out of ideas.[134] Stott wanted to see the people who lived in his parish turn to Christ; when they did not, he started the Clubhouse, tinkered with the format of guest services, and changed the emphasis of his preaching. But his fear that the guest services would become an exercise in preaching to the converted was becoming a reality and he was not sure what to do about it.[135] He could have tempered his ambitions by focusing on the middle classes who still came to church, but he had little interest in a bland, homogeneous congregation. There was Schroder's vision of preaching the gospel in fresh ways for a changing culture, and Stott went on to call evangelicals worldwide to do just that, but it was a very hard task to actually do it at home in London. Stott talked about being radical, but it was difficult to adjust to a new culture that he found disturbing and depressing.

Michael Baughen, by contrast, was much more enthusiastic about adapting church life to the 1960s and 1970s. Ten years Stott's junior, he insisted on the use of first names on the church staff. He was the founder of the Jubilate group that composed and published fresh hymns. When he arrived at All Souls, he was quick to adjust services that he saw as fusty. Older members of the church were upset, and some complained that the church was being run only for its youth, but Baughen persevered.[136] He was also keen to change the church's interior, telling the congregation that he had seen people fleeing when they had seen the pews and communion table.[137] Under Michael Baughen, All Souls was at the forefront of a major change in Anglican evangelicalism where churches became less formal and more contemporary in a range of different ways, including worship, dress, and church furnishings. Some of the roots of British popular music lay in clubs within a mile of All Souls, but it was only as jazz, folk, skiffle, and eventually rock became part of middle-class youth culture that aspects of these types of music started making their way into churches like All Souls.[138] Along with many other evangelical churches, All Souls adapted to many of the cultural changes taking place around them, and continued to thrive in the later decades of the twentieth century.

When Stott became rector of All Souls in 1950, he dreamed that the church would be a model of evangelism and part of a national movement of revival. In the mid-1950s, it seemed as though his dreams were coming true, as his guest services bore fruit and the church flourished. The church continued to attract hundreds every Sunday throughout his time there, but there were not enough conversions to sustain his hopes of revival. Stott grew disappointed and distracted. For if the flourishing and well-trained congregation of All Souls could not make a major impact on its parish, how could it be a model for other churches? Moreover, the stagnating response of the educated classes and the decline of deference meant there was no use passing off lack of success with the working classes with reference to the hope that a growing number of evangelical leaders would be able to turn the country around in the future. By almost any measure, Stott's ministry at All Souls was a success, but over time it became nearly impossible for him to see a way to the conversion of England. This helps explain why Stott devoted more of his time to ministry overseas, to places where God was obviously at work.

But Stott's years at All Souls had been crucial. They had given him a taste of success, and helped his rise to prominence. Being rector of a parish at the heart of one of the most powerful cities in the world before the age of thirty marked him out as one to watch. Even if they had never heard him in their home country, evangelicals visiting London would invariably go to All Souls in the hope of hearing Stott preach. In addition, the fact that Stott had been the senior minister of a church for two decades gave him a credibility with other pastors that he would otherwise have lacked. In all these ways, Stott's years at All Souls laid the groundwork for his global renown.

4

Anglicans

JOHN STOTT WAS a cradle Anglican. The Church of England was the church of his birth, the church of his school, the church of his college, and the church of his ordination. Stott was an Anglican before he was an evangelical, growing up in a culture where it was assumed that if you were English you were Christian and you were Anglican unless you said otherwise. At his conversion, Stott rejected the idea that one was a Christian simply by virtue of churchgoing and moral decency, but he continued to see a strong link between Anglicanism and Englishness.[1] For Stott, the Church of England was "beloved."[2]

This chapter charts the story of Stott's growing involvement in his church. In the 1950s, he showed minimal interest in national church affairs, but this changed dramatically in the following decade. The shift illuminates important cultural changes in British society and Stott's evolving ambitions. Once he had decided to throw himself into church politics, Stott worked on the unity and policy that evangelicals would need to make an impact. How he did so and how he fared are major parts of this chapter. The story tells us a great deal about Stott, about the Church of England, and about the nature of evangelical religion in that church and beyond. Ironically, it also helps explain why Stott eventually made his greatest mark outside England.

Beginnings

During the 1950s, Stott was committed to the Church of England primarily because he believed it offered unparalleled opportunities for evangelism. Most people in England still identified with the established church, however vaguely, and it seemed logical that these people were most likely to come to Christ through the church of their baptism. Stott loved the music, the liturgy, and the theology of Church of England but, like Eric Nash, he loved it most because he believed it was "the best boat to fish from." Stott did not go as far as T. S. Eliot, who said that "the idea of a Christian society ... can only be realized, in England, through the Church of England," but in practice he held a similar position.[3] He longed to see people converted, and saw the Church of England as the most likely means for that to happen.

However, Stott thought the Church of England was in a sorry state. There were too few clergy, he believed, and the clergy there were had often been so emasculated by modern theology that they did not know or preach the gospel. Many parish churches were poorly attended, even in the 1940s and 1950s. So although the national church looked like a perfect tool for evangelism, it was a dull one. Stott's solution came straight out of Nash's book: more evangelical clergy. It was all well and good to dream of parish evangelism across the nation, as Stott had in the 1950s, but Stott knew that in practice that required lots of evangelical ministers.

In the mid-1950s, there were signs of hope. In 1954, Stott told the All Souls congregation that "one of the most encouraging signs of the Holy Spirit's working at the present day is the number of young men, particularly in the University Evangelical Unions (associated with the Inter-Varsity Fellowship), who are offering themselves for Ordination." "Perhaps no one need is greater for the welfare of our beloved Church of England," he went on, "than that the men now offering for Ordination should be men of God."[4] But as encouraged as he was, Stott wanted more. Less than a year later, he lamented that "the annual number of men offering [for ordination] is woefully short of the needs of the country, let alone the world."[5] Stott wanted lay people to be involved in ministry, but he believed that the health of the church was dependent on its leadership.[6] And from the heart of the British Empire, it made sense to say that Anglican clergy were vital for meeting the spiritual needs of the world. Stott regularly asked men at All Souls to consider ordination, and between 1957 and 1975 thirty-five entered the Anglican ministry.[7]

It was a good time to encourage young men to serve in the Church of England. Overseas mission, long a favored destination for devoted evangelicals, was losing much of its luster in the postwar years as the British Empire dwindled. Before the war, evangelical Anglican newspapers had been filled with advertisements from groups as diverse as the Church Missionary Society, the Barbican Mission to the Jews, the Zenana Bible and Medical Mission, and the Colonial and Continental Church Society, but after 1945 such adverts were much less common. More and more of those going into vocational ministry were drawn to ordained ministry in England.[8] The conservative evangelical Bible Churchmen's Missionary Society sent out forty-nine clergy in the ten years after 1925, but only nineteen in the 1950s.[9] The growing number of evangelical clergy in England after the war was in part a reflection of the declining commitment to overseas mission. But evangelicals in the Church of England were thrilled. Those who watched the ordination statistics began to think that the future of the church belonged to them.[10]

Stott also wanted to ensure that evangelical clergy held fast to their evangelical beliefs. The Church of England was not a comfortable place for conservative evangelicals. Their views were often the object of ridicule from other members of the church, as the fundamentalism controversy of the mid-1950s had shown. There was always a danger, therefore, that evangelicals would lose their nerve and go theologically soft. So at the high point of the fundamentalism controversy, Stott started the Eclectic Society in 1955 to encourage these young evangelicals to stick to their theological guns. If ever there was a time when Anglican evangelicals might have made a decisive shift to a more populist stance, unconcerned with what their social and ecclesiastical peers made of them or did to them, it was in 1954–55. But Stott did not want to forsake the church that he knew and loved, and he continued to believe that the Church of England was key for the spread of the gospel in England. Despite all the interdenominational camaraderie of the Billy Graham missions, Stott decided to start this new organization to nurture Anglican evangelical leaders. Stott was never going to be a British Billy Graham—his address at a large evangelistic meeting in Bristol in January 1955, for example, received no attention in the local press.[11] But he was an insider in the English establishment and was determined to work as one.

The name for the new society was significant. Suggested by one of Stott's assistants at All Souls, it was borrowed from an eighteenth-century society of evangelical moderates who wanted to shape the Church of England from the inside.[12] This was in contrast to another group of eighteenth-century evangelical Anglicans, led by John and Charles Wesley, whose innovative ideas finally led to a break with the established church and the formation of the Methodist church. Nash had prayed that God would raise up another Wesley to bring revival to England, and in his biography of Stott Dudley-Smith suggests Nash might have felt his prayer was being answered in Stott.[13] But Wesley was never one of Stott's heroes. As Dudley-Smith points out, Stott's imagination had been captured by CICCU hero Charles Simeon, an evangelical from Cambridge who worked to increase evangelical influence in the Church of England in the late eighteenth and early nineteenth centuries and who had been a member of the original Eclectic Society.[14] Stott was a much more conventional character than John Wesley. Yes, Stott tinkered with tradition in his guest services at All Souls and irritated his bishop on occasion. But he did not want to strain the structures of the established church, as John Wesley had. He wanted to use them.

The Eclectic Society flourished. It soon had to subdivide, and by 1966 there were seventeen groups across the country, with more than one thousand members.[15] It was obviously meeting a need for fellowship among evangelical clergy, and a good deal of credit accrued to the person who had recognized the need and filled it. Stott was already a rising star among Anglican evangelicals by 1955, but the Eclectic Society increased his visibility and his stature. The leadership of the liberal evangelicals in the Church of England at this time was graying, and Stott was well positioned to lead a new movement of the growing numbers of conservative evangelical clergy coming out of Nash's camps and the IVF.[16] He could have worked through existing structures, such as the theologically broader Fellowship of Evangelical Churchmen, but instead he chose to form his own organization. He decided who joined (at least in the early days), ensuring that they were theologically conservative and loyal. Limiting members to clergy under forty kept out senior evangelicals, whose presence would have diluted his leadership. As the society spread, Stott became the doyen of the conservative evangelicals. According to the *Church of England Newspaper*, he had "an affection and loyalty from hundreds of young clergymen" that had to be "seen to be believed."[17]

The success of the Eclectic Society emboldened Stott to launch other ventures. Of greatest significance here was the founding of the Church of England Evangelical Council and the Evangelical Fellowship in the Anglican Communion in 1960–61. The context was the 1958 Lambeth conference, which brought together bishops from Anglican churches all over the world. This gathering "saw the Anglican communion discover and affirm itself as an international and inter-racial Christian fellowship," and several evangelical Anglicans saw a need for more effective international cooperation to further the evangelical cause in the communion.[18] This led to the formation of the Evangelical Fellowship in the Anglican Communion (EFAC), and the Church of England Evangelical Council (CEEC) was founded at the same time to be the English member of this international fellowship. Stott was a prime mover behind both. Whereas the Eclectic Society was a private affair, here were two organizations designed to defend evangelical belief in the church.

This seemed essential to Stott and other evangelical Anglicans in the early 1960s. They were very worried that changes being made to the internal law of the Church of England (known as canon law) would reflect the theology of the dominant Anglo-Catholic wing of the church, and as Protestant and law-abiding sorts this filled them with horror. Under Jim Packer's leadership, Latimer House in Oxford was becoming a theological think tank for evangelical Anglicans, but Stott and others felt more was needed. Marcus Loane, an Australian bishop and author of the very Protestant book *Masters of the English Reformation*, played an important role in encouraging English evangelicals to take a stand on the doctrines of the Reformation.[19] An article introducing EFAC to the readers of an evangelical journal stressed that evangelicals could no longer "afford the luxury of isolation" in view of Anglo-Catholic teaching that threatened the "Protestant and Reformed" heritage of the church.[20] Talbot Mohan, one of EFAC's founders, raised the specter of "the accelerating process of the catholicizing movement."[21] Stott's tone was less fearful, but as he introduced the EFAC and the CEEC to the readers of the All Souls magazine, the emphasis was still on the need "to bear witness with courage and clarity to the great Biblical and Reformation principles."[22]

The rationale for the EFAC was clear enough, but the decision to form a new organization, the CEEC, to be its English member group was more curious. There were already several organizations that were English, evangelical, and Anglican, notably the Church Pastoral Aid Society (CPAS), Church Society, and the Fellowship of Evangelical Churchmen, but there is no record that Stott or the other EFAC founders negotiated with any of them, let alone suggested that they should be the English part of EFAC. Some of the reason for this was that these organizations had slightly different briefs; one of the CEEC's founders saw no conflict with his position as Secretary of CPAS.[23] But it is still remarkable that Stott, along with Oliver Barclay (his old friend from Cambridge), Talbot Mohan, and several others decided to form a new organization so easily. The result was a rigorously conservative organization that they could control. To get it, they simply took an informal group to which they all belonged and rebranded it as the Church of England Evangelical Council.[24] Significantly, this former group was the firmly conservative Inter-Varsity Fellowship's Church of England Group. There were definitely other streams of evangelicalism in the established church. But for people like Stott conservative evangelicalism was what really mattered, and the founding of this new organization with its implicit claim to represent genuine evangelicalism in the Church of England was a political move. In no way was the group representative of the breadth of evangelical belief in the Church of England.

They soon ran into difficulties when they approached evangelical bishops whom they wanted to sponsor the organization. Three out of four simply refused, recognizing the hubris of a new group that was not "sufficiently representative of evangelicalism," and although the fourth agreed he was soon wanting to pull out for the same reason.[25] Stott expressed his fear that "we might appear to others as representing an extreme wing of the Church of England," and he was right.[26] Desperate not to lose their one episcopal supporter, the members of the council discussed changing its name to make it sound more representative. Stott suggested dropping the definite article, and the council accepted his proposal without dissent.[27] The change mollified the bishop, but Church of England Evangelical Council was linguistically awkward and it proved impossible to keep the definite article and the claim it made out of the title. Three years later it reverted to the Church of England Evangelical Council.[28]

Stott had still not made his mark in the debates of the Church of England: he remained preoccupied with student missions and his ministry at All Souls and had little time for ecclesiastical politics. But his feet were wet, and before long he would become much more involved in Anglican affairs. The turning point was 1962.

1962

Anniversaries of the English Reformation were very important for evangelical Anglicans. Celebrating key moments of the Reformation provided them with regular opportunities to remind each other of the noble and very Protestant tradition to which they belonged. In 1936, it was the four-hundredth anniversary of William Tyndale's martyrdom; in 1938 the four-hundredth anniversary of Henry VIII's decision to place an English Bible in every parish church; in 1961, the three-hundred and fiftieth anniversary of the publication of King James I's Bible.[29] One group of no-nonsense Protestants urged people to celebrate Reformation Sunday with extra gusto in 1958 because it marked the four-hundredth year since the death of Catholic Queen Mary.[30] As 1962 dawned, many evangelical Anglicans knew that it was the three-hundredth anniversary of the last revision of the Book of Common Prayer, and this particular anniversary was loaded with significance. On the bright side, the last major victory for Anglican evangelicals had been in 1927–28, when the British Parliament had rejected a revised version of the Prayer Book and retained the older, more Protestant book of 1662. More ominously, the church was still dominated by Anglo-Catholics who remained intent on revision. Evangelicals worried that if a revised prayer book went through, they would no longer be at home in their church.[31] And here another event from 1662 seemed portentous, for in that year hundreds of committed Protestant clergy (including one of Stott's heroes, Richard Baxter) had been forced out of the Church of England because they refused to agree to new demands for uniformity in religious practice in Charles II's England.

Protestantism was not just a matter of religious conviction in Britain. For a long time, it had been at the heart of people's understanding of what it meant to be British. Since the reign of Elizabeth I, England and then Britain had defined itself as a Protestant nation, and the wars it fought against Catholic Spain and France were part of a struggle between truth and error, good and evil, liberty and despotism. A desire to counter Catholic gains in the Americas helped spur British expansion in the New World.[32] As late as the 1920s, it was possible for people to see a revision of the church's Protestant Prayer Book as "an Act of National Apostasy."[33] By 1960, however, such sentiments were fading fast. There were not many who still believed the story that Britain had become great since the sixteenth century because of its stand for the truths of the Reformation. Stott was one who did.

Stott and his fellow evangelicals wanted to call their church back to its Protestant roots. Stott contributed to a series of books celebrating the Reformed theology of the Prayer Book.[34] In 1962, the CEEC wanted to make a statement on prayer book revision and decided to publish its own series of books. Under Stott's editorship, this eventually became the *Christian Foundations* series, twenty-two books that each presented an evangelical perspective on some area of Anglican doctrine and practice. When the idea originally came up in the CEEC, the intent was to publish a contemporary evangelical equivalent of the nineteenth-century *Tracts for the Times* that had put John Henry Newman and the Catholic Oxford Movement on the ecclesiastical map and changed it completely.[35] However, in the end the *Christian Foundations* series was very different from the *Tracts for the Times*. For while Newman was combative, even rash, and risked alienating the church authorities, the new series made reserved statements of theological positions that their authors argued were authentically biblical and historic.[36] Sent to numerous bishops in the Anglican communion, these books were not punchy pieces of propaganda, but rather sober apologia for the acceptability of conservative evangelical beliefs.[37] Stott and his friends were in the strange place of feeling on the backfoot yet believing that they were the representatives of genuine, Protestant Anglicanism.

The best insight into Stott's own thinking in 1962 comes from a series of sermons he preached at All Souls under the title "Evangelical Principles, or Christ's Controversy with His Contemporaries." Later published as *Christ the Controversialist*, these sermons argued that "the great theological principles for which evangelical churchmen stand today were clearly enunciated by Jesus nearly two millennia ago."[38] The take-home message of the sermons was that evangelical Protestants followed Jesus while Catholics (Roman or Anglo-) were like the Pharisees and the Sadducees in their attitudes toward things like Scripture, worship, morality, and salvation. On worship, Stott enthusiastically celebrated Thomas Cranmer, the principal author of the Book of Common Prayer.[39] In a sermon on authority he drew a sharp contrast between Catholic reliance on church tradition and the evangelical and Reformed commitment to Scripture.[40] In the published version of the sermons, he went so far as to call pre-Reformation Catholic priests "despotic."[41] Marcus Loane also came to speak at All Souls in 1962, and Stott recommended his *Masters of the English Reformation* to the congregation.[42] Stott was thoroughly Protestant. He did not align himself too strongly with any particular strand of Protestantism, notably refusing to sign up to the Calvinist theology of the Puritans that was popular among evangelical leaders such as Jim Packer and Martyn Lloyd-Jones.[43] Rather, he followed his hero Charles Simeon, who believed that systematic theology of any sort tended to lead its advocates to twist the meaning of Scripture. However, Stott was in no doubt about the historic teachings of the Protestant Reformation and the dangers of Catholic doctrine.

The year 1962 was very significant for Stott: "If every schoolchild knows what happened in 1066," he wrote in the parish magazine, "every church member ought to know the importance of the year 1662."[44] However, 1962 proved to be the year when Stott was forced to realize how quickly England was severing its Protestant roots.

In July 1962, every member of the British parliament received a letter from England's two Anglican archbishops, Michael Ramsey and Donald Coggan. As the two processes of canon law and prayer book revision inched forward, the archbishops raised the question of how such changes should be tested and approved. Historically, any changes to the law or liturgy of the Church of England required the approval of parliament, and it was parliament's opposition that had doomed the 1927–28 revised prayer book. So now the archbishops wrote to ask for permission to depart from the Book of Common Prayer and experiment with new services without official sanction from parliament.[45] This was worrying indeed to Anglican evangelicals who had come to see parliament as their ally against Anglo-Catholic reformers in the established church. So Stott and three other leading evangelicals decided to write a letter of their own to the members of parliament.

One can only imagine the ire with which Ramsey and Coggan read the evangelicals' letter. The authors challenged the archbishops' contention that the new services had the support of "the great majority in the Church," arguing that the church's councils were obviously unrepresentative. Parliament still had a role to play, therefore, to counterbalance "clerical domination" and "protect lay-folk from abuse." They spoke of how the archbishops' proposal would be controversial at a time when the church was in such a state of "doctrinal confusion," which suggested a not-yet approach to revision yet seemed disingenuous in view of the profound unlikelihood that the Church of England would ever not be in a state of doctrinal confusion. The established church had "a religious responsibility for the whole nation," they went on, and "since its Protestant character was fixed at the Reformation it ha[d] exerted a continuous influence for good upon our English life and character." Therefore, "any weakening of the historic links between the Church and the nation would be deplorable."[46]

Stott knew that the letter was unlikely to win him friends in the church hierarchy, but he hoped that it might win influence in parliament and beyond. What he found was that almost no one cared. As far as the press was concerned, there was almost total silence. *The Times* carried an outline of the letter's contents, but no leading article or correspondence followed.[47] *The Daily Telegraph* said nothing. There was no impassioned discussion in the *Church Times* or the *Church of England Newspaper*.[48] In parliament, there was a debate on Church of England affairs the following month that made reference to the evangelicals' letter, but what stood out was not harsh, Protestant polemics—despite the efforts of Captain Orr from the Northern Irish constituency of Down South—but rather the way in which (as *The Times* put it) the debate was marked by "tolerance, faith, hope, and charity."[49] The bulk of the MPs in the house that day saw no problem in allowing the Church of England to remain established while having greater control over its forms of worship and internal discipline.

To make matters worse, Eric Fletcher, an MP who said that Stott and two of the other signatories on the evangelicals' letter were personal friends, charged them with threatening to cause disestablishment. If the church approved changes, Fletcher argued in the House of Commons, and the group he called "the extreme evangelicals" then asked parliament to intervene, that would be what produced an insistent demand for disestablishment.[50]

We know that Stott read the debate because Fletcher sent him a transcript the following week, and we know that Stott was considering an appeal to parliament because he said so in an article in the *Church Times* in March 1963.[51] But what the response to the letter and the parliamentary debate had made abundantly clear was that such an appeal would have little point, for they demonstrated that the old, Protestant platform had little resonance in 1960s Britain, little attraction, and few supporters in the place that mattered, the House of Commons.[52]

Stott and his friends were facing a sea change in British cultural and national identity. Protestantism had been one of the strongest pillars of British identity in the eighteenth and early nineteenth centuries, and the prayer book debates of 1927–28 showed that it was still standing. But the independence of most of Ireland, the fighting of two World Wars alongside the old, Catholic enemy, France, and the crumbling of Britain's great empire had done much to erode this pillar, and it disappeared almost completely during the 1960s.[53] Talbot Mohan recognized this at the time and quietly lamented it, saying that "the Englishman has abandoned his inherent and perhaps unreasoning antipathy to Rome."[54] This trend away from Protestantism as a focal point for British national identity accelerated during the 1960s, as both British imperial power and Anglican attendance declined markedly. John Wolffe has suggested that the two declines were likely related, and there is good reason to think that the decreasing need for a sense of national mission in Britain's reduced circumstances contributed to a weakening of Christian sentiment in Britain.[55] As the imperial tide receded, people were faced with growing questions of what it meant to be British, and with church attendance now a minority interest there was little hope that Christianity, still less Protestantism, would be central to that identity. One evangelical leader suggested at the time that "a healthy church is more likely in a land where there is a confident national awareness," but such confidence had been in dwindling supply in Britain ever since the Suez Canal crisis had laid bare Britain's imperial impotence in 1956.[56] There was now little hope for those who wanted to drape themselves in the Union Jack and talk about the importance of Protestantism. Although the 1950s awakened evangelicals' hopes of revival, the 1960s brought a rude reaffirmation of their cultural marginality.

This was very unsettling for Stott and other evangelicals. For hundreds of years, English Protestants had looked to parliament for support, often with success. The sense that Britain was a Christian nation with a Christian government that cared about the morals and faith of the nation ran deep. But now it seemed that parliament did not care that much. In truth, the idea that parliament had always been firmly Protestant was a myth—it had offended determined Protestants regularly since the sixteenth century, not least when Richard Baxter and others felt they had to leave the church in 1662. But it was now obvious to Stott that playing the parliament card or the Protestant card was not going to work.

However, the danger of a catholic drift in the Church of England had not gone away. Stott therefore needed to find news ways of combating it. His answer was to become more heavily involved in the debates of his church. From 1962 on, there was a marked increase in Stott's engagement in national church affairs.

There were no other good options. Secession was a possible step, and one that a few Anglican evangelical clergy took around this time, but Stott had no interest: the Church of England was still strategic and beloved. Alternatively, he could have stayed in the church and ignored what its councils handed down, but after the founding of CEEC and EFAC this would have seemed like admitting defeat. Indeed, the arguments he had already made against the archbishops' proposals had already all but committed him to becoming more involved—one of his reasons for appealing to parliament was that the councils of the church did not represent the views of the laity, but those councils were fast becoming much more representative in the 1960s.[57]

Stott also decided to devote himself to church affairs for more personal reasons. This was the period when his ministry at All Souls was falling on leaner times and when the revival he had hoped for failed to materialize. But there were more and more evangelical clergy in the Church of England, and so winning back the ground lost to Anglo-Catholics in previous generations seemed a realistic goal. If the conversion of England was not going to come through parochial evangelism in the short run, might it come in the long run through making the institutional church more evangelical? By the late 1960s he was telling people to get involved in the church and not sit around waiting for revival.[58] It is likely that Stott was also motivated by a desire for greater responsibility within the Church of England. Such a transition to a ministry in the wider church was expected for talented Anglican clergy, who typically did not stay in parish ministry for very long.

In 1959, Stott became one of the Queen's chaplains, a largely honorific appointment with few responsibilities and no authority. But the appointment showed that he was not beyond the pale and as the most prominent leader of conservative evangelicals in the Church of England it was realistic for Stott to hope for a bishop's crook and mitre. By 1969 he believed he would probably be offered them some day.[59] This put him in a very different position from most evangelical leaders in places like the United States, who had no hopes of ecclesiastical promotion. Where evangelicals were not in an established church with a clear career ladder, the ability to win a hearing was all that mattered. Billy Graham exploited the democratic culture of the United States to gain a huge following and the ear of presidents. By contrast, Stott's desire to make his mark led him to pour his energies into the internal politics of his church. Back in the late 1950s and early 1960s, Stott's superiors still saw him as an irksome character: when he was hauled before the Bishop of London and told to stop allowing non-Anglicans to participate regularly in communion at All Souls, he refused to comply.[60] But from the mid-1960s, charitable and constructive engagement with non-evangelical Anglicans became his modus operandi. He saw that bishops had power and wanted to have that sort of influence himself. Stott never became theologically vague out of a desire to ascend the church hierarchy, but his growing conviction that ecclesiastical involvement was right and necessary meshed nicely with his own hopes for promotion.

In 1662, one of Stott's heroes, Richard Baxter, had decided that he could not accept the new deal in the Church of England and left the church. Three hundred years later, Stott responded to the changing relationship between church and state in a decreasingly Protestant Britain by deciding to throw himself into ecclesiastical politics.

Rallying the Evangelicals

Stott knew that he could not save or change his church on his own. So he started to rally his fellow Anglican evangelicals to more active engagement in the debates and politics of the Church of England. This was a difficult task. Many conservatives had long been wary of non-evangelicals in their doctrinally diverse church who they were sure were wrong and who they suspected were not even Christians. This had been Stott's own position. But as the Church of England became increasingly democratic, especially after the opening of the church's new representative body, the General Synod, in 1970, involvement and success in the church's debates seemed the only way to ensure that the church continued to feel like home.

Getting people involved, however, was only part of the challenge. For Stott knew that evangelicals were adept at squabbling, and that reaching agreement on what evangelicals should be arguing for was going to be difficult. Stott dealt with these questions in a memorandum to the CEEC in 1965. He began by noting "our disastrous evangelical disunity," which he believed was the greatest obstacle to evangelical influence in the church. He described three groups that were prone to quarrel: academics, who liked theological principle and worried when people started talking about what was expedient; diplomats, who called for realistic compromises; and Protestants who wanted to defend the doctrines of the Reformation. "We shall never influence the Church of England for the gospel," Stott went on, "unless the three streams to some extent converge and form a confluence."[61]

None of this was news to the CEEC. But his next move would have shocked some of those who read the initial memorandum, for what Stott called for was "a common policy," and for the CEEC to be "*exclusively devoted* to the formulation of policy." Evangelical church politics had often been about a conference here and a clique there. Influence was to be gained incrementally, and the best ideas would win. But here Stott was recommending something much more deliberate and structured, something more akin to mainstream politics where parties organized to achieve their ends. Unity and therefore success could be theirs if the movement's leaders on the CEEC worked out what evangelicals should be arguing for, and then other Anglican evangelicals toed the line.

The key event for this strategy became the National Evangelical Anglican Congress, scheduled for 1967. Here, hundreds of evangelicals from across the country would gather to show their strength and affirm a common policy. The congress was not Stott's idea, but when others suggested it in 1964 he responded enthusiastically and was soon chairing the organizing committee.[62] Here again Stott and others opted to create new structures rather than work with or build on old ones, for Anglican evangelicals already had a conference that gave evidence of their growing strength, namely the Islington Clerical Conference. As with the founding of the CEEC, critical here was the desire of Stott and others for their own, decidedly conservative entity. Islington brought together people from across the evangelical spectrum; Stott, the CEEC, and others involved in the planning of the Keele congress wanted it to give a clear, conservative evangelical message.[63] But by omitting the adjective conservative from the title of the National Evangelical Anglican Congress the organizers were claiming the evangelical heritage for themselves and implicitly excluding others. At least one person recognized this at the time and criticized Stott for it.[64] Stott, however, was unapologetic. That he and the other organizers of Keele were able to pull this off was a testimony to the growing strength of the conservatives, the waning of the liberal evangelicals, and the willingness of many to follow where Stott, Jim Packer (by now the most talented theologian in the movement), and others led.

Several things helped Stott as he worked to motivate Anglican evangelicals to get involved in their church. The first, ironically, was a handful of noisy secessions by Anglican evangelical clergy in the mid-1960s. Two issues pushed them over the edge. One was the 1964 Vestments of Ministers Measure, which made garb with decidedly Catholic connotations legal wear in the Church of England. The other was growing reluctance to fulfill the national church's historic role of baptizing children without asking too many questions about the spiritual state of the parents.[65] However, although these departures rattled evangelical Anglicans, they also encouraged most of them to reaffirm their commitment to the established church. At the Islington Conference in 1965, "the air was thick...with protestations of undying loyalty to 'our beloved Church.'"[66]

Then there was a conference sponsored by the ecumenical British Council of Churches in Nottingham in 1964. The British Council of Churches was the British arm of the World Council of Churches, and both sought to foster unity among the major Protestant churches. For conservative evangelicals, these ecumenical organizations were the epitome of theological relativism. In the mid-1950s Stott had taken part in a series of conversations designed to find common ground between supporters of the British Council and more skeptical evangelicals, but he pulled out of what he saw as a pointless endeavor. But when several conservative evangelicals went to the conference in Nottingham in 1964 they discovered that they had more in common with their non-evangelical brethren than they had anticipated. They found that people listened to what they had to say.[67] Getting involved in their own church would surely be no harder. This conference was also the high tide of ecumenism in twentieth-century Britain, setting as it did the target of uniting all Britain's churches by 1980. However Pollyannaish this resolution may seem with hindsight, it was a powerful encouragement to serious discussion between different denominations, and one that gave extra incentive to Anglican evangelicals to shape the future of their church.

Some of the evangelical clergy at the 1964 conference were representative of a younger generation who had been converted, nurtured, and ordained in the era after defensiveness had given way to growing confidence in the Anglican evangelical community, and they were therefore more open to and optimistic about involvement in the Church of England. Protestantism was not a rallying cry to which these younger evangelicals responded, but they were keen to be conscientious members of their church.[68] As early as 1963 people were recognizing the emergence of this new group in the evangelical fold, and with one of their number, John King, as editor of the *Church of England Newspaper* there were plenty of opportunities for them to air their views.[69]

The most dramatic moment in Stott's struggle to get Anglican evangelicals on board with CEEC's vision for greater evangelical influence in the Church of England was his confrontation with Martyn Lloyd-Jones at the Evangelical Alliance's National Assembly of Evangelicals in October 1966. Lloyd-Jones was one of the most influential evangelical leaders in the country. He was the pastor of Westminster Chapel in central London, where his long, erudite sermons introduced many to the Puritans and their Calvinist theology. He was an imposing figure in the Inter-Varsity Fellowship. He was also Welsh, and his distaste for the established church helped spark the square-off with Stott in 1966.

The Evangelical Alliance, a loose fellowship that united evangelicals from every denomination, had invited Lloyd-Jones to share his views on evangelicals and the ecumenical movement at a large public meeting in London. John Stott chaired the meeting. Like Stott, Lloyd-Jones was disturbed by the decline of Christianity in Britain: "We do not seem to count as the church once counted in this country," he said. He was also concerned about the rising tide of ecumenism, and criticized those who, like Stott, were "content to be an evangelical wing of a territorial church, hoping to infiltrate and show others they are wrong." Lloyd-Jones did not make his solution entirely clear in his address, but he called for "something new," "a fellowship, or association, of evangelical churches." He bemoaned the fact that evangelicals were divided in different churches that more often than not reflected only "an accident of birth": an obvious reference to the English Anglicans among others. "We are living in one of the great turning points of history," Lloyd-Jones declared, and called his listeners to respond by coming together in a firmly evangelical expression of ecumenism.[70] Stott interpreted this as a call for people to leave their denominations, and was worried as he sat by Lloyd-Jones and listened.

On Stott's view, Lloyd-Jones was wrong, but he was a very persuasive and highly respected preacher. Stott also worried that his own presence on the platform might lend support to Lloyd-Jones's position. If some of the Anglican clergy present responded to Lloyd-Jones's appeal and left the Church of England, it would be a blow to his vision for evangelical supremacy in the established church. As he announced the closing hymn, Stott said he hoped that no one would make any rash decisions. Scripture and tradition, he said, were against Lloyd-Jones's position.[71]

This quarrel was pivotal for British evangelicalism, and it has been a matter of debate ever since. Most of discussion has centered on the theological dimensions of the clash. The debate has divided along partisan lines around the central question of who had moved from their earlier position, Lloyd-Jones or the evangelical Anglicans, and thus fractured the shaky conservative evangelical consensus.[72] The debate is not very illuminating: the truth is that both sides had moved, though in both cases in line with their previous positions. Lloyd-Jones's views on ecclesiastical independency were becoming stronger at the same time as Stott, Packer, and others became more committed to ecclesiastical involvement.[73] John Brencher's study of Lloyd-Jones has brought clarity to the debate, especially its analysis of the 1966 blow-up in terms of Lloyd-Jones's desire to emulate those who had taken uncompromising, lonely stances in Christian history, such as Athanasius and Luther.[74]

However, the British cultural and religious context is vital for understanding what happened at the meeting in 1966. Both Stott and Lloyd-Jones had to respond to major changes in British culture in the 1960s. They were committed Protestants at a time when Britain was looking less and less Protestant. To make matters worse the Roman Catholic Church, fresh from its face-lift at the Second Vatican Council of 1962–65, was making ecumenical noises. In addition, Lloyd-Jones had to face the growing irrelevance of nonconformist Christianity in Britain, which had once given Welsh Christians a significant voice in national life. More than twenty years Stott's senior, Lloyd-Jones was less willing to dispense with the Protestant banner and was very worried by the theological relativism and incipient Catholicism that he saw in mainstream ecumenism. He wanted a new ecumenical movement made up of evangelicals, and he knew that the Anglicans' cultural attachment to the Church of England made that much more difficult. Stott still held to Reformation theology, but he also still dreamed of national influence and had no desire to leave his church and go with Lloyd-Jones into the cultural wilderness at the height of his career.[75] This wider religious and cultural context goes a long way to explaining why this particular issue became explosive at this time. Lloyd-Jones and Stott made different responses to the unnerving reality of a post-Protestant Britain. The culture was changing, and Stott wanted to move with it.

Stott's public challenge to Lloyd-Jones steadied wavering Anglican consciences. Yet again, conservative evangelical Anglicans had been invited to look at the possibility of leaving their theologically mixed church and decided to stay put.[76] And at their head, bravely facing up to the call for secession, was John Stott. It was a victory for Stott's campaign to encourage evangelical Anglicans to get involved in their church and a confirmation of his leadership.

But how important were Anglican politics by the late 1960s? Two years before the Keele congress, Stott said that he wanted conservative evangelicals to have the chance to "speak to the Church and nation."[77] But as the gathering approached, Stott trimmed his aspirations, speaking only of a desire to address the church.[78] For although the evangelicals believed they could gain more influence in their church, that church was moving further to the margins of English life. The Protestant pillar of national identity was crumbling, the establishment was still under attack, and to make matters worse this was the decade when the Church of England saw its sharpest numerical decline on record. Stott was calling conservative evangelicals to leave their comfortable, subcultural, evangelical "ghetto" (to use the word Stott used at the time) and get involved with the life of their church just as that church was itself becoming a subculture.[79] It was not a recipe for great national influence, and certainly not for immediate progress toward the conversion of England. The move toward the established church was a conservative one. Ironically, Stott became more involved in the Church of England at the same time as he was lambasting the corrupt establishment in his university evangelism.

The National Evangelical Anglican Congress took place at the University of Keele in April 1967. It brought together a thousand delegates, just under half of them lay people, and gave Anglican evangelicals an opportunity to affirm their doctrinal commitments and to discuss the challenges facing them in church and society. But the conference was a very different one from that initially envisaged by Stott. His vision was of a conference where people came to listen to what he and other CEEC leaders had to say. The speakers would tell the rank and file what evangelical policy was to be, along the lines of the memorandum he had submitted to the CEEC back in 1965. But as the congress approached, a growing number of younger clergy made it clear that they were not happy with this plan. For them, Keele was the new establishment, another example of the sort of old-school hierarchical thinking that they and many other younger people were busily trying to bury in the second half of the 1960s. Leading the charge were some of the young men in Stott's own Eclectic Society. They wanted the congress to include more discussion and to produce an official statement. The idea of a statement was one that Stott warmed to quickly—it would make for a clear expression of policy. Discussion carried more risks, but Stott wanted to keep these younger evangelicals on board and so helped to persuade the rest of the organizing committee on both scores. Stott saw again that evangelicals were not easy to corral. The result was a very different conference. But could greater participation lead to similar conclusions, and perhaps even greater enthusiasm?

At the congress, the delegates discussed six major topics: the church's message, mission, structures, worship, unity, and relationship to the world. A lengthy statement had been drawn up before the congress began, but this was subjected to tortuous revision during the event; Stott was one of the authors at the center of this process.[80] This was his first experience of crafting a conference statement, and it became one of his specialties and an important part of his international influence through the statements of the Lausanne movement. At Keele, the result was a vindication of Stott's program, for it made very strong expressions of commitment to the necessity of involvement in the established church. "We are deeply committed to the present and future of the Church of England," ran section 87; and, to reassure themselves and others in the church, the statement continued: "We do not believe secession to be a live issue in our present situation."[81] Reflecting their commitment, the statement took up numerous matters facing the church at that time and presented a concise, conservative evangelical viewpoint on each, including subjects such as liturgical revision, taking the Eucharist with non-Anglicans, the proposed union of Anglican and Methodist churches, and infant baptism. In each case the statement was in line with what the CEEC desired. At several points, the statement disagreed with the dominant position in the church. This was most noticeable on infant baptism, where it argued that such should only be open to the children of professing Christians and spoke of indiscriminate baptism as a "scandal."[82] The content of the document was contentious, but on the whole it was widely welcomed. It represented a desire on the part of those present to get more involved in the internal debates of the Church of England rather than criticizing from the sidelines or crying out to parliament.[83]

Stott was thrilled as he returned to London. In his parish magazine, he reported that the All Souls delegates had returned "full of excitement" from the congress, where a "remarkable spirit of unity, good humour and serious purposefulness" had prevailed.[84] He wrote to Michael Ramsey (who had given the opening address at Keele "in the hope of doing some good," as he put it) and told him of how he had returned to London "full of thanksgiving to God for His mercies to us."[85] Ramsey had not stayed for the whole event, but Stott was glad to be able to tell him that the congress had "ended on a high note of common resolve to play our part better in the Church of the future."[86] In 1965, Stott had told the CEEC that he wanted unity and policy. Keele had given both. It was a major triumph.

The Coalition Unravels

Before the congress the *Church of England Newspaper* had predicted a split between younger clergy who were eager for the sort of engagement Stott advocated and their more traditional senior counterparts.[87] These suggestions increased Stott's apprehension before the congress and his joy afterwards. The split did not happen, even with the free discussion that had been allowed. But given the constant tendency of evangelicals to argue and part ways, a major question for Stott after Keele was whether the divisions had been healed or merely papered over.

The younger, more open clergy were very happy after Keele. John King called it "exhilarating" and spoke of "sacred cows" that had been "nipped unceremoniously in the rear and have galloped off, making through traffic possible."[88] But Keele soon generated dissatisfaction among those who had been happy with the status quo and who worried about greater involvement in the Church of England. They worried for what was to them a clear and crucial reason: gospel truth. The desire of Stott and others to influence the Church of England demanded a commitment to constructive dialogue, but this implied that conservative evangelicals, who for so long had been sure that they had the truth about God and his good news, could learn from others in the church whom they had derided for so long. Many conservative evangelical Anglicans, like Eric Nash and Basil Atkinson, had been involved with the IVF movement and other groups whose links to fundamentalism produced people more prone to dogmatism than dialogue. But now penitence for past isolation and openness to others were to be the order of the day. It was no surprise that many found this hard to stomach. After all, they had been reared on the conviction that only evangelical Anglicans were true Anglicans, for only they preached the gospel of the Bible and of Reformation Anglicanism.[89] "Many of us find the Church of England a doubtful enough institution to belong to at the best of times," wrote clergyman John Rosser in a letter to the *Church of England Newspaper* a few weeks after Keele, "but to help us we were taught that authentic Biblical Anglicanism was Evangelical Anglicanism. Now it seems we can learn from others. From whom?"[90]

The theme was a recurring one in the letter pages of the paper. Another correspondent asked whether evangelicals had been wrong in saying that they were the ones who stood for the true Church of England: "If we were wrong, why aren't we told plainly that we were wrong and that in reality the English Church always has been officially and legally a happy agglomeration of conflicting views—Scriptural, aScriptural, and unScriptural?... I am finding modern Evangelical gymnastics most confusing."[91] For many, the decision to get more involved in the Church of England seemed to be tantamount to a confession that the evangelical gospel was not *the* gospel. Certainty, not humility, was the more usual intellectual virtue for conservative evangelicals.

An invitation to attend the 1968 assembly of the World Council of Churches (WCC) in Uppsala, Sweden, forcibly brought home for Stott the tension between these conservative evangelicals and their more open counterparts. The Keele statement had made a commitment to ecumenical dialogue, but here Stott was being asked to take a concrete step that he knew would alienate large sections of the English evangelical community.[92] For them, the WCC was theological liberalism writ large, and the council's preoccupation with radical political issues in the mid-1960s made it even easier for conservative evangelicals to write it off as deluded and dangerous. Stott later reported that he felt "in a real quandary... anxious not to contribute to the increasingly self-conscious rift between evangelicals on this matter," but after a good deal of heart-wringing and consultation with several friends, Stott accepted the invitation.[93] He wrote a long letter to the general secretary of the WCC to explain the terms on which he did so. The heart of the letter was a quotation from the Keele statement which, while welcoming dialogue with people from other theological traditions, made very clear that this did not carry the implication that all such traditions were equally true:

> Our desire to engage in dialogue... does not mean that we think all points of view equally valid, or all theological and ecclesiastical systems equally pleasing to God. It means only that we, who know ourselves to

be prone to error and infected by sin, wish to join in conversation with others who are similarly affected, yet learn from the Bible what God by His Spirit has to say to us all.[94]

The length of the letter suggested the complexity of Stott's position, which involved holding to the rightness of evangelical faith, on the one hand, and a willingness to learn from others, on the other.

Stott knew that not all would be pleased with his decision to go, and so in an article in the *Church of England Newspaper* written after the assembly, he decided to quote from this letter in self-explanation and, no doubt, in self-defense.[95] But he also knew that not everyone would be persuaded. The suspicion was growing that the new, more open policy bred theological wooliness and doctrinal compromise.

In 1968, Stott acknowledged that some felt that he and other supporters of Keele had "betrayed ... the evangelical faith."[96] He was certainly in a different place from the young clergyman who had given up on a series of discussions with the British Council of Churches a decade earlier. Over time, Stott had become much more open to other points of view. He was now convinced that engaging with non-evangelicals was the right thing to do. So he refused to retreat, even in the face of pressure from conservative stalwarts such as his old Cambridge friend Oliver Barclay. Barclay was now the General Secretary of the Inter-Varsity Fellowship, and together with the renowned Anglican preacher Alan Stibbs he visited two meetings of the CEEC in 1970 and 1971 to warn Stott and others that they were going down a dangerous road. Stibbs was almost in tears after one of the meetings.[97]

These divisions made concerted action very difficult. In 1973, Stott put on a brave face and said that he was happy that Anglican evangelicals held differing views. It showed that they were not a party with a whip, he argued; and it was a sign of maturity as they showed their willingness to subject all their traditions to the judgment of Scripture.[98] But in practice the challenge for Stott and his colleagues on the CEEC was to try to hold together people of differing convictions with no power other than that offered by loyalty, persuasion, and success. Stott may have been a hero to hundreds of evangelical clergy, but getting them to work together was another matter. Yet, as he had recognized back in 1965, this was what was needed in order to achieve greater evangelical influence in the established church.

The CEEC devoted itself to defining evangelical policy. Stott was at the heart of this effort, especially after his appointment as president in 1967.

Whether people would follow where the CEEC led was another matter, and for the skeptics in particular the key question was whether the new strategy worked, whether greater evangelical involvement led to greater evangelical truth and influence in the church. It was not going to be easy. Evangelicals were still weak at every level of the church's councils, and after 1970 the new and more representative General Synod was happy to ignore those outside its chamber. The result was that there were few victories to celebrate.[99] Their greatest triumph, the narrow defeat of the proposed scheme to unite the Anglican and Methodist churches, was achieved only because of a tactical alliance with Anglo-Catholics who opposed it for very different reasons—hardly the sort of thing to win over the doubters.[100] More typically, the evangelical leaders in the CEEC put their names to unsatisfying compromises.[101]

Even had evangelicals kept ranks, it is unlikely that they would have had much more success. They entered debates whose terms had been set while conservative evangelicals had been politically weak in the Church of England. Anglo-Catholics and other members of what John Maiden has called the Center-High consensus in the church had set the terms, and it proved very difficult to alter them.[102] For example, when it came to designing new services, many of the starting points were taken from the revised prayer book of the 1920s.[103] The lines of the playing field had been drawn by others, and so it was the evangelicals who were accused of partisanship, however hard they sought to justify their positions.[104] Even taking part in the debates posed a challenge, for it meant laying aside the language of the revival meeting and taking up the language of the cloister. It was predictable that Stott and those who moved with him would begin to sound less gospel-centered and more liberal to those who continued to speak their native evangelical dialect. In such circumstances, it was much more likely that evangelicals would be influenced in Catholic directions than that the body of the church would be influenced by the evangelical minority.[105] To make matters worse, the decline of Protestant sentiment in England meant that Stott and his companions could no longer play the anti-Catholic card that had historically been so effective for English evangelicals.

There were therefore few triumphs for the new post-Keele policy, and those who had been skeptical from the beginning became more vocal in their criticism. The CEEC acknowledged the grassroots worries and noted that there were "certain superficial similarities between post-Keele evangelicalism and the earlier liberal evangelicalism" before reassuring themselves that they did not fit the liberal evangelical bill.[106] They were right—the CEEC had not moved away from traditional conservative positions on the nature of the atonement and biblical inspiration as the liberal evangelicals had done in the 1920s. But Stott and the CEEC had become more open to other ideas, and many evangelical Anglicans were still worried about the path that their leaders were taking.[107]

There was a steady stream of criticism from the more conservative wing of the movement. Alan Stibbs publicly criticized Stott's line on the new Communion service.[108] "Have we approached problems within the Church of England as bargainers rather than as reformers?" asked another evangelical in the church press.[109] John Rosser eventually decided that the leading evangelicals had compromised too much and left the Church of England in protest.[110]

But it was not just the conservatives who caused problems for Stott: so did those who were prepared to go farther down the path of compromise. John King, for example, was much less reticent about the need to be political in the church and insisted that compromise was necessary; evangelicals could not claim that they were the only legitimate Anglicans.[111] Colin Buchanan, who later became Bishop of Aston, was similarly frank about the fact that they would have to settle for less than the ideal.[112] The demise of the liberal Anglican Evangelical Group Movement a few months after Keele created more problems. As the conservatives softened their polemics and got involved in church and world, they became increasingly attractive to other evangelical clergy who were looking for a group in the church where they could belong.[113] The Keele party was the main and vibrant option. It became less conservative as a result.

Ten years after Keele, Anglican evangelicals gathered in Nottingham in April 1977 for a second congress. Before the Keele congress, Stott had said that the evangelical wing of the church had been growing in "numbers, scholarship, cohesion and confidence."[114] By 1976, however, as Stott began to publicize the Nottingham congress, cohesion had dropped from the list.[115] As the second National Evangelical Anglican Congress approached, much of the confidence was also notably absent. The *Church of England Newspaper* ran a series of articles reflecting on the ten years since Keele, with titles such as "Dedicated, energetic but slightly puzzled...," "Still not too late if...," and "A feeling of profound unease."[116] In some ways, the congress was a rerun of Keele: John King in the *Church of England Newspaper* suggesting a possible split, and John Stott working to ensure that this did not happen, but in reality the tone was very different.[117] The wide eyes of Keele had given way to suspicious and anxious glances.

The most obvious division at the congress was between two groups that had been barely visible at Keele. One was a large contingent of charismatic evangelicals, who were intent on raising their hearts and hands in worship. They did not make many significant contributions to the theological debates, but the liturgical openness that they showed heralded an important shift among many Anglican evangelicals away from service books and toward more informal and contemporary forms of worship.[118] The other group was made up of academic theologians, who wanted the conference to agree to theological statements that would command the respect of a church that often saw evangelicals as trite and intellectually lightweight. By the end of the first night, reports were coming in that the sessions were above the heads of most of the delegates.[119]

Stott was never going to side with the charismatics—he had decided against their doctrine and their demeanor a long time ago—but the extent of his support for the academics was striking.[120] Stott had effectively been out of parish ministry for over six years by the time of the Nottingham congress, and he had left some of the immediate concerns of the pew behind. Many laypeople had little interest in debates on the Series II Communion service or different philosophies of biblical interpretation, and the danger for Stott was that he was cutting himself off from a large part of the constituency he was attempting to unite.[121] According to the *Church of England Newspaper*, Stott "dismissed the criticism that the [congress] papers used difficult language with a nonchalant shrug." Hermeneutics was "a perfectly simple word," coming from the Greek word *hermeneuia* meaning interpretation, and therefore referred to the science of interpreting the Bible. "Then why not say so?" was the response of many in the audience.[122] Stott may have left the evangelical ghetto, but he was joining a clerical and academic ghetto that had even fewer links to the wider culture.

The diversity at Nottingham was so obvious that some began to question what it was that held all these very different people together. At a congress press conference, John King asked Stott to tell him what exactly it meant to be an evangelical and reported in a special edition of the *Church of England Newspaper* distributed at the event that Stott had looked somewhat dazed in response. King then said that many would like a straightforward answer to this question. Stott rose to the challenge and at the end of the congress gave a rallying address under the title, "What is an Evangelical?" For Stott, there were two defining marks: evangelicals were Bible people and gospel people.[123] But the conciliatory address was predictably vague, and both Colin Buchanan and more conservative voices expressed dissatisfaction with Stott's and the congress's conclusions on this basic matter.[124] One clear sign of how much had changed since the early 1960s was the failure of two attempts to include a reference in the congress statement to the Thirty-nine Articles, the key sixteenth-century statement of the Protestant doctrine of the Church of England.[125] In the absence of such concrete commitments, could such abstract ideas as "Bible people" and "gospel people" hold the coalition together? More than that, was there any point in the continued existence of a coalition that seemed to have achieved little in the preceding decade? And did Stott have the willingness or the ability to rally his increasingly disparate troops?

The outlook was grim after Nottingham. Morale was low, and more evangelicals were wondering whether the decision to get involved in the church had been a bad one. Public soul-searching became the order of the day and before long people were talking about an Anglican evangelical identity problem, the phrase cemented by Jim Packer's 1978 booklet *The Evangelical Identity Problem: An Analysis.*[126] There were two issues in the debate. The first was whether "evangelical" continued to be a useful term of self-description or whether it would be better to dispense with it altogether.[127] The second was the ongoing question of whether the Keele turn had been wrong, and whether the movement had drifted toward the dreaded liberal evangelicalism as a result.

Dick Lucas believed it had. Lucas was the rector of St. Helen's Bishopsgate in the heart of London's financial district, and a forthright leader of the conservative wing of Anglican evangelicalism. He was worried about doctrinal decay, and in an address to the Islington conference in 1979 targeted the young academics as responsible for encouraging "a new liberalism" in evangelical ranks.[128] Colin Buchanan was predictably more optimistic, saying that what they were seeing was attributable to the change in dynamics from being shoulder-to-shoulder in the last ditch to now being in a strong position in the field, when people begin to fan out.[129] Tom Wright, later Bishop of Durham, was getting his feet wet in church affairs during this period, and in 1980 sought to move the debate forward in a booklet on *Evangelical Anglican Identity*. His contribution was to emphasize the importance of the church for evangelicals, saying that the Reformers themselves "refused to water down the church to a mere agglomeration of like-minded Christians." Therefore because evangelicals were "Bible people and Gospel people" they were "*compelled* to be *Church* people."[130] Wright's determination to emphasize the rightness and goodness of the visible church put him closer to Buchanan than Lucas. Trying to hold the center were the likes of Packer and Dudley-Smith, who insisted that there was no major crisis and called for continued, watchful advance down the path they were already on. Dudley-Smith tried to calm frayed nerves by saying that every movement had "growing pains," and that this, rather than a "crisis," was what they were experiencing.[131]

Stott agreed with this last approach to the problem. He still hoped to hold everyone together. He was firmly against dropping the evangelical label and gently chastised those who were depressed about the state of the movement.[132] With the preface to the 1979 edition of the *Crockford's Clerical Directory* suggesting that the evangelicals were the most likely group to shape the future of the Church of England, a preface that also mentioned Stott's great influence on the movement, it seemed to him that some were giving up on the coalition just as victory was at last on the horizon.[133] To make matters worse, Jim Packer announced in the summer of 1978 that he was leaving England to take a post at Regent College in Canada. Packer had many reasons, but one was a sense of unease about the direction that Stott and others were taking Anglican evangelicals. Stott marked his departure in 1979 with an article entitled "Enormous Contribution to the Cause of Christ," and Stott knew that losing him was an enormous blow.[134] Packer was a highly respected, heavyweight, traditional anchor that pulled against more liberal ideas. He had been the brains behind much Anglican evangelical policy. Yet Packer had felt sidelined by Stott and the CEEC for some time, and in the end he was prepared to leave them.[135] His move was one more sign that the evangelical party in the Church of England was in trouble.

In March 1979, Stott gave a state of the party address. He sought to allay fears, explain what was going on, and encourage people not to give up. Perhaps the most striking thing about this address was how Stott explained some of the evangelicals' malaise with reference to context. He reflected on how the decline of the Student Christian Movement meant both that more liberally-minded people were joining university Christian Unions, and that these groups did not have to define themselves over against theological liberalism to such an extent.[136] Speaking against the backdrop of the Islamic revolution in Iran and the rise of Margaret Thatcher in Britain, he suggested that Christians were also increasingly attracted to more authoritarian leaders, "such as in Iran at the moment."[137] His growing love for hermeneutics encouraged him to explain the rifts in the evangelical Anglican coalition with reference to people's cultural places and perspectives, a very different intellectual position from the one he had held in the 1950s. Then, he had believed that the truth of Scripture was clear and all one needed to understand it was a willingness to submit to its authority and a brain, but by the late 1970s things looked much more complicated. In reality, there had always been significant diversity among evangelicals; what Stott was seeing was merely its increased visibility as evangelicals started to try to work together on matters of church policy. But for Stott in the 1970s, hermeneutics became a helpful way of explaining the glaring differences of opinion among people supposedly committed to the authority of Scripture. As he put it in a diary in 1981: "It is increasingly clear to me that hermeneutics is Issue No. 1 in the church today, & not least for evangelical Christians. Our differences are largely due to different ways of reading and understanding Scripture."[138] Stott had lost his simple confidence that those who read and respected the Bible would agree; hermeneutics allowed him to retain the hope that one day they might.

Stott's message was conciliatory, but it satisfied few. His stress on the primacy of evangelical over Anglican identity would have alienated people like Tom Wright who had a deeper theological commitment to the Church of England. As for charismatics, they were hardly likely to be won over when part of the blame for the current lack of emphasis on the revealed truth of God was laid squarely at their feet. Some conservatives would have been disappointed by Stott's frank confession that while he used to think the only Christians in the world were evangelicals, he thought this no longer. All in all, one gets the impression that Stott was attempting to square a circle that could not be squared unless everyone came to join him on the middle ground. But the preceding decade had made it clear that this was not going to happen.

There were some encouraging signs in the late 1970s and early 1980s. The publication of *The Myth of God Incarnate*, a book that offered radical interpretations of traditional orthodoxy regarding the deity of Christ, allowed the evangelicals to forget their differences for a while and unite against theological opponents.[139] And in January 1982, the first Anglican Evangelical Assembly met in London, the result of years of discussions between the CEEC, Church Society and CPAS aimed at forming one central and more representative body.[140]

But continued difficulties overshadowed these bright spots. The most visible was the sacking of the editorial board of the evangelical Anglican journal *Churchman* in 1983. The journal was owned by Church Society, an organization that stood for Reformed doctrine in the Church of England, and in the early 1980s it moved with conservatives like Lucas to an even more robust stance. In 1982 Church Society appointed David Samuel as its new head. Samuel was the director of the Protestant Reformation Society, and for him any hesitancy about the Reformation was simply "the spirit of Antichrist!"[141] He had achieved notoriety for his editing of the 1979 book, *The Evangelical Succession in the Church of England*, which argued that Anglican evangelicalism was going off its theological and historic rails.[142] Shortly after Samuel's appointment, *Churchman* published articles on biblical inspiration by James Dunn, which heavily criticized the belief in the inerrancy of the Bible common among conservative evangelicals. Dunn was a rising academic star, who went on to become Lightfoot Professor of Divinity at the University of Durham. As a student, he had been a very conservative evangel- ical—he was shocked when one of his evangelical friends bought a Sunday newspaper—but as he continued with his theological studies he concluded that the evangelicals were wrong on some important points, including the nature of Scripture.[143] So in the pages of *Churchman*, this former insider launched a swingeing critique on the doctrine of inerrancy, which he argued was "exegetically improbable, hermeneutically defective, theologically dan- gerous, and educationally disastrous."[144] The journal's editorial board then came under severe pressure from outraged conservatives. Stott and the CEEC tried to intervene and bring reconciliation, but to no avail. The results were a new editorial board for *Churchman*, and a new journal, *Anvil*, which promised to be more patient of diversity and more prepared to hammer out fresh approaches.[145] Stott declared that he would subscribe to both, but nothing could hide the sharp diversity of Anglican evangelicalism.[146]

A return to Protestant roots made sense to many Anglican evangelicals. Some had never given them up, but they became more prominent at a time when there was widespread dissatisfaction with the recent past. The late 1970s and early 1980s were grim in Britain, with the economy struggling and lots of industrial unrest. The optimism of the 1960s had evaporated. Many were nostalgic for the past and looking for stable foundations for society. Margaret Thatcher's leadership as Prime Minister was both cause and effect of a desire for strong, conservative leadership. When Samuel and others made stern declarations about John Calvin, Protestant Britain, and Bible truth they were speaking a religious version of the idiom of the day and won a hearing.[147] *Churchman* introduced its new editorial board in 1984 with words such as "staunch," "outspoken," and "defender," words that were redolent of a fundamentalism that matched the tough political lan- guage of the day.[148]

Stott's retirement from active engagement in Anglican evangelical politics came soon after. In December 1984, he stepped down from the chair of the CEEC. With some pathos, the minutes stated simply that "the Chairman spoke briefly of his 'objective in working for the unity of our Evangelical constituency in truth and love.'"[149] It is hard not to feel his disappointment. His replacement by Jill Dann, a woman who was a member of the General Synod, was a sign of how much things had changed since a group of IVF men with little experience of church politics had formed the CEEC back in 1960.[150]

Leading Anglican Evangelicals

On the face of it, Stott's attempt to unite Anglican evangelicals around a theologically conservative program to change the church was a failure. The party he built fractured, and the new leaders who emerged were more interested in their own particular agendas than in salvaging Stott's coalition. So, for example, Dick Lucas poured his energy into encouraging conservative, biblical preaching and had no truck with charismatics.[151] Just as Lloyd-Jones had seemed behind the times in 1966, so now Stott seemed out of place. One correspondent in the *Church of England Newspaper* had seen him as an evangelical version of the 1960s and 1970s Labour Party leader Harold Wilson, who worked extraordinarily hard to keep his chaotic party together, but in the 1980s leadership was now defined by the brusque style of Margaret Thatcher.[152] The no-nonsense Lucas served a church in the City of London, one of the chief beneficiaries of Thatcher's policies. Stott recognized the shift in his 1979 address on the identity problem, but after years of working for evangelical unity and experiencing the joys of fellowship with Christians who saw things differently from him he had no interest in becoming a partisan. Stott was less willing to adjust to cultural change than he had been twenty years earlier.

Still, Anglican evangelicals made important strides under the leadership of Stott, Packer, and the CEEC. Their work ensured that their church was one in which they wanted to stay, which given their fears of rampant Anglo-Catholicism in the 1960s was no mean achievement. The deals they made may have been condemned as compromises by conservatives, but they allowed many to remain in the Church of England with a good conscience. Indeed, Anglo-Catholicism was running out of steam during this period, and a growing number of evangelicals committed to the Church of England did eventually lead to growing influence in church affairs.[153] More evangelicals became bishops, and even archbishops, and although they were never as conservative as some other evangelicals might have wished, they were evidence that the work that Stott and others did to defend their position did much to relegitimate evangelicalism in the established church. By the 1990s, conservative evangelicals were an undeniable, awkward, and combative force in the church, most obviously in the way they challenged archbishops and bishops on the ordination of women and sexual ethics. And although much of the explanation for this lay in the continued success of evangelical and charismatic Anglicans at the parish level—their thriving congregations represented an ever-larger proportion of practicing Anglicans—the work of Stott and others in the 1960s, 1970s, and 1980s was critical for the growing power of evangelicals in the Church of England and the worldwide Anglican Communion by the end of the century.

Why did unifying Anglican evangelicals prove so difficult? The diminishing social significance of Christianity, the fundamental changes taking place in the Church of England's relationship to the state, sharply declining Anglican practice, enormous liturgical change, the clergy's ever-dwindling income and prestige, the jettisoning of Protestantism as a plank of national identity—all of these made it a disorientating time for Anglican evangelicals, a time that made uniting look necessary but its achievement extraordinarily difficult. Making the task even harder was the individualist streak that had always been strong in evangelicalism, an expression of Christianity that prioritized the individual's relationship with God. This has made evangelical unity a difficult proposition in every age, as seen, for example, in the tensions between John Wesley, Charles Wesley, and George Whitefield, and the denominational explosion among North American evangelicals and then globally since the eighteenth century. As far back as 1947, a leading article in an evangelical Anglican newspaper claimed that "almost as many cliques and factions share the title 'Evangelical' as split the official party groupings at Westminster," but unlike those parties, there was rarely a compelling reason for evangelicals to bury their differences and stick together.[154]

Moreover, there were reasons why uniting Anglican evangelicals proved an especially difficult proposition. Mark Noll has argued that a polity of disestablishment and evangelical religion share certain important affinities that foster the flourishing of evangelicalism.[155] Stott and his fellow Anglican evangelicals were part of an established church. As Anglicans, they were meant to submit to their lord bishops, but their evangelical individualism often led to conflict. Thus evangelical strength in the parishes has rarely been accurately represented on the bench of bishops. There have been two obvious directions to go for Anglican evangelicals: either toward greater conformity to their church or toward a greater emphasis on the evangelical conscience that balks at ecclesiastical constraint.[156] It was therefore no surprise that Stott ran into serious problems in his attempts to unite people infused with such a heady mix of deference and insubordination. Stott may have been able to hold the center for himself with a degree of success, but to hope that a host of others would be able to do the same was perhaps expecting too much. The antihierarchical individualism of some, which in his earlier career Stott had reflected so faithfully, and the attractions of a historic church and its hierarchy for others, which from the 1960s allured Stott, finally put paid to the attempt to forge an effective coalition.

Stott's task was made even harder by the nature of the authority at his disposal. The reality was that other than that conferred by persuasion and voluntary (and always retractable) submission, he had none. Not only were there few victories to celebrate, or spoils to divide, there was nothing that Stott could do to keep other evangelicals in line. Others might refer to him as the bishop, or archbishop, or cardinal, or patriarch or even the pope of the evangelicals, but he had none of the tangible means of power and control associated with any of these offices.[157] Indeed, there is a fascinating contrast here between Stott and Pope Paul VI. Paul VI had been in favor of the Second Vatican Council and the changes it brought in the Roman Catholic Church but he was soon concerned by the activities of those who saw the council as the beginning of a process of exploration rather than an instrument for settling the relevant questions. His response, particularly after the furor surrounding his opposition to artificial birth control in *Humanitae Vitae* in 1968, was to sit tight, keep his encyclical pen idle, and rely on the power structures of the church to maintain order and unity.[158] By contrast, being an evangelical leader was more like being a political leader, where loyalties could and did shift with a host of different variables, and yet without the power and impetus for unity that comes from the obvious and distributable rewards of electoral success. Stott's coalition was undone by other Anglican evangelicals demonstrating the same initiative, self-assurance, and determination to rally people of like mind that he had when founding the Eclectics and the CEEC. One example of a new initiative that upset Stott was Reform, a decidedly conservative association of Anglican evangelicals who, among other things, opposed the ordination of women. Stott was frustrated with the leaders for not talking with the CEEC and therefore "weaken[ing] the evangelical cause by further division," but this was precisely the sort of lack of deference for established structures that Stott had embodied earlier in his career.[159] The Keele coalition had become the new Islington, the new evangelical establishment, and there were plenty ready and able to challenge its dominance.

Stott did not always get his ecclesiastical politics right. Real questions remain over whether Stott was wise to take up the technical talk of hermeneutics as a central plank of his program from the late 1970s, alienating as it did both those less interested in theological terminology and those of a more conservative bent (including Jim Packer) who worried that hermeneutics would let theological liberalism and relativism in by the back door.[160] His refusal to stand for General Synod may well have been very costly when a lead by him would have encouraged dozens of other evangelicals to join what became the ultimate power in the Church of England. But in view of the challenges he was facing, what is remarkable is not that the coalition eventually fell apart, but that it had held together for so long. Stott was the primary uniting force, and his ability to keep together a group renowned for its unruly individualism in an era of intense change, with few victories and little in the way of spoils, was remarkable.

It was especially so given that during these years Stott was spending more and more time overseas. As early as 1971 he asked the CEEC whether they wanted him to continue as chairman, given that his travel schedule meant he would miss up to a third of their meetings every year. Six years later, he was missing half, and asked them again. If he was trying to bow out, he was not successful: the CEEC wanted to keep him, and appointed Dudley-Smith as co-chair.[161] But one could hardly blame Stott for his willingness to step down. Anglican politics provided little cheer and lots of irritation for him, as his correspondence makes clear. There was not much evidence to suggest that England was about to turn a spiritual corner. By contrast, his work overseas was invigorating and took him to parts of the world where the church was flourishing. When in 1975 the president of the Eclectics told Stott that he longed for him to spend more time with evangelicals in England, Stott made it clear that he believed his ministry should now be exercised "chiefly" in the Third World.[162] His experiences with the CEEC had confirmed his preference for preaching over politics. Abroad, he saw new places, preached to adoring crowds, and enjoyed bird-watching. Being an Anglican clergyman could still be an asset overseas at a time when it seemed a liability in satirical, post-imperial England. The American InterVarsity Christian Fellowship loved the BBC accent, the dog collar, and the liturgical poise that he brought to the closing communion services at their missions conventions. Back in England, by contrast, his fruity accent was as much a cause of ridicule as respect.

If Stott had been asked to be an English bishop in the 1960s or early 1970s, things might have been different. He would likely have accepted and dug in to his diocese. However, the invitation never came. Much of the reason was surely the opposition of Michael Ramsey, who had censured Stott and his ilk in the fundamentalism controversy and who as Archbishop of Canterbury had the strongest voice in the selection process.[163] But that only held until Ramsey's retirement in 1974, when Stott, at fifty-three, was still young enough for an appointment. By that time, however, Stott was well established as a global figure, more concerned with the church worldwide than Anglican affairs at home. Overseas, he was more an evangelical than an Anglican, and his enduring association with the International Fellowship of Evangelical Students damaged his reputation among people like Ramsey, for whom that organization conjured up images of zealous undergraduates at places like Cambridge. In this regard, the problem for Stott was that he was too talented: he stayed much closer to student ministry than other evangelical Anglicans because he was in such demand as a preacher. He was also still too uncompromising: his 1970 *Christ the Controversialist* spoke of the dangers of more catholic and liberal doctrine. He could have become a bishop in Australia, but he was decidedly lukewarm about overtures from Down Under. By the time that his name came up for serious consideration for the diocese of Winchester in 1985, he felt the position would mean "chang[ing] the whole direction" of his ministry and so refused to allow his name to go forward.[164] As with Jim Packer, Stott gave himself to Anglican politics but in the end tired of them. Neither had an obvious, appealing role to fill in England. Both were in demand elsewhere. The result was that two of England's most gifted evangelicals spent most of the end of their careers serving the church beyond England's shores.

5

Society

IN APRIL 1982, the London Institute for Contemporary Christianity opened its doors. Its aim was to help Christian professionals to think biblically about their work and be a more effective Christian presence there as a result. The institute was Stott's brainchild. He wanted to see "the penetration of the secular world" by Christians whose faith shaped every aspect of their lives.[1] This was Stott's final initiative to reach England for Christ. He had led student missions, reached out to his parish, defended evangelical truth in the established church, and written books to galvanize the evangelical community. But now he turned his energies to the intersection of gospel and society, the question of how to relate Christianity to the modern world. The London Institute was a major venture. It was an institution, something that if successful could spread Stott's influence dramatically and long outlast him. He was the institute's first director, and he publicized it throughout England and the world. He taught there regularly. Stott had become convinced that Christian engagement with wider social issues was crucial to the success of the gospel in England and beyond.

The timing was hardly auspicious. Stott embraced this idea when most commentators agreed that England was already a secular society. For Stott, however, that was the point. If British Christians did not do something, their country would slide yet further from where they wanted it to be. This chapter is not a story of revival. The London Institute for Contemporary Christianity did not make contemporary London Christian. Yet Stott's call to his fellow evangelicals not to flee society but to get stuck in made a difference. England did not become as secular as many had predicted in the 1960s, and part of the reason was the decision of many evangelicals to care for people's social lives, as well as their spiritual ones.

This chapter explains Stott's decision to add social action to his list of things to do, looks at the ethical positions he came to and what he did about them, and discusses his impact. It also explains how Stott's growing ministry outside England began to shape his work back home.

Philanthropy

Stott grew up in a family of great privilege, but it was one that cared for people on the lower rungs of the social ladder. The Stotts were paternalists, people who believed that their position in society brought with it a responsibility to look out for the less fortunate. John received extra doses of this belief at Rugby. In 1936 the school sent him to Whitehaven, an industrial town in northern England hit hard by the Depression, where he rubbed shoulders with working-class men for several days. For a while, he considered offering baths to the homeless in Rugby, and on one occasion he approached an Irish laborer in the town and encouraged him to say his prayers.[2] Stott knew he was privileged, knew that the gap between him and the lower classes was huge, and had little idea what to do about it. He pondered the problem as a conservative son of the establishment who read its newspaper, *The Times*, and believed the problem should be addressed within the existing social structure.

Stott's evangelical conversion at sixteen doused the flames of his emerging social conscience. Historically, many evangelicals had embraced the need to reform society, but conservative evangelicals in England had little interest in social action in the 1930s. In part, this was a frightened response to Christianity's diminished importance in national politics. Evangelicalism had shaped British culture in the nineteenth century but was marginal by the start of the twentieth. Since that time, it had been a big temptation for English evangelicals to focus on their own holiness rather than social righteousness. Crucial in this regard was the annual convention at Keswick in the Lake District, where the Bible teaching convinced many that what God really cared about was hearts and souls, not bodies.[3] The convention's clientele was middle- and upper-class churchgoers (many of them Anglicans), people who had other reasons for being conservative and disinterested in social change. The peacefulness of the lakeside setting was disturbed by thoughts of spiritual battles on the mission field, and only rarely by attention to suffering closer to home. Stott never went to Keswick as a young man, but the Cambridge Inter-Collegiate Christian Union and All Souls Langham Place both had strong links to the convention. Eric Nash was also a supporter. Stott revered Keswick, and its wariness of social reform was part of the culture that shaped Stott's beliefs.[4]

Theologically conservative evangelicals were suspicious of social reform because they feared that it would distract them from the work of evangelism. Their chief bogey was the social gospel, a movement that called Christians to fight the social ills of their day. Many evangelicals saw this as a watered down version of the true, heaven-and-hell gospel. On their view, faint-hearted Christians advocated social action because it was more palatable than preaching sin and salvation. Important here was the spread of the theology associated with the Scofield Reference Bible, which divided cosmic history into tidy periods, or dispensations, and taught evangelicals that the next chapter was the doom of the world. The proper conclusion was that in the current dispensation only winning people for Christ mattered: the ship of society was sinking, and the Christian's task was to rescue people, not fix the ship.[5] Stott embraced all of this, armed with a Scofield Reference Bible given him by Nash.[6] So there are no stories of Stott wanting to bathe the homeless or care for domestic servants during his years in Cambridge. Before his conversion he had expressed his faith in paternalism, but now he expressed it almost entirely in evangelism.

By the time he arrived at All Souls in 1945, however, Stott was coming out of Nash's shadow. He had moved away from the more Manichean versions of a condemned world for which the end was nigh, and although introducing people to Christ remained priority number one he was open to the idea that ministry meant more than preaching. London surely made an impact. For unlike Cambridge, where one could forget the other half who lived beyond the beautiful center of the city, in London it was much harder to escape the reality of poverty.[7] Stott visited homes in the poorly heeled parts of the parish and he started a club for boys who were very different from his friends at Rugby. His greatest desire was that they would accept Jesus as their savior, reporting "glad[ly]" in the parish magazine "that many boys [had] decided to become Christians."[8] But Stott's compassion extended to other aspects of their lives. He took joy in offering these boys from smoggy London "a first-rate holiday in new, healthy and happy surroundings."[9] His concern for them brought together his longing for conversions with the love of nature and concern for others' physical well-being that he had learned from his parents.

This concern for people's more tangible needs continued after Stott became rector of All Souls in 1950. He oversaw the creation of a home for the elderly in the parish and supported the church's school for local children.[10] In 1957, he helped start a Social Action Committee to address needs in the parish, although the committee could not find many that were not already taken care of with the exception of prostitution (which they were "at a loss to know how to deal with").[11] And there was the Clubhouse, which served a whole array of needs from childcare for toddlers to Christmas dinners for the lonely.[12] Philanthropy was a part of the ministry of All Souls, even if it always came second to evangelism.

Stott was interested in broader social issues, and started a reading group in 1958 called Christian Debate to address them. But he had little vision for engaging these issues beyond his parish. So when Stott turned to issues of race and class in a sermon at All Souls, he was concerned primarily with discrimination within the congregation:

> In our parish there live the so-called rich and poor, the university grad-
> uate and the pupil from the secondary modern school, British and for-
> eigners. In theory we glibly claim to be one in Christ, but are we in
> practice? Let me ask you these straight, personal questions. Are you
> British? If so, how many overseas visitors have you ever invited from
> the congregation into your home? Are you fairly well-to-do? Then
> how many less fortunate people from the parish have you entertained
> in your home? Are we a fellowship, or a conglomeration of cliques?[13]

However, this lack of engagement with wider social issues made some sense in the 1950s. Social debate was subdued during that decade. Political disagreements did not disappear, but there was significant consensus on many issues. All the major parties had accepted the implementation of the welfare state by the early 1950s, and the twin traumas of obvious imperial and industrial decline still lay in the future.[14] Radicalism was muted, and the idea of England as a more or less harmonious Christian community lived on. It had received a fresh lease on life from the success of the war, the coronation, and the welfare state, all of which could claim Christian roots.[15] Prostitutes were beyond the pale, but for the most part Stott and many like him saw England as a functional and healthy society. It was, more or less, a Christian country.[16] It did not need a major overhaul.

What change was needed would come, Stott believed, primarily through evangelism. "If every church in the country of every denomination were mobilized for aggressive evangelism," he wrote in 1955, "the face of the country would be changed."[17] So the Clubhouse did care for people in Fitzrovia, but for Stott and those who worked with him salvation, not social services, was what would really change their lives and their community. The training for those who visited the elderly was in evangelism, not social work.[18] For Stott, the spiritual was social. Stott remained fundamentally conservative but his vision was, in its own way, a radical one—society would be transformed as people turned from sin to God and lived the righteous and compassionate life he required. Stott was hopeful that England would become more Christian as people responded to the good news of the gospel.

Embracing a Social Gospel

By the mid-1960s, however, Stott's hope was faltering. Earlier chapters have told the story. Fewer people were responding to the gospel at All Souls and the universities. To make things worse, growing sexual license and more liberal statutes on divorce, abortion, and homosexuality made it feel as though England was not a Christian country after all.

This was unnerving. In a sermon on "Church and Nation" in 1968 Stott said bluntly that England was "in disgrace," and so was the church. Both were under "God's judgment."[19] Up to this point, it had been possible for Stott to see most English people as tethered to Christianity by social norms, and his evangelistic efforts could make use of those links. Christian paternalism was plausible: All Souls could provide help for those who lived in the parish with some confidence that it worked hand in hand with a sympathetic state. But by the late 1960s, it seemed that state and society were taking advantage of the new divorce laws to split from Christianity and the church. Things were made even more disorientating by the fact that Conservative members of parliament and church leaders such as Archbishop Michael Ramsey had lent support to the legislative changes. There was no grand culture war in which Stott could line up on the side of traditional mores. English society had made one of its most dramatic shifts since the Reformation, right in the middle of Stott's career.

Stott's response was to decide that the church's mission did include a mandate to reform society. The change came in 1967-68. In a 1966 sermon in Berlin, Stott spoke on Christ's post-resurrection Great Commission to the disciples and emphasized that "the commission of the Church...is not to reform society, but to preach the Gospel."[20] Stott had long believed that Christians should care for the poor and the sick, but these tasks were peripheral to the church's principal work of witness. But in 1967–68, just as much of the liberalizing legislation was making its way through parliament, Stott came to the conclusion that Scripture taught that social action was an integral part of the Great Commission. He now thought Christians should do more than meet people's needs. They should make their voices heard in the debates of their day. In short, Stott was adding politics to philanthropy.

The first clear sign that Stott's thinking was changing came right after the National Evangelical Anglican Congress at Keele in 1967. Before the congress, Stott's attention was focused solely on the need for evangelicals to get involved in their church. At a press conference he said that evangelicals "want[ed] now to emerge from our ghettos...and to take a positive and responsible part in the work of the Church in this country, especially during this era of revolution."[21] But one of the speakers at Keele advocated a broader remit for the church in a revolutionary age, and Stott was persuaded. The speaker was Norman Anderson, Director of the Institute for Advanced Legal Studies at the University of London. Anderson had been a missionary in the Middle East in the 1930s. His language skills attracted the attention of the British government, who recruited him to work on colonial affairs. At the Keele conference, Anderson argued that "Evangelicals, pietists, and monastics have frequently held an unbiblical doctrine of separation from the world," and he called for Anglican evangelicals to get involved in the issues facing society in their day.[22] The congress statement contained a paragraph that paraphrased Anderson's argument, and it had made an impact on Stott. In contrast to his comments before Keele, when he had called for evangelicals to get involved in the church, after 1967 Stott spoke regularly of the need for them to attend to their "wider responsibilities in the church *and the world.*"[23]

Stott received an extra jolt at the World Council of Churches' 1968 assembly in Uppsala, Sweden. Martin Luther King, Jr. had been due to address the delegates, and after his assassination earlier that year the emphasis on injustice of every form was acute. Reporting on the event, Stott said he had been "helped and moved by the heavy emphasis which was laid on the needs of the 'Third World,'" which was a big change for someone who in the late 1950s and early 1960s had visited Africa and Asia and responded with relative equanimity to refugees, apartheid, and anti-colonial activism.[24] From this point on, Stott argued that the world's concerns required a Christian response. Social action was not optional. Now when he traveled to places like Africa he agonized over the suffering he saw.[25] When the second edition of *Basic*

Christianity appeared in 1971, it included an extra paragraph on the need for Christians to serve an unjust world. Christians should care, Stott wrote, "for the needy and neglected people of the world—the poor and hungry, the sick, the victims of oppression and discrimination, slaves, prisoners, orphans, refugees and drop-outs....An enormous amount of work is waiting to be done."[26]

None of these ideas were new in 1967–68 and they were not new to Stott. There were evangelicals calling for greater involvement in society before 1967, and the Church of England Evangelical Council had already spent time discussing abortion and homosexuality.[27] It is too simple to say that he was persuaded by Anderson's paper at Keele, for he had read it before the congress began. Rather, Stott's thinking at Keele was shaped by his fear, mentioned in the previous chapter, that the congress would produce a split between older, more conservative evangelical Anglicans and their more adventurous younger counterparts. Anderson was part of the older generation, but most of those calling for greater engagement with the issues of the day were young clergymen.[28] For Stott, then, heeding their call and including their concerns in the Keele statement was a way of keeping them on board. And once these concerns were in the statement, Stott was always going to support them. The next chapter looks at a similar situation in the mid-1970s, when the Keele debate between senior, evangelism-centered evangelicals and younger ones committed to social action was replayed on a global stage in the Lausanne movement. "If we didn't find room for the concerns" of "the younger, rising evangelical leadership," Stott reflected later, "Lausanne was doomed."[29] Stott's commitment to social concern was genuine, but it was spurred by his desire to build effective evangelical movements.

In truth, Stott's commitment to getting involved in the debates of his church all but required engagement with social issues, for many of the debates in the Church of England were social debates. During this period the Church Assembly, the principal representative body of the church, discussed everything from world poverty to race relations to government social services.[30] It made sense that Keele committed evangelical Anglicans to involvement in both church and state. Stott wanted evangelicals to make their voices heard, and as they did so they took up the language that others were already using in their church, much of which had political overtones.[31] So when Stott repeatedly urged evangelicals to get "involved," he was using a word that had become commonplace among Anglicans to describe the need for Christian engagement with social issues.[32]

For Stott, however, as important as anything was the fact that he saw in social engagement a way to reinvigorate evangelism. Stott wanted to show that the gospel was not past its sell-by date. If he could show that the Bible had answers for modern people's modern problems, that might serve as a way to increase people's willingness to consider Christ. The heart of the evangelical message could not change but its dress could, and should. In 1970, Stott reflected on his recent experiences at university missions in Liverpool, Helsinki, and Lund and compared them to earlier missions he had done. At Cambridge in 1952, Stott wrote, the mission was essentially eight services in Great St. Mary's, the university church, complete with hymns, prayers, a lesson, and Stott in full clerical dress, whereas from the time of his missions in North America in 1956–57, the pattern had been a lecture series held in a secular venue, with the object of attracting "the secular student." "But now," Stott went on, "this approach is not secular enough; it has little or no appeal to the way-out student, who has little or no inclination to listen to lectures about Christianity." Stott then went on to refer to an initiative called the Traveling Circus, which connected the gospel to contemporary issues on university campuses with folk singing, records, and films.[33]

Stott never took up folk singing, and in the end he was not particularly optimistic about these novel forms of outreach anyway. The buzz of success that Stott had experienced in the 1950s never returned. Besides, he was in the process of moving on to other things. Once he had given up responsibility for the day-to-day life of All Souls in 1970, he could speak about evangelism in general more than practical terms. Stott was thinking that a bishop's mitre would come his way, and bishops were more concerned with grand social issues than with parochial evangelism. At a time when he was at a loss for how to reach English people on the local level he preserved his hope that England could be Christian once more by talking in more general terms about Christians being salt and light in society. As his evangelistic renown faded, he stayed on the leading edge of conservative evangelicalism by joining the charge toward social and political involvement.

Stott's decision that Christ's commission to his followers included a mandate to reform society thus made a great deal of sense. The change was in line with his long-standing concern for others' well-being, with his vision for successful evangelism, and his desire to see evangelicalism flourish. It fit well with his move away from parish ministry and his hope for a more senior role in the Church of England. Yet this should not obscure the extent to which this was a radical departure. Reinterpreting the Great Commission was no small thing.

Stott was persuaded to do so because he believed it was necessary for the success of Christianity in England and the world. He had to distance himself from his instinctual conservatism. And he became a very different person as a result.

The Principled Floater

Stott started to drift left. Both in England and abroad, the debates Stott entered were dominated by voices with a socialist timbre. In the developing world, where Stott spent more and more of his time after 1970, anticolonialism was alive and kicking. Marxism was in vogue among those who lambasted the capitalist imperialism of the West. When Stott visited college campuses in places like Latin America, he met students who found these ideas very attractive. He told the story of students in Quito who heard a Catholic bishop speak of the radicalism of Jesus and said that if they had heard of this Jesus they would never have become Marxists.[34] By the mid-1970s, Stott was making use of the Marxist language that was becoming more common in universities worldwide. He spoke of churches in Europe and North America "which are more bourgeois than Christian, and exhibit not the revolutionary ethic of the kingdom of God but the prudential ethic of middleclass [*sic*] respectability."[35] He led at least one mission under the title "The Revolution of Jesus Christ."[36] As he opened his eyes to global poverty, he was ready to hear the critique of Western capitalism that non-Western Christians made. He made his already spartan lifestyle even more so and urged others to do the same, both out of conviction and in the hope that the church might win the attention of people "disillusioned with materialism."[37] All this placed him on the left of most American evangelical leaders, who were keen to defend capitalism during the Cold War. Billy Graham's wife and mother-of-five Ruth Bell Graham saw this peripatetic bachelor's call for Christians to live more simply as "a bit self-righteous and precious."[38]

In England too, Stott gravitated to the left and thought he saw opportunities for evangelism. Speaking on Radio Merseyside in 1973 Stott argued that many of the views of Jimmy Reid, the Communist leader of Glasgow's shipyard workers, were very Christian, before suggesting that there were things that Jesus could offer that Marx could not.[39] In church debate, Stott was pushed left as he adopted much of the language that others were using. One of his favorite phrases, "holy worldliness," he borrowed from Alec Vidler, a well-known theological radical.[40] When Stott denounced the pietism of evangelicals, calling it "such a concentration upon our own interior spiritual life and evangelical fellowship as to neglect our responsibility for the secular world," he sounded very like the very liberal Joseph Fletcher, who in *Situation Ethics* characterized pietism as a preoccupation with one's own affairs and a resultant tendency to "frown…upon all Christian involvement in questions of economic, racial, or political justice."[41] In the nineteenth century, the French politician François Guizot noted that many move from youthful radicalism to conservatism by middle age; for Stott, it was the other way round. In the end, this pushed him to the left of most Anglican evangelicals: he read the left-leaning *Guardian* while they read the reliably conservative *Daily Telegraph*.[42]

One contemporary historian, Edward Norman, was sharply critical of Anglican clergy at this point, accusing them of modish accommodation to the liberal mainstream in England. He was frustrated by clergy who had been educated at exclusive boarding schools and knew nothing of the working classes, and yet naively believed that their lefty language would endear them to "the masses."[43] In 1963, playwright Michael Frayn divided Britain's middle classes into carnivores, who were confident that "if God had not wished them to prey upon all smaller and weaker creatures without scruple he would not have made them as they are," and herbivores, "gentle ruminants, who look out from the lush pastures which are their natural station in life with eyes full of sorrow for less fortunate creatures, guiltily conscious of their advantages."[44] Stott's experience and his reading of the Bible made him one of the latter, and subject to Norman's censure.

However, Norman's own conservatism made him uncharitable, and it would be wrong to see Stott as a pathetic, left-leaning clergyman.[45] Norman was not very interested in the variety of things that Christian leaders were attempting to do by adopting the language of the left.[46] In Stott's case, he was more interested in relating to students in places like India than blue-collar workers at home. And although some clergy may have pontificated about the needs of people they hardly knew, Stott spent countless hours listening to students during his evangelistic missions overseas (his knowledge of British workers was a good deal more shaky). In addition, there were issues on which Stott remained resolutely conservative. He was open to critiques of capitalism in large part because the Hebrew prophets routinely vilified those who exploited or ignored the poor; but if Stott believed that the Bible contradicted liberal mores, he went with the Bible.

Homosexuality was one such issue. There was no way Stott could get around the biblical texts on the subject, and submitting to the Bible's authority was of greater importance than any potential evangelistic edge. In his chapter on the subject in his major book on social ethics, *Issues Facing Christians Today*, Stott said he was writing not for non-Christians, "who reject the lordship of Jesus Christ, but rather [for] those who earnestly desire to submit to it, believe that he exercises it through Scripture, want to understand what light Scripture throws on this topic, and have a predisposition to seek God's grace to follow his will when it is known."[47] Stott stressed that everyone sinned sexually, acknowledged that there was a difference between homosexual orientation and practice (the former was blameless), and noted that not every sin was a crime, but in the end argued that God's Word proscribed homosexual acts. Many of his readers would have agreed: when some English clergy had called for the decriminalization of homosexuality in the 1950s and 1960s, many ordinary members of the Church of England were horrified.[48] But Stott was addressing an educated audience, most of whom had spent time in the more liberal atmosphere of British and other universities, and so he was especially sensitive on this issue. He was no closeted cultural warrior. As David Brooks recognized in his *New York Times* column on Stott, he could be courteous and uncompromising.[49]

Faithfulness to the Bible, then, trumped cultural accommodation for Stott. But as Christian Smith has argued for American evangelicals, a combination of engagement and distinctiveness has served Christians well in a pluralistic society. Steely opposition to the wider culture and swimming with the cultural flow were not the only two options, and for sustaining vitality they were not the best ones. Like evangelicals across the Atlantic, Stott and English evangelicals found that it was possible to thrive on "distinction, engagement, tension, conflict, and threat."[50]

Stott's position on gender was also conservative. In brief, Stott defended a degree of difference between genders, within a rubric of full equality, and to argue that part of that difference consisted in male leadership. Here was an issue on which Stott's interpretation of Scripture changed over time. He always took seriously the Bible's teaching on male headship, but what that meant altered. In an article in 1963, for example, he interpreted 1 Corinthians 11 to mean that man had authority over woman, following up his exposition with the bald statement, "You may not like this, but it is the plain teaching of Scripture."[51] By the mid-1980s, however, he had toned down his language and was talking about male responsibility.[52] When it came to the ordination of women, he balanced these convictions about equality and headship: writing in 1984, he was in favor of female clergy, but only in a congregation that had more than one ordained minister and where the woman concerned would not have ultimate authority. Female senior ministers or bishops were, therefore, out of the question—although by then Stott lived not only with a queen as head of his church but with Margaret Thatcher as head of his country's government. By 2006, with many female senior ministers and several female bishops in the Anglican communion, he had softened further: male headship was still the ideal, but there was "no a priori reason why women should not be ordained or consecrated [as bishops]." Yet his position seemed confused, for he still believed male headship was "the ideal arrangement."[53] Stott's desire to be faithful to the ancient text and thoroughly up to date made things very tricky. On this issue, the Bible's emphasis on human equality and the diversity of what it said about women in the church gave Stott more interpretive room than he had in the case of homosexuality, but his commitment to interpreting the Bible as straightforwardly as possible would not permit him to endorse functional equality without qualification.

It is noteworthy that Stott's position on women's ordination stood in the middle of divergent evangelical positions on the matter. There were evangelical Anglicans who supported the ordination of women, and others who opposed it strongly. Different parts of what he said were acceptable to people on each side, while both were ultimately unsatisfied. It is not credible to think of Stott deliberately crafting his position this way in order to allow him to broker evangelical unity: the Bible was God's Word and interpreting it too serious a business for that. However, when he was working on the issue for a new book in 1995, he wrote to Dudley-Smith and said that he felt as though Dick Lucas, Jim Packer, and "liberal feminists" were all looking over his shoulder as he wrote.[54] His determination to see the good and the right on each side led him to a position that was right in the middle of the road. Stott's position was the product of a mind that had long been striving to bring evangelicals together.

Stott also changed his mind on abortion. In an article published in the *Church of England Newspaper* in 1971, Stott demurred from the contemporary Roman Catholic position that the fetus was a full human being from the moment of conception and argued that it was still only a "potential human being" while in utero. This meant that "an abortion would seem to be morally permissible when the mother's life (perhaps interpreted to include her physical and mental health) is gravely at risk. For then the choice is between an actual human being and a potential human being."[55] However, he had changed his position by the time he came to write on the subject again nine years later. Psalm 139 had by then become the key text for an understanding of the fetus that emphasized actual, as well as potential humanity. "For it was you who formed my inward parts," the key verse read, "you knit me together in my mother's womb."[56] Stott was now hesitant about artificially ending a pregnancy in any but the most extreme of circumstances.[57] By the time of *Issues Facing Christians Today* in 1984, he was clear that all Christians should see conception as "the decisive moment when a human being begins."[58]

Two things stand out here. First, not only is it too simple to label Stott liberal or conservative, it is also too easy to see him as incipient liberal. Here his thinking became more conservative. Second, this is another example of how Stott's thinking was influenced by the opinions of those around him. For a range of reasons, which included better pictures of the fetus and the sharp increase in abortion rates, opposition to abortion was growing in both Britain and the United States.[59] The growing confidence of American evangelicals and their public campaign against abortion made the issue front-page news there. In Britain, many were more wary and weary of radical ideas in the 1980s than they had been ten years previously. Evangelical Anglicans and Roman Catholics exerted increasing influence among Conservative MPs on this issue.[60] Just as in Rome, where the papacy of John Paul II symbolized a renewed hesitancy about modernity, so in England radical Christian ideas were looking worn by the 1980s. The confidence of conservatives was returning.

There was one issue where Stott took a lead, namely ecology. Stott's love of birds was old and deep, and once he had sold his cello it was one of the few direct links to his father and childhood. Environmental concern was more a conservative than a progressive preoccupation in England during the mid-twentieth century, so it is not a surprise that this was one of Arnold Stott's gifts to his son.[61] Stott was a founder-member of the council of reference for A Rocha, a pioneering Christian conservation movement.[62] In "Our Human Environment," the chapter on the subject in *Issues Facing Christians Today*, Stott called his readers to "think and act ecologically." He argued that "the root of the ecological crisis is human greed," and in words that sounded like a prayer, he wrote: "We repent of extravagance, pollution and wanton destruction. We recognize that man finds it easier to subdue the earth than he does to subdue himself."[63] Stott leaned on contemporary critiques of capitalist excess, including E. F. Schumacher's *Small is Beautiful*, and there was little here that was original. Nevertheless, Stott's advocacy of environmental concern long before it became fashionable stands out as his most important contribution to evangelical ethics.

Stott was in Australia on the day Margaret Thatcher and the Conservative Party won the 1979 British general election. He confided in his diary: "I confess I was quite glad—irresponsibly no doubt—to be out of the country and therefore unable to vote. For I'm one of those prize imbeciles dubbed 'floating voters['], & in previous elections have voted for all 3 parties."[64] Stott was attentive to the Bible's calls for economic justice and sexual probity, and this made him politically awkward for right and left. He was a centrist, a position that reflected his understanding of the Bible and served his missions of evangelism and evangelical unity well. Like Robert Runcie, the Archbishop of Canterbury of the day, Stott was either a Conservative wet (to use the snarling epithet directed by Margaret Thatcher against those in her party who were not fully on board with her economic ideals) or on the most moderate wing of the Labour Party.[65] Stott would have agreed with the author who suggested that God himself, after all, might have been called a wet.[66]

Action

If coming up with robust Christian social thought was a challenge for Stott, figuring out what Christian social action might look like was even more so. The obstacles in England were enormous. The churches' lack of support in the country as a whole, especially among the working classes, made it easy for political leaders to ignore the clergy.[67] In the mid-nineteenth century, Anglican evangelicals had made up 14 percent of the population of England and Wales, but for the late 1980s, the figure was more like 0.5 percent for Britain as a whole.[68] During Margaret Thatcher's years as prime minister in the 1980s "the so-called moral leaders in their palaces and pulpits were deposited outside the walls," seen as "a discardable class whom government found it could easily do without."[69] The way elections worked and the positions of its dominant parties in the twentieth century also militated against Christian influence. The first-past-the-post system made it easy for politicians to ignore the active Christian minority in most parliamentary constituencies and made it impossible for Christian groups to band together nationally in an attempt to gain representation. Moreover, religion no longer marked a major dividing line between political parties in twentieth-century Britain, as it continued to do in much of continental Europe, making it even harder for Christian activists to make their voices heard.[70] There was a tiny political party called the Christian Party;

its obscurity was testimony to realities it faced.[71] Evangelicals found it almost impossible to win the attention of politicians.

Stott made a few forays into politics. After the 1977 National Evangelical Anglican Congress in Nottingham, Stott sent letters on behalf of the congress to the Chancellor of the Exchequer on tax concessions for charitable giving, to the Foreign Secretary suggesting trade restrictions on countries that did not implement UN covenants on human rights, and to the Minister for Overseas Development on the government's contribution to global aid.[72] The Minister for Trade, who had received a copy of the last of these letters, did write directly to Stott, but all he got from the other three were polite but dismissive letters from their lieutenants.[73] One of Stott's acquaintances was Sir Geoffrey Howe, who served as Chancellor of the Exchequer, Foreign Secretary, and Deputy Prime Minister under Margaret Thatcher, but this does not seem to have led to any influence for Stott.[74] Stott was a little more active in lobbying and protesting. He spoke at rallies put on by an evangelical social morality organization, the Festival of Light (he had to wrestle protestors for the microphone at one rally), and by the Society for the Protection of the Unborn Child, and he lent his support to campaigns for fair trade with the developing world.[75] Even here, however, such efforts were the exception rather than the rule. One leader of an evangelical social policy organization expressed his regret over Stott's lack of speaking on and engagement with policy issues in Britain.[76]

If Stott had been a bishop, he would have done more. Bishops continued to get attention in the press for their public pronouncements, and Stott said that he "would have loved the opportunity" to use that sort of influence.[77] Yet even for bishops the road was a hard one. In March 1981, Margaret Thatcher gave a speech at the Church of St. Lawrence Jewry in the City of London on the theme of politics and Christianity. Britain, on her view, remained an admirably Christian country, but she did not admire Christians who took sides "on those practical issues over which many good and honest Christians sincerely disagree."[78] Thatcher had Anglican bishops in her sights, some of whom had criticized her economic policies. She was not alone in her criticism of clerical politicking. Edward Norman was equally skeptical, and three years after Thatcher's speech, a volume of essays appeared under the title *The Kindness that Kills: The Churches' Simplistic Response to Complex Social Issues.*[79] Some of the explanation for this hostility was political: many bishops leaned left, not right. But part was a more instinctive irritation with bishops presuming to interfere in politics. In any preceding century, few would have

seen this as odd: bishops had frequently been influential and respected participants in public life. But in the second half of the twentieth century, increased
specialization and professionalization meant that what the clergy saw as ful-
filling a historic, moral duty appeared to others as ill-informed trespassing. At
a time when more people were willing to plead "That's not my discipline," it
was unsurprising that church leaders talking about social problems appeared
presumptuous.

Stott therefore knew that it would be almost impossible for him to make
an impression on the front line of social and political debate. He concluded
that his greatest contribution would come through using his calling as a
preacher and a writer to help others use their influence in society.

So Stott poured his efforts into creating the London Institute for
Contemporary Christianity. Building on the success of the London Lectures
in Contemporary Christianity, which Stott had started as an annual, endowed
lectureship in 1974, the institute opened in 1982.[80] It was modeled in part on
Regent College, a Christian college in Vancouver, Canada, that educated lay
people for Christian service. The institute offered short courses to part-time
students from Britain and overseas. The aim was to train university graduates
and professionals (the emphasis on the educated and the potentially influential remained) to understand their vocations from a Christian perspective so
that they could be better Christians in the workplace.[81] Stott took advice from
numerous people, including some whose social and political views were very
different from his own. He consulted Conservative member of parliament
Michael Alison, later Margaret Thatcher's Parliamentary Private Secretary,
who thought that capitalism was the answer to world poverty not part of the
problem.[82] Brian Griffiths, Head of the Policy Unit at 10 Downing Street
under Thatcher, served on the institute's council, despite being a thoroughgoing monetarist who was much more keen than Stott about wealth creation.[83]
Closer to Stott was Roy Clements, chair of the institute's council in the mid-
1980s and pastor of Eden Baptist Church in Cambridge, who though critical
of the economic policy of Thatcher's governments sought the middle ground
politically.[84] This was an attractive place for ministers like Stott and Clements,
both of whom were committed to fostering evangelical unity. Indeed, the
small size of the evangelical community in England seems to have encouraged
some of its prominent leaders to emphasize unity and adopt more or less centrist positions in the hope of having any political influence at all.

In an interview just before the institute opened, Stott spoke of it as
"a culmination of these last 15 years in which I have begun to struggle with

contemporary issues and preach about them," and said he had "seen the need to encourage other people to do the same things."[85] The opening was the beginning of a busy five years for Stott as the institute's director, during which he worked hard to secure students and its long-term viability. Unlike Canada or the United States, there was little free trade in education in Britain, and with the government footing the bill for almost all undergraduate and post-graduate education most people had little vision for paying to learn. Using the highly successful Regent College in Vancouver as a model was inspiring, but the educational context in Canada was very different. The three principal visionaries behind the institute—Stott, James Houston, the president of Regent College, and Andrew Kirk, a theology professor from Argentina—were British men who had spent significant time overseas and seen the potential in private, Christian higher education. But in England, the institute was a risky proposition, and it struggled to stay afloat.

Stott also preached and published on social issues. By 1984 this had led to a 340-page book on the subject, *Issues Facing Christians Today*. This chapter has referred to the book numerous times. It covered everything from nuclear disarmament to apartheid. It also provided an extensive rationale for Christian social involvement that sounded like autobiography as Stott traced the reasons for evangelical reticence and then reengagement. Stott wanted his work to make a contribution to society's debates, but he recognized that his typical reader would be an evangelical layperson, not a member of parliament. So he challenged Christians to get involved in their world and work for its improvement to the glory of God. This comes across clearly in the final chapter, entitled "A Call for Christian Leadership." At first blush, the chapter seems incongruous: it did not deal with one of the major questions vexing the mind of the average citizen. Yet it was the climax of the book. Stott dreamed of a new generation of Christian leaders who would take on the challenges of their day and see God's kingdom come. He wrote:

> The world can be won for Christ by evangelism, and made more pleasing to Christ by social action. Why then does this prospect not set our hearts on fire? Where are the Christian people today who see the *status quo*, who do not like what they see (because there are things in it which are unacceptable to God), who therefore refuse to come to terms with it, who dream dreams of an alternative society which would be more acceptable to God, and who determine to do something about it?[86]

An earlier chapter carried the same theme:

> Secular society may do its best to push us on to the circumference of its
> concerns. But, refusing to be marginalized, we should seek to occupy a
> sphere of influence for Christ. Ambition is the desire to succeed. There
> is nothing wrong with it if it is genuinely subordinated to the will and
> glory of God. True, power can corrupt. True also, the power of Christ
> is best displayed in our weakness. And indeed we shall continue to feel
> our personal inadequacy. Yet we should determine by his grace to infil-
> trate some secular segment of society and raise his flag there, maintain-
> ing without compromise his standards of love, truth and goodness.[87]

Stott wrote *Issues Facing Christians Today* to stir up evangelicals to godly
ambition in society.

The cultural context that Stott assumed when he wrote the book was very
different from that of the 1950s, when England had still looked like a Christian
country. Society now seemed much more secular. But Stott did not see this as
an insurmountable obstacle. He argued that Christians could form their own
counterculture and influence society by being a distinctive community.[88] It
was significant that Stott used the term "counterculture" and not subculture:
the prototypical counterculture, the youth culture of the 1960s, had started as
a minority movement of rebellion and gone on to alter the face of entire soci-
eties. Stott believed that cultural marginality did not entail cultural irrelevance, and in this sense, the dream of the 1940s and the 1950s lived on. Here
again we see Stott's optimism, an optimism that was in short supply in Britain
when he wrote the book in the early 1980s. "It's a heart-rending moment,"
author Kingsley Amis mused at the time, "when you realise you've got to give
up the notion of building The Just City."[89] Other evangelicals resigned themselves to a more or less subcultural existence, focusing on preaching to those
who would still listen (including the boarding-school educated minority,
whose compulsory chapel attendance made them one of the least secular
groups in the country). But Stott's belief in a living and active God helped
him hold on to the hope that England could be Christian, even if the march
of social change in his lifetime had not gone in the direction for which he had
longed and worked.

His plan was thus to use his gifts of teaching and preaching to expose
people to the Bible's concern for social issues and then urge them to get to
work. A comparison with another evangelical initiative emphasizes Stott's

distinctive approach. The Nationwide Festival of Light was formed in 1971 to stand for Christian morality in the face of perceived threats to it, especially pornography. Thousands attended a rally in London, which was a public demonstration in the mould of nineteenth-century evangelical protest movements.[90] It styled itself as a "Christian counter-attack" against barren secularism.[91] It was the closest thing in Britain to America's Moral Majority. Stott was a friend of the Festival of Light's leader, Raymond Johnston, lent his support to the movement, and wanted the London Institute to cooperate with it, but his basic approach was very different. Individual education rather than mass mobilization was the strategy Stott adopted.[92] The influence of Rugby and Nash lived on.

Impact

The fact that Stott's vision for Christian social action was all about getting others moving makes it difficult to assess his influence. There was no major revival, no invitations to 10 Downing Street, and the London Institute never gained much prominence or acclaim. However, there is evidence that English conservative evangelicals became more involved in society and politics, and the wholehearted commitment of one of their primary leaders to the cause was critical. Former colleagues John Gladwin and Michael Baughen went on to become evangelical bishops with a social conscience. Evangelical Anglican Conservative MPs, such as Stott's old friend Michael Alison, were important voices in the party's debates over abortion and in the shaping of the 1988 Education Reform Act, which insisted on a special role for Christianity in public education. The London Institute continued to help Christians, especially non-British ones, to think about their role in society.[93] By the 1970s, the honeymoon of Britain's welfare state was coming to an end. As it became apparent that governments were not able to take care of everyone's every need, a large gap opened up once more for Christian philanthropy. Evangelical organizations proliferated, tackling problems such as racism, AIDS, urban poverty, and hardships for the disabled.[94] In all this, Stott's fingerprints were visible.

Christianity continued to provide inspiration for politicians on left and right, including people as diverse as Tony Blair and Conservative shadow Home Secretary Ann Widdecombe. The Labour Party's Christian Socialist Movement and the Conservative Christian Fellowship both flourished during the 1990s.[95] Blair's ideas were shaped by Catholicism, but evangelicalism was important too.

Conservative Party chairman Brian Mawhinney paid tribute in his memoirs to Stott's influence on his thinking.[96] Christendom did not return, but the continuing influence of Christianity in British society and politics should temper assertions about a secular society.[97] And Stott was the most important person persuading evangelical Christians that they should get involved.[98]

There was one moment when Stott made a significant impact on government policy, but it was in America, not Britain. At the close of the twentieth century, an organization called Jubilee 2000 launched a campaign to encourage wealthy countries to cancel the debts of poorer ones in the developing world. Tony Blair became involved and worked to persuade the U.S. government to get on board. In 1999 the Americans did, and it appears that a short letter from John Stott, sent to prominent Christians in the United States, was instrumental. The then Chancellor of the Exchequer, Gordon Brown, told fellow Labour politician Stephen Timms about how persuasive this letter had proved among members of congress. Timms also heard that Tony Blair had said that Stott's letter was worth more than any of the high-profile anti-poverty rock concerts.[99] Stott would have liked to have had this kind of influence in England. But after the heady days of the 1950s, his desire to see England become a Christian country again lived on more by faith than sight. His influence overseas, however, only grew.

Stott went from being a young preacher with little time for social problems to a major advocate of Christian social action. The unsettling 1960s were crucial, both because Stott felt the need to find new ways of winning a hearing and because his desire to forge effective evangelical movements needed to include the younger and less conservative evangelicals. He never became a partisan, but selected his positions on his understanding of the Bible. However, he did not read the Bible in a cultural vacuum. The time he spent with Christians from Africa, Asia, and Latin America often nudged him toward left-wing economic positions. But he never gave up his primary work as a preacher, in part because England was unenthusiastic about clergy in politics but also because he still believed this work was vital. "We still insist," he wrote in *Issues Facing Christians Today*, "that evangelism is the major instrument of social change. For the gospel changes people, and changed people can change society."[100] Stott was in his mid-forties when social action became a major plank in his ministry, a fairly old dog for new tricks. But he incorporated it into his existing commitments to create a vision for the gospel and social outreach that many found compelling.

6

World

JOHN STOTT WAS very English. He was raised the quintessential, upper-class English gentleman and loved his country. In the end, however, that love was never fully requited. Stott did not receive the recognition in England that he desired, whether from his parishioners in London or from those who appointed bishops. If he had, it is unlikely that he would have spent quite so much time overseas. Yet he was happy to do so. He saw God at work there and saw more work to be done. He was also feted in a way that he no longer was at home. After Stott had turned over his leadership roles in the Church of England Evangelical Council and the London Institute for Contemporary Christianity in the mid-1980s, he was free to devote even more of his time to ministry around the world. This work dominated the years of his semi-retirement between sixty-five and eighty-five. Stott's ambition was global. He wanted to see God's kingdom come throughout the earth and for a long time had been turning his gifts to this end.

Stott had never been particularly parochial. As a child, he had French governesses, and he was writing in French by the age of seven. As a teenager, he traveled alone to France and Germany to work on his language skills. After his conversion he started to read biographies of famous missionaries, such as James Hudson Taylor. As a theological student during the war, he composed prayers for other countries, including a decidedly Protestant one for Spain, "where of all the evangelical Churches existing before the civil war only 8% remain open, where education is in the hands of Roman Catholic priests and where all circulation of the Scriptures is forbidden."[1] When Stott arrived at All Souls in 1945, he found a church committed to God's work overseas: the senior minister had been a missionary in northern Nigeria and the parish magazine carried regular extracts from the China Inland Mission publication *China's Millions*, with titles such as "Missionaries Still Needed."[2] This was standard fare for English evangelicals, who knew their world maps much better than their neighbors did. Stott was part of a Christian culture where people could name provinces in China.

Yet it is striking just how strong Stott's commitment to the world became. If one's heart is where one's treasure is, Stott's heart was definitely overseas. He provided some financial backing for the London Institute for Contemporary Christianity, but most of the money he earned and raised went to the organizations he set up to serve the church abroad. The Evangelical Literature Trust, John Stott Ministries, and the Langham Trust provided good evangelical books to Christian leaders in the developing world, funded theological training for some of them, and put on seminars to teach pastors in places like Papua New Guinea and India how to preach the Bible. Of all the organizations that Stott had started and been involved with, these were the ones he tended most carefully as he aged. Stott's desire to see the global church grow in evangelical truth and biblical understanding became his dearest hope. This chapter charts the development of these global ambitions, and the way in which Stott became one of the most influential Christians in the world.

A New Type of Evangelical Hero

Stott's commitment to ministry overseas was a natural extension of his work in England. It all started with students. The year after he left Cambridge, Stott headed off to Switzerland to speak at a camp for Christian students from France, Belgium, Holland, and Switzerland. The following year he visited groups of students in Paris, Lyon, and Grenoble.[3] These groups were part of the continental equivalents of the Inter-Varsity Fellowship. In France this was the Groupes Bibliques Universitaires (GBU), and GBU leaders invited Stott because he spoke French and because he had experience working with students in England. News of him had traveled along the sort of informal international networks that had characterized the evangelical movement since the days of John Wesley and Jonathan Edwards. Key here was the International Fellowship of Evangelical Students (IFES), an organization founded in 1947 to link groups like the Inter-Varsity Fellowship and the GBU. After Stott's highly successful missions at Cambridge and Oxford, IFES networks ensured that he was in demand for similar events in other countries. The first major trip took place from November 1956 to March 1957, when Inter-Varsity groups in America and Canada invited him to conduct a series of evangelistic events from the University of British Columbia to Harvard. The second was in the summer of 1958, when he went to Australia for missions in Sydney and

Melbourne. The following year it was Cape Town and Johannesburg. And so it went on, with missions in places as diverse as Aberystwyth, Ceylon, Helsinki, Ibadan, Malaya, Manila, Nairobi, Sierra Leone, and Vellore. In time, Stott also became a star Bible teacher for IFES groups around the world. His renown in the United States, which would later become crucial for the funding of his international ministry, stemmed largely from the keynote addresses he gave at Inter-Varsity Christian Fellowship's triennial missions conventions in Urbana, Illinois. Here, thousands of students from across the country gathered every third December to learn more about God's mission in the world. Stott spoke five times in the 1960s and 1970s, giving the main Bible expositions on four occasions.

Stott's fame also grew among evangelical Anglicans, whose own networks spread word of Stott's successful ministry in central London. The visit to Australia in 1958 set the pattern, as he spoke at conferences for clergy and shared his vision and strategy for parish evangelism. Before and after the founding of the Evangelical Fellowship in the Anglican Communion (EFAC) in 1961 Stott did much to encourage Anglican evangelicals wherever he traveled, and as Dudley-Smith has said it was his visits that "made EFAC a reality in many places" at a time when there were precious few opportunities for its members to get together.[4] Stott's evangelism among students took him to current and former English colonies where the Anglican church had put down roots, and by the early 1960s he was one of the world's most well-known Anglican evangelicals.

It is a little difficult to imagine the star quality that attached to people who regularly traveled overseas in the 1950s and 1960s. Long journeys required a liner or several airplanes and were very expensive. Only important people made such trips, and the British media gave lots of attention to the odysseys of the Queen and the Archbishop of Canterbury. When the Queen returned from her first tour of the Commonwealth in 1954, the BBC covered nothing else from the moment the royal yacht saw land to her arrival at Buckingham Palace. Thousands turned out to welcome her home.[5] It was not an age of exotic exploration, but the newness of swift intercontinental travel made it almost as glamorous. As an Englishman, Stott was a celebrity overseas, a rare representative of the homeland for thousands of English emigrants and their families. So when visiting Australia in 1958, Stott found that his hosts were "immensely proud of any connections they may have with England which is always affectionately known as 'the old country' or even 'home,' whether they have ever visited it or not. Many homes boast pictures either of the Royal

Family or of Churchill."[6] When he was in southern California in 1961, the Anglican cathedral in Los Angeles invited him to preach at a special service, complete with consuls reading the Scripture lessons and four members of the Royal Canadian Mounted Police. After the service, Stott said he had been "literally mobbed by hundreds of folk wanting to shake hands: 'I come from Yorkshire,' 'I was born in Newcastle,' 'my home was in Tunbridge Wells,' 'my grandfather lived in Leicester' etc. etc." It was the same story in Australia.[7] After 1959, Stott wore the distinctive red cassock of a chaplain to the queen, which made him even more special. The fact that Stott hailed from London was also a bonus. The city enjoyed iconic status in many parts of the world including the United States. When Billy Graham was planning his 1954 England crusade, his English associates suggested a test run in a smaller city before attacking London. Graham, however, insisted that it take place in the capital. "I could not interest the masses of Americans," he wrote, "in a campaign in a city that they do not know and are not burdened for. I could get millions on their knees in America for London."[8]

The result was that Stott became a new type of evangelical hero for the jet age. "Our rector is enabled, by the aeroplane, to do what none of his predecessors have done," wrote one of his assistant ministers in the All Souls magazine, "and that is both to encourage the missionary interest of us all, and also to exemplify its importance by devoting himself to the work of a missionary, as well as that of a pastor." It was, he continued, nothing less than "a modern apostolic ministry."[9] Of course, all this burnished his reputation in England. English conservative evangelicals were awed by the only one of their number who had a truly global ministry. Like Billy Graham and later John Paul II, Stott took advantage of the airplane to extend his ministry to every continent, and although he never had the stature of Graham or the pope, he cut an impressive figure. Stott's single-ness and then his retirement from All Souls allowed him to travel relent-lessly. He visited dozens of countries in the 1980s alone, with almost twenty trips to the United States.[10]

Stott took his ascent to global prominence in stride. He had, after all, been prepared for things like this. When Stott was at Rugby in the 1930s, the British Empire was as large as ever, and Rugby's blend of duty, service, national loy-alty, and Christianity gave its boys a sense that Britain had good and godly work to do in the world. Cambridge reinforced this notion. The Church of England assumed it. And while the demise of the empire after the Second World War now appears inevitable, Britain continued to see itself as a global power into the 1960s.[11] So there would have been few raised eyebrows when in 1952 All Souls hosted the Empire Youth Sunday for the borough of St. Marylebone. "Uniformed youth organizations will parade," the readers of the parish magazine learned; "Our own young people are strongly urged to support this service in strength."[12] Stott invested Anglican clergy with global significance, and this is how he came to see his own calling.[13] He became an answer to his own prayer, written early in his ministry, that God would "raise up among us those who shall be heralds and evangelists of Thy Kingdom, and shall build up Thy Church in every land."[14]

So the linguist who as a schoolboy had been groomed for the diplomatic corps became one of the best-known Christians in the world. One sign of Stott's stature was the three plenary addresses he gave on the Great Commission at the mammoth World Congress on Evangelism at Berlin in 1966. The Great Commission was Jesus' last words to his disciples, his command for them to take the gospel to the ends of the earth, and it had long been one of the best-known texts of Scripture in evangelical communities committed to missionary endeavor. It was an honor to be given the task of explaining it at such a high-profile event. The Billy Graham Evangelistic Association organized the congress, and it was Graham who in the following decade provided the impetus for the Lausanne Congress on World Evangelization. With thousands of dollars pouring in from Graham's American donors, it dwarfed IFES and EFAC; indeed, EFAC piggybacked on the congress by arranging a concurrent and for them very rare meeting when many people's airfares had already been paid.[15] For Stott, Lausanne provided the opportunity to become a different sort of diplomat, a statesman for the growing global evangelical movement.

Leading Lausanne

In July 1974, 2,500 evangelicals from 150 countries and 135 denominations arrived in Lausanne, Switzerland, for the International Congress on World Evangelization.[16] The gathering was testimony to the decades of missionary work that evangelicals had done on every continent, but there was little sign of complacency. The central purpose of the congress was to galvanize evangelicals to finish the task, to ensure that the gospel finally reached every corner of the earth. Its theme, emblazoned above the podium, was "Let the Earth Hear His Voice." In addition, Lausanne was a conservative evangelical response to the World Council of Churches (WCC), an organization that had been set up in 1948 to unite the historic Protestant churches. By the 1970s, however, the WCC had become the home for some decidedly radical theological voices, and Graham, Stott, and others wanted to show the world and the churches that there was a vibrant, more orthodox alternative.[17] At the congress itself, however, evangelism held center stage. A large digital display registered the world's growing population throughout the event. Delegates gathered in small groups to discuss how to spread the Christian message in particular countries or demographics. The congress produced a 1,500-page book documenting its discussions and resolutions.[18]

This was the biggest stage of Stott's life. Here were thousands of evangelicals from all over the world, most of whom lay outside the IFES and Anglican communities in which he was already well known. Stott had two jobs at Lausanne. The first was to deliver a plenary address on "The Biblical Basis for Evangelism." The second was to chair the committee charged with producing the official congress statement, what became known as the Lausanne Covenant. Neither was an easy task. Subsidized airfares and conference conviviality eased many tensions, but they could not mask the differences that existed among the world's evangelicals.

The most obvious disagreement was on an issue where Stott had himself changed his mind, namely whether God wanted his people to be involved in social reform. By the time of Lausanne, Stott had come to the conclusion that God called his people to care about society and politics, as well as evangelism. Many at Lausanne agreed with him, especially people from churches associated with the WCC, where social and political issues were high priorities. However, the belief that preaching the gospel was all that really mattered was still common, especially in the United States. Talk of social action brought to mind the dreaded social gospel, which many saw as a chief culprit in the theological drift of America's historic denominations.[19] So when an American evangelical missions executive saw a Brazilian church considering membership in the WCC, he worried that it would "get detoured into this type of social gospel that will ultimately kill them."[20]

The argument surfaced even before people arrived in Switzerland. All the main speakers had to send in preliminary versions of their addresses so the delegates could read them beforehand. Samuel Escobar, a Peruvian who was head of the Canadian Inter-Varsity Christian Fellowship, used his paper to condemn American and European evangelicals for their lack of concern for the poor. A tragicomic mistake made Escobar's paper even more offensive to conservative Americans. Escobar did not get his paper in on time, and when it arrived Lausanne's associate director Paul Little hastily phoned him to check whether he really wanted the paragraph critical of Western leaders in the text. Escobar said yes, and listed some of the people he had in mind, including Richard Nixon. Inadvertently, the names made it into the version sent to delegates.[21] Even without this blunder, Escobar's words were strong enough. He raised the question of whether evangelism could be a form of imperialism.

> Those who advocate this view can well point to the way in which Christians, evangelicals in particular, oppose the violence of revolution but not the violence of war; they condemn the totalitarianism of the left but not that of the right; they speak openly in favor of Israel, but very seldom speak or do anything about the Palestinian refugees; they condemn all the sins that well-behaved middle class people condemn but say nothing about exploitation, intrigue, and dirty political maneuvering done by great multi-national corporations around the world.[22]

Another nettle for the Americans was René Padilla, who was the IFES general secretary for Latin America. Padilla had graduated from the impeccably evangelical Wheaton College in Illinois, but he had no compunctions about accusing American missionaries of communicating American culture as much as the biblical gospel and of propagating the gospel as though they were marketing merchandise. He also rebuked those who had a gospel that was not good news for the poor. "There is no place for statistics on 'how many souls die without Christ every minute,'" Padilla wrote, "if they do not take into account how many of those who die are victims of hunger."[23]

Stott's own position was close to that of Escobar and Padilla, and in his own address he tried to persuade the delegates of his position. The core of his message was terse definitions of mission, evangelism, dialogue, salvation, and conversion. He made numerous contrasts with contemporary understandings of these concepts common in the WCC while insisting that evangelicals had things to learn from their brothers and sisters connected with that organization. The Church of England was a member of the WCC, and after his trip to the WCC's assembly in Uppsala in 1968 Stott saw himself as a broker between evangelicals and this ecumenical movement. At the WCC meetings in Uppsala in 1968 and then Nairobi in 1975, Stott had urged that organization to pay more attention to Christ's commission to preach the gospel to those who did not know him. By contrast, at Lausanne Stott wanted evangelicals to take social action more seriously. The twist in Stott's message to the congress was his argument that the Great Commission itself demanded that Christians pay attention to people's physical and social needs, as well as their spiritual ones. He did this by focusing not on the standard version of the commission, namely Jesus' command to go and make disciples of all nations as recorded in Matthew's gospel, but rather on John's account of Jesus telling his disciples that as his Father had sent him, so he was sending them. And just as Jesus' mission had involved caring for people's bodies, as well as their souls, so should that of the church.[24]

Not everyone was convinced. And there were Americans at the podium whose gospel had a very different hue. Donald McGavran, a professor from Fuller Seminary in Pasadena, California, was one. McGavran had served as a missionary in India, but he had been frustrated at how few conversions there were. So he began to plant churches, and concluded that part of the problem for the missionaries had been their focus on social action at the expense of evangelism.[25] In his paper for Lausanne he decried the "pernicious notion" that evangelism was a form of "Eurican imperialism" (to use McGavran's awkward neologism for Europe and North America; the rest of the world was reduced to "Latfricasia") and asserted that "world evangelism has nothing to do with Eurican imperialism, past or present."[26] McGavran was not opposed to social concern, but the priority he gave to evangelism was overwhelming.[27] The watchword was church growth. McGavran's colleague at Fuller Seminary, Ralph Winter, addressed the congress under the title "The Highest Priority: Cross-cultural Evangelism." He outlined three different types of evangelism, E-1, E-2, and E-3, which represented differing cultural and linguistic distances between the evangelist and the non-Christian culture in question.[28] He argued that the church's task should be divided up not by nations but by these particular cultural and linguistic groups. There was no need for delegates to draw the conclusion that the cause of world evangelism would be well-served by the neologistic conceptualizing and people-group statistics of the professional missiologists from Pasadena, for McGavran said as much when he urged his listeners to "read extensively on church growth" and, if necessary, to "translate materials on the growth of churches into your language."[29]

These disagreements made Stott's work as chair of the group charged with drafting Lausanne's covenant extremely tricky. The drafting committee started with a preliminary version, but delegates were encouraged to submit their comments as the conference went on. Suggestions flooded in, and it is testimony to Stott's powers of expression, compression, and ability to function on little sleep that he and his small committee were able to craft a comprehensive and comprehensible statement by the time the congress closed. Pressure came from delegates who set up the Theology and Radical Discipleship Group, which wanted to push the congress and its covenant toward a strong statement on the importance of social action. Stott listened to their concerns, and agreed with many of them, but he did not want to alienate those who wanted an overwhelming emphasis on evangelism.

The final product included sections on the authority of Scripture, the person of Christ, the Holy Spirit, spiritual conflict, culture, leadership, and several on evangelism. Stott's voice was prominent, with parts sounding very much like the 1967 Keele document (for example, the emphasis on penitence for shortcomings in the past). Evangelism retained center stage, and in case anyone needed clarification the covenant stated: "In the church's mission of sacrificial service evangelism is primary." But social responsibility received its own section, with the crucial sentence reading: "Although reconciliation with man is not reconciliation with God, nor is social action evangelism, nor is political liberation salvation, nevertheless we affirm that evangelism and socio-political involvement are both part of our Christian duty." The covenant denounced "every form of alienation, oppression and discrimination."[30]

As Stott stood up and presented the covenant on the final day of the congress, he looked every bit the sage leader that the divided world of evangelicalism seemed to need. This was the moment, one contemporary said, that "established [Stott] as the key figure in contemporary world evangelicalism."[31] Some evangelicals referred to Stott as their pope, and it is easy to see why. He was not the greatest evangelist or even the best-known evangelical—Graham held those palms—but for many Stott served as a one-man magisterium for evangelical belief. Translated into more than twenty languages, the Lausanne Covenant became the closest thing that evangelicals had to an agreed statement of faith and practice, and Stott, as its chief architect, received the plaudits. He had become an evangelical icon.

In the months that followed, however, Stott realized that he had not carried the day. This became clear as a group of evangelical leaders began discussing how to continue the work begun at Lausanne. Plans were afoot even before the congress closed, and a survey revealed that 90 percent of the delegates wanted the congress to give birth to some sort of organization.[32] Yet after agreeing to join the committee responsible for determining what that might look like, Stott discovered that the powers that be in this American-led

movement had not really accepted the covenant's dual emphasis on evangelism and social action. Jack Dain, an Australian Anglican bishop who was the
Executive Chairman of Lausanne, wrote to Stott asking for comments on a
draft brief for the committee. Stott was disappointed that it used the phrase
"international network for world evangelization." He told Dain:

> I myself am very reluctant to see any network for the specialist and
> exclusive purpose of evangelism. It seems to me that it would be a great
> step forward, and fully in keeping with the spirit of Lausanne, if we
> could accept from the beginning that as evangelicals the responsibil-
> ities God has laid on us are broader than evangelism. We cannot
> segregate one responsibility, concentrate on it as a kind of evangelical
> speciality, and neglect the rest.[33]

Stott was adamant that Lausanne should be about social action, as well as
evangelism.

The committee had already been stacked against him, however. Padilla
and Escobar were not invited. They had not even made the shortlist.[34] Padilla
wrote to Paul Little, the American in charge of convening the group, saying
"A friend of mine comments that with regard to the selection of representatives from Latin America we've taken a step backwards some 10–15 years!" So
as Stott arrived in Mexico City in January 1975 for the first meeting of the
continuation committee he knew it would be an uphill battle.

Billy Graham addressed the meeting on the first night. "What I counsel…," he said, "is that we stick strictly to evangelism and missions, while at
the same time encouraging others to do the specialized work that God has
commissioned the Church to do."[35]

Stott stayed awake for several hours that night, formulating his response
to Graham's proposal. By morning, he had decided to confront Graham, who
was bankrolling the meeting and the movement. As business began, Stott
stunned everyone by saying that he would resign from the committee if
Graham's vision for the movement prevailed.[36] Stott demanded that the
Lausanne Covenant's emphasis on the social implications of the gospel be
reflected in the organization's ongoing work. Stott and Graham had known
each other since Graham's crusades in England in the mid-1950s and they had
become personal friends. But Stott's challenge was still bold.

Why did he do it? He certainly believed that the church's mission was
about more than evangelism. But this cannot be the primary explanation, as

others on the committee believed this and yet would have been happy with an organization devoted to evangelism. Stott was especially keen to speak out on this point in the absence of friends like Padilla and Escobar, who might forget about Lausanne if evangelism were the only focus.[37]

The committee was shocked. Many in the room disagreed. For them, social concern had occupied just one paragraph of the covenant and little of the congress's discussions, whereas evangelism had dominated both. Many evangelicals still saw the world very much as Stott had done back in the 1950s: caring for people's physical needs was important, but getting them saved was much, much more so. But losing Stott would have been a big blow. Some felt he was blackmailing the committee. In the end, they locked Stott and Peter Wagner, a Fuller Seminary professor who wanted Lausanne to focus on strategies for evangelism, in a room and told them to come up with a compromise. The result was a weak reference to "the total biblical mission of the church" in the committee's statement of purpose.[38] Graham made sure that his relationship with Stott was not breached, writing to him in April to say that "there is no man that I respect, love, admire and would gladly follow more devotedly than I would you."[39] It was a mark of Graham's humility that he did not use his enormous capital to press his point at the meeting at Mexico.

As Stott left and headed north for engagements in the United States, his conscience was troubled. Threats were not his normal way of getting things done. Part of the difficulty was that he was used to being in charge. He was the leading figure at All Souls, in the Eclectic Society, in the CEEC, at Keele, and in the EFAC, and he seemed unsure what to do when he was not in the driving seat. He recognized at the time that his indelicate behavior could look like "personal power hunger," yet exonerated himself from the charge.[40] So did Dudley-Smith, saying that any idea that Stott was "challenging Billy Graham for the worldwide evangelical leadership" was "ludicrously far from the truth."[41] But was it? His desire to stand up for his fellow evangelicals in places like Latin America and Asia was genuine, but that does not mean his actions were entirely disinterested. Evangelical leadership had been plural and fluid ever since evangelicalism became a recognizable movement in the eighteenth century. So whilst Stott was not trying to usurp Graham and establish himself as the best-known public face of global evangelicalism, he did see himself as the leading thinker and statesman in the movement—especially after his triumph at Lausanne. This was a role he wanted to play and believed he should play, for the sake of Christ's kingdom.

But the line between godly and selfish ambition was sometimes hard to tell, hence, the uneasy conscience.

Stott's behavior in Mexico is illumined by wider Anglo-American relations in the postwar period. It was significant that the people Stott faced down were from the United States. In one letter after the Mexico meeting he wrote almost gleefully of "opposing the Americans!"[42] By the late 1960s, Britain had lost its empire but had not yet found a role, as US Secretary of State Dean Acheson memorably put it. The nation's decline rankled with the British upper classes. They tried to salvage their self-esteem with the idea that Britain should play Greece—that smaller, more historic, and more intelligent democracy—to America as Greece had done to Rome. It became a popular idea.[43] The evidence suggests that Stott saw his role in global evangelicalism in similar terms. There was no way he could match Graham's preaching power or financial muscle, and much of his globe-trotting was dependent on the dollars of Graham and other Americans. But his sharp mind and first-class education meant that there was a role for him as the leading thinker of the evangelical movement.

Stott came to see himself more and more as an educator, a learned yet popular theologian who could bridge the gap between academy and pew. After his retirement from All Souls, Stott had more time to read and his intellectual rigor increased accordingly. One obvious sign of this was the increasing quantity and diversity of footnotes and endnotes in his books. This can be seen in the *Bible Speaks Today* commentaries, an extraordinarily influential series of accessible commentaries edited by Stott that helped countless pastors prepare their weekly sermons. Stott contributed several volumes, and there is a striking difference between the one on Galatians, which was essentially a series of sermons preached at All Souls in 1965–66, and his 1994 work on Romans, which included dense introductory pages on the work of biblical scholar E. P. Sanders on Paul and the law.[44] In 1971, Stott was awarded an honorary doctorate from Trinity Evangelical Divinity School in Deerfield, Illinois (although he refused to style himself Dr. until he received one from England), and he did see himself as a theologian—not in the academy (where few took his work seriously), but for the church. Understanding the relationship between evangelism and social action was thus first and foremost a "theological question."[45] His concern at a Lausanne meeting on culture was "how to popularise, and to make available to pastors, missionaries & thoughtful laymen, the fruits of this egghead debate."[46] And by the late 1980s, he was saying things like this: "In my view there is nothing more important for the re-evangelization of Europe than that we develop a Christological basis for mission."[47]

Stott also raised questions about whether hell would in fact involve the eternal, conscious torment of the lost—a staple of conservative evangelical preaching. Stott had struggled with this issue for quite some time. As a pastor he evaded the question, telling his congregation that he did not want to "be drawn into controversy about the exact nature of hell."[48] Now, however, he was as much a theologian as a pastor, and it was the theologian's job to raise awkward questions, to stake out his ground, and take flack if necessary.[49] Stott came in for heavy criticism after he published his views on this subject, and he lost credibility among American evangelicals in particular. He defended himself by saying that the true marks of an evangelical were a commitment to study the Bible and to submit to its authority not the tyranny of doctrinal traditions. However, the criticism hurt him deeply, especially when it came from the mouth of that other tower of postwar Anglican evangelicalism, Jim Packer. Stott's willingness to be candid about his questions about the nature of hell damaged his credentials as an evangelical stalwart. This made life harder for him with the theologically conservative end of Lausanne. His 1986 *The Cross of Christ* showed that he was still conservative and evangelical on this key doctrine, but by this time Stott was a different type of Christian from the one who first became famous preaching to students in the 1950s.[50]

Stott was still committed to mission, but increasingly he saw himself as much a thinker as a preacher. And it was through the Lausanne movement that Stott solidified his position as "almost by common consent, the leading intellectual in the Evangelical world."[51] Historian Adrian Hastings called him "the recognized senior theologian and thinker of world evangelicalism."[52]

So while he was not trying to usurp Graham as the most powerful evangelical in the world, Stott was prepared to stand his ground when it came to matters that impinged on his newfound role as evangelicalism's leading thinker and statesman. So at the meeting in Mexico City in January 1975 Stott stepped forward to defend his interpretation of the church's mission and to determine the course of a movement that he wanted to lead.

It would be wrong, however, to think that Stott now thought education was more important than evangelism. For him, the two were inextricably linked. He wanted evangelicals to come together and think together because he believed these were vital for the spread of the gospel. "Our muddle-headedness plays into the devil's hands," Stott told Lausanne supporters in 1980.[53] In *Christianity Today* in 1981, he called "chronic evangelical divisiveness" a "grave obstacle" to world mission.[54] One of his last books, *Evangelical*

Truth: A Personal Plea for Unity, bemoaned evangelicals' "pathological tendency to fragment," which he saw as "a major hindrance to our evangelism."[55]
It was important that Lausanne educate and unify evangelicals because the
lost were important.

Stott's strategy for bringing the world's evangelicals to a common mind
centered on a series of conferences that he organized as chair of Lausanne's
Theology and Education group. Stott had long believed that ideas and
influence would flow from leaders to those whom they led, and so for him
these conferences of evangelical bigwigs held much potential for shaping the
beliefs of churches worldwide. For example, in 1977, a conference in Pasadena,
California, brought together the Fuller missions professors with their critics
to discuss whether the Bible allowed homogeneous churches for the purposes
of evangelism, or whether this undercut the Bible's call for human reconciliation. The following year, a conference in Bermuda encouraged some honest
thinking about how culture influenced people's understanding of the gospel.
A meeting between advocates of active social responsibility and those who
were skeptical took place in Grand Rapids, Michigan, in 1982.[56] Stott was the
key figure behind and during these events, and his efforts were based on a
fundamental optimism about the possibilities for evangelical unity. Given the
commitment to the authority of Scripture that evangelicals shared, he was
confident that the Holy Spirit could bring them together.[57] Stott saw the conferences as an opportunity to bring evangelicals together to reduce stereo-
types, foster understanding, and seek this common, biblical mind.[58] At each
event, Stott worked late into the night producing the carefully worded statement that expressed the conference's findings and that he hoped would shape
evangelical thinking on these subjects worldwide.

In the end, however, unifying the world's evangelicals proved too difficult. Evangelicals did have a tendency to fragment, and trying to unite them
interdenominationally and globally made Stott's work among evangelicals in
the Church of England look easy by comparison. Lausanne provided a focal
point for global evangelicalism, an umbrella under which many could gather,
but it made clearer than ever just how diverse and divided the world of evangelicalism actually was. Stott had to confront the differences generated by a
whole variety of church traditions, including everything from the venerable
Church of England to groups who worried that Henry Kissinger might be
the antichrist.[59] Many evangelicals were involved with churches that belonged
to the WCC, which exposed them to discussions about the relationship
between missions and imperialism. By contrast, large numbers of American

evangelicals came from churches that had cut themselves off from mainline church life in the fundamentalist-modernist controversies of the earlier part of the twentieth century.[60] The exponential growth of pentecostalism in the developing world also posed particular problems for Stott.[61] Pentecostals and their close kin, charismatics, agreed with evangelicals on most things, but argued that the supernatural gifts of the New Testament era, such as healing, should be present-day realities. Their growth meant they had to be integrated into the movement if Lausanne was to retain any claim to being representative, but both the suspicions of more phlegmatic evangelicals such as Stott and the anti-institutional bent of many pentecostals made this very hard.[62] Differing educational backgrounds also contributed to the diversity within Lausanne. There was a marked difference between the many American evangelical leaders who had been educated at fundamentalist or conservative evangelical institutions and evangelicals from elsewhere whose more secular higher education had put them in touch with more liberal theology and social thought.[63]

National differences made things even harder for Stott. Many Lausanne participants were quick to see the ways in which others were influenced by their home culture—for example, Jack Dain said that some American evangelicals had "a total inability to see behind the cultural and political outlook of the typical well-to-do American Christian"—but comparable self-criticism was hard to come by.[64] It is not difficult, however, to understand many of the tensions in the Lausanne movement, accurately if not exhaustively, along national lines. British evangelicals, including Stott at first, were skeptical about this American initiative, a reflection of anti-American sentiment in Britain.[65] Many Americans believed in Manifest Destiny, global-style, in the years of the Cold War, which spurred American evangelicals' commitment to evangelize the world and explained their suspicion of anyone whose thinking bore even a hint of Marx.[66] It was scarcely surprising to hear voices from Africa, Latin America, and Asia railing against imperialism in an era of rising Third World nationalism and decolonization. Obviously not everyone's position could be accounted for by reference to their citizenship, but as Peter Wagner said with reference to America, those whose convictions did match their national setting were often deliberately choosing to live counter to their own culture.[67] Despite the participants' best intentions, national context played more of a part in the positions they came to than most people cared to acknowledge. One who did concede this was Canadian Leighton Ford, the first chairman of the Lausanne Committee for World

Evangelization, who raised the issue in a letter to Stott when they were discussing the forthcoming conference on evangelism and social responsibility. Stott had said he was "convinced that the Holy Spirit can lead us to a substantially common mind," but Ford replied, "I must admit that I am not too sanguine about evangelicals coming to agreement at this point. I hope I do not expose my lack of faith, but it seems that ecclesiastical, cultural and sociopolitical backgrounds are so mixed in with our point of view that it is unlikely one consultation would begin to solve the problem."[68]

For Stott, however, his nationality was a real asset for his leadership in Lausanne. His Englishness made him an ideal broker between evangelicals from the United States and those from the Third World. A shared heritage and American Anglophilia contributed to the esteem and affection that many American evangelicals had for Stott, who traveled frequently to North America and whose books sold there in large numbers.[69] Americans were more willing to listen to Stott than to evangelicals from Latin America and Africa saying similar things. And for non-Western evangelicals, Britain's very reduced circumstances and diminishing missionary presence meant that being English was much less of a liability than being American. Stott was thus ideally placed to win the trust of evangelicals from both North and South.

Yet Stott was working with an incredibly diverse group in a decidedly weak organization. Pastors, evangelists, churches, and mission boards could sign up to receive its publications but Lausanne never had authority over any of them. To use the words of one participant, it was little more than "an instrument of spiritual motivation."[70] Indeed, any organization with even implicit authority would have gone against almost every bone in the evangelical body. Their commitments to personal conversion, individual spiritual growth, and the right to interpret the Bible for oneself had been central to the tradition for more than two hundred years, and all of these attributes militated against any strong organization. Even Stott was happy with a weak institutional set up.[71] The result was a toothless organization that could be safely ignored.

But this suited most evangelicals just fine. Large swathes of global evangelicalism were only vaguely interested in the sorts of questions that preoccupied Stott and saw them as a potential distraction from the work of missions and evangelism. This was the basic position of Billy Graham, who in his autobiography said that Lausanne had been "something of a diversion" from the real work of evangelism.[72] In the end, Stott never convinced him that the thinking and unity Lausanne sought to generate was worth very much.

The dominance of the doers had become apparent by the time of Lausanne's second mammoth congress in Manila in 1989. Thomas Wang, Lausanne's international director by this time, was also one of the leaders of the AD2000 and Beyond movement, and the congress showcased their vision to accomplish most if not all of the remainder of the task of world evangelization by the year 2000.[73] All five members of the initial AD2000 and Beyond working group were invited to speak, and four of them comprised half the speakers at the climactic final session.[74] Stott was not the bestriding figure at Manila that he had been at Lausanne: his addresses did not set the agenda, and the congress document he helped to shape—the Manila Manifesto—was unwieldy and received with much less enthusiasm than its 1974 counterpart.[75]

In the 1990s, Lausanne wilted. Its magazine did not come out for three years and when it did it was with the news that subscription, not free distribution, would now be the order of the day.[76] Crucially, Billy Graham had lost interest in Lausanne. He had been so irritated by the expense of the Manila congress that at one point he threatened to resign as its honorary chair.[77] After the event, he ignored pleas from a movement that was now in half a million dollars of debt.[78] He had not given up on world evangelization—he had just decided that it was better served by pouring millions of dollars into conferences in Amsterdam for evangelists, people who, in his words, were "actually doing the work of evangelism."[79] For although Graham gave in to Stott at the meeting in Mexico City in 1975, he had never really agreed. The meetings in Amsterdam did what Graham had wanted Lausanne to do. Lausanne did not expire, but until it returned to prominence with a congress in Cape Town in 2010 there was no more money for the sort of expensive conferences that Stott had convened in his desire to bring evangelicals to a common mind.[80] With or without them, evangelicalism continued to be a movement characterized by individualism and activism more than consensus and reflection. Uniting evangelicalism would have required changing evangelicalism, and this did not happen.

This is not to say that Lausanne was fruitless. It provided an excellent forum for mutual encouragement and the sharing of ideas. It gave evangelicals fresh inspiration for evangelism and provided useful tools, such as the people-group vocabulary from Fuller Seminary, which became the basic evangelical framework for world mission.[81] It allowed evangelical thinkers to find people of like mind, spawning groups such as the International Fellowship of Evangelical Missionary Theologians. And although the trickle-down was less than Stott wanted, the ideas of the various consultations did make a difference in evangelical communities. Like UN resolutions, Lausanne's statements had influence even if they lacked authority.[82] More evangelicals warmed to the idea of social responsibility and the notion that culture was worth thinking about, with significant implications for thousands of evangelical churches.

Stott was clearly saddened by his fellow evangelicals' inability to get along. "We are all sinful, individualistic empire builders!" he had said in 1974, and in 1989 he spoke of "the continuing suspicions and rivalries which divide us."[83] But evangelicalism's malleability was also a strength, allowing it to spread across the globe during the twentieth century as it took root in an astonishing diversity of cultures. Emphasis on the Bible fueled a commitment to its translation into vernacular languages, and this, together with the lack of any equivalent of Rome or Mecca, made for the creation of churches with strong roots in local cultures.[84] As an evangelical, Stott saw the growth of Christianity in the developing world and rejoiced. As an evangelical intellectual attempting to deliver evangelicalism from what he saw as its besetting sins, he lamented. In *Christianity Today* in 1981, Stott wrote that while he rejoiced "at the astonishing statistics of church growth in some regions of the Third World," "euphoria should be tempered by the question of whether the growth is as deep as it is broad."[85] He was saying the same thing twenty-five years later: when asked by the same publication to evaluate the church worldwide his simple answer was "growth without depth."[86] This was disheartening. But it was also the basis for an ongoing ministry that would last well into Stott's retirement.

Built to Last: The Langham Partnership

The fading of Lausanne was not the end of Stott's international ministry. He was still in heavy demand as a preacher, and the greater visibility that Lausanne had provided only increased the flow of invitations. But over time Stott turned his energies to the training of others to preach and teach the gospel. This was Stott's vision for two nonprofit organizations that he set up in the early 1970s: the Langham Trust, which took care of Stott's post-All Souls financial needs but was soon being used to fund young evangelicals coming to study theology in the United Kingdom, and the Evangelical Literature Trust (ELT), which provided evangelical books for pastors in poorer countries.

The rationale was simple. Stott saw the growing strength of Christianity in the non-Western world first hand and wanted to see it flourish even more. For that to happen, Stott believed, good, godly pastors were needed to preach the Word of God and train believers in Bible-based living and witness. But there lay the problem, for Stott saw most of the leaders of churches in the developing world as ill-equipped. He saw lots of Christians, but not enough teachers; lots of enthusiasm, but not enough erudition. The ELT and the Langham Trust addressed these problems. The ELT provided a steady supply of free or heavily discounted good, solid, evangelical books to tens of thousands of pastors and libraries.[87] Much of the early funding came from Stott's own book royalties. The Langham Trust paid for talented young men from places like Nigeria, India, and Romania to come for theological training in the West. Eventually, it also funded Ph.D.'s for existing leaders to bolster evangelical theological education outside Europe and North America, the so-called Langham Scholars.

For a long time, these initiatives competed for Stott's attention with CEEC, EFAC, Lausanne, and the London Institute, but after he resigned his leadership positions in these during the 1980s he gave the rest of his working life to his trusts. He helped set up separate Langham trusts in the United States, Canada, and Australia. In 1996 the American arm, which was by far the most muscular, called itself John Stott Ministries to make its fundraising easier. In 2001, all these groups united with the original, British Langham Trust and the ELT to form the Langham Partnership International (although it continued to be known as John Stott Ministries in the United States). Even together, these ministries were much smaller than the Billy Graham Evangelistic Association, with their annual income standing at $1 million by 1999.[88] But they were ones that Stott could control much more reliably than he ever could Lausanne, and at this stage of his career he had had enough of the wrangling on committees that had occupied much of his work in the twenty-five years after 1960. With missionary theologian Chris Wright appointed as its international director in 2001, this was an organization that Stott was determined would outlive him. As he neared the end of his own life, his ambitions focused more and more on others, on making them more useful in the kingdom of God.

It is possible to criticize these ventures as yet one more expression of Western dominance in the worldwide church. Stott was building up indigenous evangelical leadership, but the framework was still almost entirely foreign. People were brought to study in the West, which was in part a reflection of the realities of theological education in the rest of the world, but it did reinforce the notion that some cultures were dominant and others dependent. It also meant that Ugandans, say, returned to Uganda with categories for life and theology that might sit uneasily with the people in the churches they sought to lead.[89] The books sent to pastors and seminaries also tended to be Western. Readers in Pakistan, Poland, and Ghana were introduced to the theological controversies of places like America and Australia through books such as Inter-Varsity Press's *New Bible Dictionary*. And the expository style of preaching that Stott had believed in so strongly for so long, may have been one more Western imposition: its emphasis on the sober explanation of Scripture owed much to the sort of Enlightenment rationalism Stott had first learned from his stern medical father (in the key section in his book on preaching, there were more exemplars from modern Europe than from the Bible).[90] When so much of the materials and methods were foreign, it is not hard to see these ministries as an expression of a phenomenon noted by historian Paul Gifford: that although the number of missionaries declined, dependence on the West remained a defining mark of Christianity in places like Africa.[91]

However, it would be unfair simply to criticize Stott's trusts as a sophisticated form of ecclesiastical imperialism aiming to bring enlightenment to Christians in Asia and Africa. For one, these ministries served pastors and churches in Europe, as well as the southern hemisphere.[92] When one looks at the people shaped by them, a list that includes Michael Nazir-Ali (from Pakistan, he became Bishop of Rochester in England), John Chew (a Singaporean who became Archbishop of the Anglican Church in Southeast Asia), and Michael Nai-Chiu Poon (a professor at Trinity Theological College in Singapore) one does not see stooges. And for all the paternalism embedded in his bald characterization of the church in the global South as lacking depth (after all, as Philip Jenkins has pointed out, how can Christians who are willing to face suffering and death be shallow?), Stott was willing to learn from his brothers and sisters overseas.[93] There was a humility to Stott's engagement with the Christians he met abroad: he was sensitive to cultural differences and to his homeland's imperial past, and he looked for pitfalls wherever he went. This was surely one of the reasons why he was warmly received in so many places.

A full assessment of these ministries will have to wait. Even with time, it will be difficult to tell how important they were or were not in the growth of global evangelicalism. Stott shaped Michael Nazir-Ali, but so did many others Nazir-Ali knew. Disentangling different influences on a particular person is impossible. Yet the way churches work suggests that the impact of the Langham Partnership will prove to have been significant. Evangelicals tend toward individualism, but they also lean on trusted guides when it comes to interpreting Scripture, whether that be books, sermons, or seminary professors. Aiming at the pastors who preached the sermons and the educators who taught the pastors was thus an astute method for shaping evangelicalism. One scholar of global Christianity has spoken of Stott as the preeminent intellectual inspiration for evangelicals in Africa and Asia, calling him their "pope."[94] We will never know the extent of Stott's influence, whether as a writer, a preacher, or one who equipped preachers. But through the millions of books published and the millions of sermons preached by those who read the books, he touched as many lives as his Rugby and Cambridge peers who went into British politics.

Stott had come a long way from the culture of his youth. But in many respects he had changed very little. The Bible, for so long so central for evangelicals, remained as important as ever. Having spent countless hours poring over it as he prepared his own sermons, he spent countless more equipping others to do the same. Another fixed point was his preoccupation with leaders. Rugby had taught him to be one, Nash had urged him to see their significance for the spread of the gospel, and Stott was still convinced in his eighties. Langham's work was unapologetically focused on the development of evangelical leaders. It also prioritized the life of the mind. Langham was about getting people to read as much as anything else, whether by sending books to them or helping them to pursue formal education. Stott still believed that mature Christianity meant educated Christianity, and it was this lack of education that made the churches of the South lack depth.[95] Above all, Stott remained confident in his ability to lead and make things happen. His own education had done its work. There are two ironies here. One, the Rugby that had been so suspicious of Nash had done a great deal to equip Stott for evangelical activism. Two, despite Stott's own anxieties about the evangelical individualism that made unity so hard, he remained very willing to plot his own course and set up whatever structures were needed to make it possible. This was authentic evangelicalism. To the end, Stott was always as much a doer as a thinker.

Conclusion

IN HIS COMMENTARY on Jesus' Sermon on the Mount, John Stott reflected on the place of ambition in the Christian's life:

> In the end, just as there are only two kinds of piety, the self-centred and the God-centred, so there are only two kinds of ambition: one can be ambitious for oneself or for God. There is no third alternative.
>
> Ambitions for self may be quite modest (enough to eat, to drink and to wear, as in the Sermon) or they may be grandiose (a bigger house, a faster car, a higher salary, a wider reputation, more power). But whether modest or immodest, these are ambitions for myself—*my* comfort, *my* wealth, *my* status, *my* power.
>
> Ambitions for God, however, if they are to be worthy, can never be modest. There is something inherently inappropriate about cherishing small ambitions for God. How can we ever be content that he should acquire just a little more honour in the world? No. Once we are clear that God is King, then we long to see him crowned with glory and honour, and accorded his true place, which is the supreme place. We become ambitious for the spread of his kingdom and righteousness everywhere.
>
> When this is genuinely our dominant ambition, then not only will *all these things...be yours as well* (i.e. our material needs will be provided), but there will be no harm in having secondary ambitions, since these will be subservient to our primary ambition and not in competition with it. Indeed, it is then that secondary ambitions become healthy. Christians should be eager to develop their gifts, widen their opportunities, extend their influence and be given promotion in their work—not now to boost their own ego or build their own empire, but rather through everything they do to bring glory to God. Lesser ambitions are safe and right provided they are not an end in

themselves (namely ourselves) but the means to a great end (the spread of God's kingdom and righteousness) and therefore to the greatest of all ends, namely God's glory.[1]

This book has been the story of Stott's ambitions. He lived what he taught here. He saw no conflict between seeking God's glory and seeking excellence and success. What is absent in this passage is any sense that serving God could become a mask for selfish ambition, an accusation hurled at Christian leaders for centuries. Nor is there any comment on the possibility for self-deception or mixed motives. Elsewhere, Stott acknowledged that things were more complex. "Pride and vainglory," he wrote, were a temptation for "all Christian leaders."[2] In the conclusion to *Calling Christian Leaders*, one of his final books, he lamented the power hunger of evangelical pastors.[3] At a dinner marking his retirement from the presidency of the Evangelical Fellowship in the Anglican Communion, he said that he "long[ed] to see in myself and among all evangelicals more gentleness, more patience, more humility, more Christlikeness."[4]

Pride was thus a snare, but the evidence shows that Stott was not a fake. He strived to live what he preached. He shared the Christian good news with sailors and shut-ins, as well as doctors and students. He worked at humility, even if he never attained perfection in this or anything else. Yet Stott was still extraordinarily driven. He believed what he said in his commentary on the Sermon on the Mount: that the one who prays for God's kingdom to come, as he did, is free to have subsidiary dreams. So he pursued his godly ambitions for England and the world without apology.

Were they fulfilled? Stott certainly saw significant fruit from his ministry. Hundreds of students became Christians, All Souls flourished, evangelicals gained ground in the Church of England, Christianity remained a vital force in British politics, and the churches of Africa, Asia, and Latin America gained more leaders with more learning. There was always a sense in which Stott remained unsatisfied: for example, there never was a large-scale turning to Christ in his parish, let alone England, and evangelical unity remained elusive. Yet to judge Stott by his own lofty intentions is not very helpful.[5] They had to be great because God was great, as he said in the passage on ambition quoted above. Stott prayed big and hoped big. It would not have made sense to him to desire the conversion of 5 percent of his parish. Moreover, there was a theological reason why Stott never expected his dreams to be fully realized: perfection awaited the return and rule of Christ.[6]

What is remarkable is how unprepared Stott was to settle down once he had experienced the sort of success that many ministers would have been tempted to envy. Being a successful university evangelist and pastor of a large church were not enough. To use his words, Stott's desires to "develop [his] gifts, widen [his] opportunities, extend [his] influence, and be given promotion" were extremely strong. There were times when Stott could have relaxed and enjoyed life yet chose not to because of his longing for God's work to go marching on. The way he gave his substantial book royalties for the education of church leaders from the non-Western world is a case in point. Also impressive was how troubled Stott was by the fact that All Souls had made little impact on the working-class residents of the parish. He could have rejoiced in and busied himself with all the upper- and middle-class people in the church, but instead he pushed himself and them to reach out to the church's poorer neighbours. He was not willing to settle for a large, vibrant, yet relatively homogeneous congregation. The gospel demanded more. Indeed, here Stott might have appeared more successful if he had been less ambitious: focusing on the well-educated people already in the church and making it more attractive to others like them could have made for a more triumphant handover to Michael Baughen in 1970.

Stott's life was driven by his ambitions, but it was also shaped by the circumstances in which he found himself. These circumstances do much to explain why Stott became more famous outside England than inside, why he was celebrated more in *Time* than in *The Times*. Stott was ordained at a time when a hierarchical vision of British society was still compelling for many, and with the probity of the postwar era it was reasonable to think that Anglican clergy could lead England back to faith (with some help from their loyal churchgoers). When in 1949 the Anglican diocese of London staged a mission to reach their city for Christ, there was nothing strange about the pictures of dozens of surpliced men streaming into St. Paul's cathedral for a commissioning service.[7] But as Britain's power declined in the 1960s, hierarchy became as much a target as a treasure. The Church of England and its ministers were easy to hit. It became much harder for Stott to think that the residents of his parish would listen to him and that he could win them for Christ. In certain parts of the country at least, the Church of England seemed like a boat from which one was likely to catch only certain types of fish. To make matters worse, the idea that Britain was on a steady path of secularization became a common one in the 1960s, and this theory had a dispiriting impact on evangelicals like Stott.[8] In truth, All Souls and many churches like it continued to thrive, but the absence of revival and the fear of decline help explain Stott's decision to retire from All Souls and focus on other parts of the world where the church was flourishing. Stott's principal ambition was to bring God as much glory as he could, and as he saw opportunities galore in the thriving churches of Africa, America, and Asia, he felt the call to spend his energy there. By the 1980s, he was preaching most of his sermons abroad. Stott did not lose all hope for England, but he traveled as much as he did because he wanted to be an answer to Jesus' prayer that his followers would "bear much fruit."[9]

Did Stott's career shape the world or merely reflect it? Was he really one of the most influential people in the world, as *Time* magazine suggested in 2005? Evangelicals will warm to the idea. They have always liked heroes, and the history that inspires them almost always celebrates great and godly leaders. In this version, Stott becomes a bolt from the blue who almost single-handedly revived the fortunes of the moribund world of English evangelicalism and went on to change the shape of global evangelicalism.[10] Stott was certainly influential in England and overseas, but this view fails to do justice to the strength of interwar evangelicalism in England, to the hard work of all sorts of very ordinary evangelicals during the postwar years, or to the very complex ways in which people everywhere from Uganda to the United Kingdom are influenced and molded. It is easier for evangelicals and for *Time* magazine to emphasize Stott's significance for African Christianity than that of African pastors, or long-dead Australian missionaries for that matter, but the picture is a distortion.

Yet the way that evangelicals celebrate their leaders did ensure that Stott's significance was very substantial. Tens of thousands heard him preach. Millions read his books, which were translated into dozens of languages. Many became Christians through his ministry. He became one of the best-known and best-loved preachers in a Christian movement that was growing very fast during his lifetime. There can be no question that he did influence many students to commit their lives to Christ, many young men to become pastors, many clergy to get involved in the Church of England, many evangelicals to address social issues, and many Christian leaders to get more education. He was not a great, original thinker, he did not have much political influence, and he did not establish any impressive institutions. But he became an evangelical hero in many parts of the world—a real live evangelical equivalent of a saint. A sign of his iconic status was the struggle for his mantle among evangelicals with different approaches to recent debates over homosexuality in the Anglican Communion.[11]

However, evangelicals had other famous preachers, notably Billy Graham. Was there anything that made Stott special? To answer that question, one must look again at how Stott became so well known. Stott first became an international star through the International Fellowship of Evangelical Students (IFES). It was this organization that gave Stott the opportunity to preach at universities all over the world and made him a household name among educated evangelicals. Stott had the right gifts at the right time, just as IFES was becoming a global movement and intercontinental air travel convenient and affordable. His fame and influence owed much to the novelty of the latter: he was one of the first Christians with a truly global reputation and presence, which was well established years before Pope John Paul II became the global Christian par excellence. Yet it was how Stott used these opportunities that explains his significance. During Stott's own days as a student at Cambridge, Douglas Johnson, the first head of IFES's English arm, the Inter-Varsity Fellowship, had encouraged Stott to use his brain. And having graduated with a first-class degree, Stott went on to show and tell thousands of students that it was possible to love God with all their mind, as well as all their heart. Around the world, he was known as the evangelical preacher with a top-drawer degree from Cambridge. So just as Billy Graham showed millions of Americans that one could be a conservative evangelical and civil, John Stott was living proof that one could be an evangelical and intelligent. Conservative evangelicals in the North Atlantic world had dug themselves into defensive positions by the 1930s as they took their stand against new learning of various sorts, including evolutionary theory and biblical criticism. But as young men after the Second World War both Stott and Graham believed that they needed to redraw the lines for the sake of the gospel. For Graham, this meant sanding down some of fundamentalism's rough edges to win a wider hearing for the gospel. For Stott, it meant the attempt to reestablish the intellectual credibility of historic Christianity. People should accept, proclaim, and defend the gospel with their minds switched on. Revelation and reason could be happily married.

Stott was certainly not the first person to argue this: the evangelical movement had always had proponents of intellectual exertion. Nor was Stott the only one making this point in the 1950s and 1960s. Three things made Stott special. The first was his preaching. Authoritative, erudite, and famously clear, it became a gold standard of thoughtful Christianity. The second was his successful academic career at Cambridge University. This made it easier for him to convince Christians and non-Christians alike that the faith was robust. Lots of preachers argued that Christianity was reasonable, but Stott's background made him convincing. He was also living proof that evangelicals could flourish at the culture's heights, emboldening others to scale them. Thirdly, Stott's IFES connections gave him the perfect opportunity to tell thousands of university students from dozens of countries that their minds mattered (to borrow the title of one of his books).[12] Many listened. IFES nurtured large numbers of evangelicals who were very evangelical and very thoughtful, and much of the credit needs to go to John Stott, their major international figurehead during the movement's formative years.[13] Pope John Paul II showed Catholics that it was possible to be devout, intelligent, and theologically conservative, and Stott showed evangelicals the same thing. Anti-intellectualism has not disappeared among evangelicals, and Stott's lack of influence among pentecostals and charismatics, who were the fastest growing and perhaps the most intellectually suspicious parts of Christianity during the second half of the twentieth century, was a major limitation of his ministry and therefore his influence. But the development of a more intellectual stream within evangelicalism, with Stott as its international standard bearer, was a significant development in world Christianity in the second half of the twentieth century.[14]

From the late 1960s, Stott also told evangelicals that engaging their countries' social and political questions also mattered. This was treacherous ground for evangelicals who had been reared on stories of the dangers of theological laxity and the social gospel, so it made a real difference that one of evangelicalism's most trusted leaders was now giving social action a green light. Again, people listened. One of the most significant developments in world Christianity in recent years has been the increased involvement of evangelicals in social and political action, and central to that story have been two groups that Stott molded on precisely this point: IFES and Lausanne.[15] Moreover, the politics of these evangelicals has been radical, as well as conservative. Stott's career and influence show that the equation of evangelicalism with social conservatism is too simple.

Was John Stott one of the one hundred most influential people in the world in 2005? Time will make it easier to answer the question, even if a definitive response will never be possible. But *Time* was surely right to recognize the importance of Christian leaders in its list. With all the recent emphasis on Islam, it has been easy to forget the ongoing importance of other faiths for global affairs and people's lives. Christianity remains a powerful motivator for millions worldwide, even in Europe, where 8 percent of the population is evangelical or charismatic.[16] Few did more than John Stott to shape global Christianity in the twentieth century.

Notes

INTRODUCTION

1. "The People Who Influence Our Lives," *Time*, April 18, 2005, 46–134; at 99.
2. David Brooks, "Who is John Stott?" *New York Times*, November 30, 2004, 23.
3. David B. Barrett, George Thomas Kurian, and Todd M. Johnson, *World Christian Encyclopedia: A Comparative Survey of Churches and Religions in the Modern World* (New York: Oxford University Press, 2001), 22.
4. For a good introduction, see Mark A. Noll, *The Rise of Evangelicalism: The Age of Edwards, Whitefield, and the Wesleys* (Downers Grove, Ill.: InterVarsity Press, 2004).
5. David W. Bebbington, *Evangelicalism in Modern Britain: A History from the 1730s to the 1980s* (London: Routledge, 1989), 2–17.
6. See, for example, Paul Freston, ed., *Evangelical Christianity and Democracy in Latin America* (New York: Oxford University Press, 2008); David H. Lumsdaine, ed., *Evangelical Christianity and Democracy in Asia* (New York: Oxford University Press, 2008); and Terence O. Ranger, ed., *Evangelical Christianity and Democracy in Africa* (New York: Oxford University Press, 2008).
7. Philip Jenkins, *The Next Christendom: The Coming of Global Christianity* (New York: Oxford University Press, 2002), especially 141–190.
8. Email from Greg Vigne of InterVarsity Press, Downers Grove, Ill., July 28, 2010.
9. Email from Kathryn Birtton of Inter-Varsity Press, Leicester, England, August 31, 2010.
10. Brooks, "Who is John Stott?"
11. Timothy Dudley-Smith, *John Stott: The Making of a Leader* (Leicester: Inter-Varsity Press, 1999) and *John Stott: A Global Ministry* (Leicester: Inter-Varsity Press, 2001). See the foreword to the first volume, 9–17, for Dudley-Smith's

reflections on his project, where he recognizes its nonanalytic nature (quotation at 12). Dudley-Smith also produced a bibliography of Stott's work: Timothy Dudley-Smith, *John Stott: A Comprehensive Bibliography* (Leicester: Inter-Varsity Press, 1995). Inter-Varsity Press has also published a shorter, one-volume popular biography of Stott: Roger Steer, *Inside Story: The Life of John Stott* (Leicester: Inter-Varsity Press, 2010).

12. Dudley-Smith, *John Stott: The Making of a Leader*, 15–16. For a discussion of the authenticity of this comment, see Laura Lunger Knoppers, *Constructing Cromwell: Ceremony, Portrait, and Print, 1645–1661* (Cambridge: Cambridge University Press, 2000), 80. I am grateful to John Coffey for this reference.

13. Knoppers, *Constructing Cromwell*, 80.

14. I enjoyed access to John Stott's papers from 2000 to 2004. He gave me freedom of interpretation, asking only to see a list of the references I wished to make to his papers in the Ph.D. thesis I was writing at the time. Stott's papers were given to the Lambert Palace Library, although it is unclear whether they received all the papers and whether they will catalogue all those they did receive. Copies of Stott's papers relating to the Lausanne movement are also available at the Billy Graham Center Archives, Wheaton, Illinois.

15. I have not relied heavily on interviews, however, believing that original sources are a more reliable guide than recollection to the realities of, say, the West End of London in the 1960s. Stott did not wish to be interviewed for this project.

16. John Stott, *Christian Counter-culture* (Leicester: Inter-Varsity Press, 1978), 172–173.

17. John Stott, *People My Teachers: Around the World in Eighty Years* ([London]: Candle Books, 2002), 49; and Chris Sugden, "Where is the Next John Stott?" *EFAC Bulletin*, 41, Advent 1990, 3.

18. Quentin Skinner, *Visions of Politics*, Vol. 1: *Regarding Method* (Cambridge: Cambridge University Press, 2002), 47. See also Alister Chapman, John Coffey, and Brad S. Gregory, eds., *Seeing Things Their Way: Intellectual History and the Return of Religion* (Notre Dame, Ind.: University of Notre Dame Press, 2009).

19. The evangelical chronicler was Douglas Johnson, former general secretary of the Inter-Varsity Fellowship and the author of the first history of this evangelical student organization. In an interview with Keith and Gladys Hunt, Johnson said that he had been happy to omit uncomfortable parts of the story in the interests of providing an inspiring picture for new recruits. "My own feeling," Johnson said, "is that we are not called upon to wash too many things in public, which are best left unsaid." Keith and Gladys Hunt, "Discussion with Douglas Johnson," October 25, 1986, 29, Inter-Varsity Christian Fellowship Records, Collection 300, Folder 3, Box 379, Archives of the Billy Graham Center, Wheaton, Illinois.

CHAPTER 1

1. Much of the detail for these first two paragraphs comes from the early chapters of Timothy Dudley-Smith, *John Stott: The Making of a Leader* (Leicester: Inter-Varsity Press, 1999), 21–50.

2. See, for example, Lily Stott to John Stott, February 26, 1941, Stott Papers. For later comment by John Stott on the close and affectionate nature of his family, see John Stott, "The Counsellor and Friend," in *A Study in Spiritual Power: An Appreciation of E. J. H. Nash (Bash)*, rev. edn., ed. John Eddison (Crowborough: Highland, 1992), 85.

3. On these boarding schools as training grounds for the nation's elites, see the data in Ross McKibbin, *Classes and Cultures: England 1918–1951* (Oxford: Oxford University Press, 1998), 237. See also Rupert Wilkinson, *The Prefects: British Leadership and the Public School Tradition* (London: Oxford University Press, 1964).

4. "It is fairly clear that the public schools' prime function, considered from a socio-logical viewpoint, is to preserve middle-class standards. It is on them, in fact, that the middle and upper classes rely to retain their privileges and values." John Wilson, *Public Schools and Private Practice* (London: George Allen & Unwin, 1962), 62.

5. By John Stott's day, Rugby had become a more humane place under the leadership of headmaster Hugh Lyon. When a senior boy beat a junior one, he would use only a slipper or a hairbrush. C. R. Evers, *Rugby* (London: Blackie & Son, 1939), 106–134.

6. Information in this paragraph on Rugby and the public schools comes from Wilkinson, *The Prefects*; McKibbin, *Classes and Cultures*, 245–247; Wilson, *Public Schools*, 61–62; Edward C. Mack, *Public Schools and British Opinion Since 1860: The Relationship Between Contemporary Ideas and the Evolution of an English Institution* (London: Methuen, 1941), 403–404; and Evers, *Rugby*, 127–128.

7. See Dudley-Smith, *John Stott: The Making*, 57–58.

8. "Meteorological Observations," *The Meteor*, February 5, 1940, 2. *The Meteor* was a publication of Rugby School.

9. See, for example, "First House Matches. First Round, Kilbracken v. H. J. Harris's," *The Meteor*, December 13, 1939, 187.

10. J. F. Wolfenden, *The Public Schools To-day: A Study in Boarding School Education* (London: University of London Press, 1948), 66. Wolfenden went on: "As a training in tact, diplomacy, steadfastness, tolerance, courage, few jobs can equal it."

11. Sixth Levées Minute Book, vol. 3, passim, especially February 4, 1940, and February 6, 1940, Rugby School Archives, Rugby.

12. Stott, "The Counsellor," 90–91.

13. Dudley-Smith, *John Stott: The Making*, 47, 89–90.

14. Letter from a Parent, *The Meteor*, March 7, 1939, 27–28.

15. John Stott, Diary, February 14, 1938, Stott Papers. For more detail, see Dudley-Smith, *John Stott: The Making*, 91–102. In later years, Stott certainly recognized as fellow Christians people who shared neither his experience nor his theology of conversion. See, for example, John Stott's review of Owen Chadwick, *Michael Ramsey: A Life* (Oxford: Clarendon Press, 1990), in *EFAC Bulletin* 40 (1990): 7–8; and David L. Edwards with John Stott, *Evangelical Essentials: A Liberal-Evangelical Dialogue* (Downers Grove, Ill.: InterVarsity Press, 1988), 332.

16. John Stott, Diary, February 15, 1938, Stott Papers.

17. On Nash's commitment to the nurture of converts, see Richard Rhodes-James, "The Pioneer," in *A Study in Spiritual Power*, ed. Eddison, 37–39.

18. Stott, "The Counsellor," 83–84.

19. Rhodes-James, "The Pioneer," 40–41; Dudley-Smith, *John Stott: The Making*, 105; and Michael Green, *Adventure of Faith: Reflections on Fifty Years of Christian Service* (Grand Rapids, Mich.: Zondervan, 2001), 25–26.

20. Stott, "The Counsellor," 83; and Dudley-Smith, *John Stott: The Making*, 105.

21. Quoted in Dudley-Smith, *John Stott: The Making*, 217.

22. For these views, see, for example, T. Guy Rogers, "Introduction," in *Liberal Evangelicalism: An Interpretation*, by Members of the Church of England (London: Hodder & Stoughton, 1923), v–viii.

23. David W. Bebbington, "Martyrs for Truth: Fundamentalists in Britain," in *Martyrs and Martyrologies*, ed. Diana Wood, Studies in Church History 30 (Oxford: Blackwell, 1993), 417–451.

24. George M. Marsden, *Fundamentalism and American Culture: The Shaping of Twentieth-century Evangelicalism* (New York: Oxford University Press, 1980), 43, 47–48.

25. See Transcripts of Interviews with John Stott by Dudley-Smith (hereafter Dudley-Smith Transcripts), 14: 28; 16: 17. On the use of brown paper to conceal books, see Green, *Adventure of Faith*, 25. For Nash's indebtedness to Torrey, see especially David Fletcher, "The Prayer Warrior," in *A Study in Spiritual Power*, ed. Eddison, 63; and Green, "The Theologian," in *A Study in Spiritual Power*, ed. Eddison, 124–125.

26. Josiah Speers had founded the CSSM after watching the American Payson Hammond preaching to children in London in 1867; see J. C. Pollock, *The Good Seed: The Story of the Children's Special Service Mission and the Scripture Union* (London: Hodder and Stoughton, 1959), 15–16. Scripture Union leader R. Hudson Pope would read aloud to his workers from Charles Finney; see Patricia St. John, *R. Hudson Pope* (London: Scripture Union, 1967), 91. Cf. the comments

of Frank Turner on nineteenth-century evangelicals in Frank M. Turner, *John Henry Newman: The Challenge to Evangelical Religion* (New Haven, Conn.: Yale University Press, 2002), 46.

27. Richard Weight, *Patriots: National Identity in Britain, 1940–2000*, corrected edn. (London: Pan, 2003), 175–176.

28. Wilson, *Public Schools*, 70–71.

29. John G. Maiden, *National Religion and the Prayer Book Controversy, 1927–1928* (Woodbridge: Boydell, 2009), 8–9.

30. Minutes, May 4, 1931, Governors' Minute Book 1, Wrekin College, Wellington, Shropshire. Wrekin was one of the Allied Schools, which were set up by Percy Warrington as conservative evangelical counterparts to the Anglo-Catholic schools set up by Nathaniel Woodard. The minutes are unclear on the reasons for Nash's dismissal. Richard Rhodes-James has argued that his desire to see conversions was the reason; Rhodes-James, "The Pioneer," 32–33. I am grateful to Dr. Rodney Edrich, a housemaster at Wrekin College, for his help with the school's archives. On the history of Wrekin, see B. C. W. Johnson, *Wrekin College 1880–1964: A Brief History* (Shrewsbury: Wilding & Son, 1965 [?]).

31. See George M. Marsden, *Understanding Fundamentalism and Evangelicalism* (Grand Rapids, Mich.: Eerdmans, 1991), 1; and David W. Bebbington, "Towards an Evangelical Identity," in *For Such a Time as This: Perspectives on Evangelicalism, Past, Present and Future*, ed. Steve Brady and Harold Rowdon (Bletchley: Scripture Union, 1996), 41.

32. See Green, "The Theologian," 122; and David W. Bebbington, *Evangelicalism in Modern Britain: A History from the 1730s to the 1980s* (London: Routledge, 1989), 175–178.

33. See Stott, "The Counsellor," 85, 91–92.

34. For more comment on premillenialism and conservative forms of evangelicalism, see Bebbington, *Evangelicalism*, 190–196; and Marsden, *Fundamentalism and American Culture*, 124–131.

35. John Pollock, "The Ambassador for Christ," in *A Study in Spiritual Power*, ed. Eddison, 152–153.

36. Quoted in Martin Ceadel, *Pacifism in Britain, 1914–1945: The Defining of a Faith* (Oxford: Clarendon Press, 1980), 303.

37. The term "multiplication tables" was Nash's. Rhodes-James, "The Pioneer," 35.

38. John Stott, "Suggestions for Running a School Meeting," September 9, 1945, Stott Papers.

39. See Wilkinson, *The Prefects*, vii; and Rhodes-James, "The Pioneer," 35–36.

40. For more general comments on the differences between American fundamentalism and English evangelicalism during this period, see David W. Bebbington, "Martyrs for Truth"; and George M. Marsden, "Fundamentalism as an American

Phenomenon: A Comparison with English Evangelicalism," *Church History* 46 (1977): 215–232.

41. Rhodes-James, "The Pioneer," 36–37. See also Pollock, *The Good Seed*, 13–14, 22, 32, 62–73, 99–107.

42. On John Stott's Christian work with his fellow pupils at Rugby, see Dudley-Smith, *John Stott: The Making*, 102–105.

43. See, for example, John Stott, "Editorial," *The Meteor*, October 16, 1939, 145; and John Stott, "Editorial," *The Meteor*, November 7, 1939, 157.

44. John Stott, "Editorial," *The Meteor*, July 11, 1940, 73.

45. "Prizes, 1939–40," *The Meteor*, June 22, 1940, 57–58.

46. See A. S. F. Gow, *Letters from Cambridge, 1939–1944* (London: Jonathan Cape, 1945), passim, especially 60–78.

47. See, for example, John Stott to Paul Gibson, December 31, 1940, Stott Papers.

48. G. E. F. Rawlins, "My Testimony," *All Souls*, October 1963, 17. Cf. Adrian Hastings, *A History of English Christianity*, 4th edn. (London: SCM Press, 2001), 221.

49. See Robert Towler and A. P. M. Coxon, *The Fate of the Anglican Clergy* (London: Macmillan 1979), 21–41; and Dudley-Smith, *John Stott: The Making*, 103–104, 107. Cf. David Cannadine, *The Decline and Fall of the British Aristocracy*, rev. edn. (London: Papermac, 1996), 255–264.

50. John Stott, draft letter to Arnold Stott, January 31, 1941, Stott Papers. Quoted in Dudley-Smith, *John Stott: The Making*, 165.

51. See Fred Catherwood, *At the Cutting Edge* (London: Hodder & Stoughton, 1995), 34–35; Dick Lucas, "The Man of God," in *A Study in Spiritual Power*, ed. Eddison, 54; and John Laird, *No Mere Chance* (London: Hodder & Stoughton and Scripture Union, 1981), 119.

52. Conversation with Timothy Dudley-Smith, 2001.

53. Robbie Bickersteth to John Stott, November 14, 1941, Stott Papers, quoted in Dudley-Smith, *John Stott: The Making*, 177.

54. See "Why I am unable to believe that I, as a Christian, am at liberty to fight," July 1, 1940, Stott Papers, quoted in Dudley-Smith, *John Stott: The Making*, 159–160; and Stott, "The Counsellor," 85.Cf. Cynthia Eller, *Conscientious Objectors and the Second World War: Moral and Religious Arguments in Support of Pacifism* (New York: Praeger, 1991), 96–98.

55. Peter Brock, *Varieties of Pacifism: A Survey from Antiquity to the Outset of the Twentieth Century* (Syracuse, N.Y.: distributed by Syracuse University Press, 1998), passim; David A. Martin, *Pacifism: An Historical and Sociological Study* (London: Routledge & Kegan Paul, 1965), 44–45, 141, 201; Ceadel, *Pacifism*, 303; and Peter Brock and Nigel Young, eds., *Pacifism in the Twentieth Century* (Syracuse, N.Y.: [Syracuse University Press], 1999), 165. David Bebbington has provided evidence to show that many fundamentalists in Britain did fight in the

armed forces, but these secondary sources and the cases of Nash and Stott demonstrate that some very conservative English evangelicals held pacifist convictions. See Bebbington, "Martyrs for Truth," 438–439.

56. Stott wrote later that Nash "did nothing to influence" him on this point; see Stott, "The Counsellor," 85.

57. See the evidence presented in Dudley-Smith, *John Stott: The Making*, 153.

58. Caroline Moorhead, *Troublesome People: Enemies of War, 1916–1986* (London: Hamilton, 1987), 150.

59. See Dudley-Smith, *John Stott: The Making*, 152–171.

60. Many conscientious objectors were sent to serve with the Royal Army Medical Corps, so Arnold Stott would have had first-hand experience of such people. See Moorhead, *Troublesome People*, 156.

61. John Stott to Arnold Stott, April 27, 1941, Stott Papers, quoted in Dudley-Smith, *John Stott: The Making*, 175.

62. See John Stott to Arnold Stott (draft), March 24, 1940; John Stott to Arnold Stott, January 31, 1941; John Stott to Arnold Stott, April 27, 1941; and John Stott to Joy Stott, February 23, 1941, all in Stott Papers. The first three of these documents are quoted in Dudley-Smith, *John Stott: The Making*, 158, 165–166, 173–175.

63. John Stott to Joy Stott, February 23, 1941, Stott Papers.

64. On assurance as a core tenet of evangelical religion, see Bebbington, *Evangelicalism*, 42–50.

65. John Stott to Joy Stott, February 23, 1941.

66. Dudley-Smith, *John Stott: The Making*, 151, 169.

67. Bickersteth to John Stott, November 14, 1941.

68. John Stott to Arnold Stott, March 24, 1940, Stott Papers [all *sic*]: "D, *please*, don't stand in my way. I've told you sev times that my des to be ord. is not sudden & pass. Fancy—it's been stead. grow. for some year. After all I'm 19 + H of S+ am not the ignor unexp public schoolboy that you take me for. Just because I behave in a child way with y as 'Johnnieboe'you must not think thats my real self—I only do it because I know it amuse + pleas. Y." Stott later regretted the way he dealt with his parents on this matter; see Dudley-Smith, *John Stott: The Making*, 162.

69. Luke 14:25–26.

70. Lily Stott to John Stott, January 25, 1941, February 3, 1941, and February 11, 1941, Stott Papers; quoted in Dudley-Smith, *John Stott: The Making*, 164, 167.

71. Quoted in Dudley-Smith, *John Stott: The Making*, 162.

72. "Court of Inquiry Ordered," *Cambridge Daily News*, October 22, 1940, 1.

73. Arnold Stott to John Stott, May 19, 1941, Stott Papers, quoted in Dudley-Smith, *John Stott: The Making*, 176.

74. See especially Dudley-Smith, *John Stott: The Making*, 174.

75. Stott, "The Counsellor," 85.

76. The idea of Christian ministry as national service was in use by evangelical Anglican organizations during these years. See the advert for the Church Pastoral-Aid Society, *The Record*, February 6, 1942, 41.

77. John Stott to Arnold Stott, February 23, 1941, Stott Papers, quoted in Dudley-Smith, *John Stott: The Making*, 166.

78. One of the early biographers of the seventeenth-century Puritan John Preston believes that Preston, who went on to become Master of Emmanuel College, Cambridge, made just this calculation. Peter Lake, "The 'Court,' the 'Country' and the Northamptonshire Connection: Watching the 'Puritan Opposition' Think (Historically) about Politics on the Eve of the English Civil War," *Midland History* 35 (2010): 33–34.

79. Dudley-Smith records the recollection of a junior doctor who worked under Arnold Stott and who remembered his "sense of disappointment and resentment 'that John should want to go into the *church*'—with an indescribable emphasis on the final word." Dudley-Smith, *John Stott: The Making*, 154–155.

80. Gow, *Letters*, 191, 227, 241.

81. "Where is Cambridge Vice?" *Cambridge University Journal*, November 25, 1939, 6.

82. Gow, *Letters*, 153, 155–156.

83. Joel A. Carpenter, *Revive us Again: The Reawakening of American Fundamentalism* (New York: Oxford University Press, 1997), 16–22.

84. The schools being the so-called Clarendon Nine (nine leading public schools which were studied between 1861 and 1864 by the Royal Commission on the Public Schools under the Earl of Clarendon: Charterhouse, Eton, Harrow, Merchant Taylors, Rugby, Shrewsbury, St Paul's, Westminster, and Winchester), and Stowe and Wellington. Information provided by Jonathan Smith, Archivist, Trinity College, Cambridge.

85. For more on the dynamics discussed in this paragraph, see David W. Bebbington, "Evangelicalism in its Settings," in *Evangelicalism: Comparative Studies of Popular Protestantism in North America, the British Isles and Beyond*, ed. Mark A. Noll, David W. Bebbington, and George A. Rawlyk (New York: Oxford University Press, 1994), 374–375.

86. C. S. Lewis, "Learning in Wartime," in C. S. Lewis, *The Weight of Glory* (Grand Rapids, Mich.: Eerdmans, 1965), 43–54.

87. Dudley-Smith, *John Stott: The Making*, 125, 173, 189.

88. Lucas, "The Man of God," 55.

89. John Eddison, "The Man We Knew," in *A Study in Spiritual Power*, ed. Eddison, 22.

90. Grant Wacker makes this point about American Pentecostals in *Heaven Below: Early Pentecostals and American Culture* (Cambridge, Mass.: Harvard University Press, 2001), 31.

91. For testimony on this point, see Green, *Adventure of Faith*, 78; Norman Anderson, *An Adopted Son: The Story of my Life* (Leicester: Inter-Varsity Press, 1985), 142–143; and Teddy Saunders and Hugh Sansom, *David Watson: A Biography* (London: Hodder & Stoughton, 1992), 37–41. See also David Goodhew, "The Rise of the Cambridge Inter-Collegiate Christian Union," *Journal of Ecclesiastical History* 54 (2003): 73.

92. John Eddison, "The Compulsive Worker, but a Rare Spelling Mistake," in *John Stott: A Portrait by his Friends*, ed. Christopher J. H. Wright (Leicester: Inter-Varsity Press, 2011), 26.

93. John Stott to Arnold Stott, April 27, 1941; quoted in Dudley-Smith, *John Stott: The Making*, 173.

94. See the letters in Dudley-Smith, *John Stott: The Making*, 189–192.

95. See Arnold Stott's letter in Dudley-Smith, *John Stott: The Making*, 189–190.

96. Gow, *Letters*, 153.

97. John Burnaby, *Religion, Learning and Research: An Inaugural Lecture* (Cambridge: Cambridge University Press, 1953), 23–24.

98. See J. S. Whale, *Christian Doctrine: Eight Lectures Delivered in the University of Cambridge to Undergraduates of All Faculties* (Cambridge: Cambridge University Press, 1941), 85–96. For Stott's appreciation of Whale's lectures, see Dudley-Smith Transcripts, 3: 40–41.

99. Dudley-Smith, *John Stott: The Making*, 201.

100. Dudley-Smith Transcripts, 3: 38–42, and 4: 34–37; referred to and quoted in Dudley-Smith, *John Stott: The Making*, 179–183, 194–196.

101. Oliver Barclay, *Evangelicalism in Britain, 1935–95: A Personal Sketch* (Leicester: Inter-Varsity Press, 1997), 57.

102. Minutes, October 15, 1941, October 7, 1942, and July 28, 1943, CICCU Executive Committee Minute Book 3, Add. 8722 A2/3, Cambridge University Library; and Minutes, May 16, 1945, CICCU Executive Committee Minute Book 4, Add. 8722 A2/4, Cambridge University Library.

103. Minutes, June 7, 1944, and June 21, 1944, CICCU Executive Committee Minute Book 4.

104. Minutes, June 28, 1944, and October 6, 1944, CICCU Executive Committee Minute Book 4.

105. Stott, "The Counsellor," 85–86. Although Stott kept letters and other material from this period of his life, he did not preserve his letters from Nash, which makes it impossible to determine to which period of his life Stott was referring. Stott probably destroyed the letters, which is rather odd, given the major role

Nash played in his life. The most likely explanation is that he did so as he moved away from Nash's strain of evangelicalism.

106. The best account is: Martin Wellings, *Evangelicals Embattled: Responses of Evangelicals in the Church of England to Ritualism, Darwinism and Theological Liberalism 1890–1930* (Milton Keynes: Paternoster, 2003), 273–281. See also an important recent article by Justin Thacker and Susannah Clark, "A Historical and Theological Exploration of the 1910 Disaffiliation of the Cambridge Inter-Collegiate Christian Union from the Student Christian Movement," forthcoming in *The Evangelical Quarterly* and available at: <http://www.eauk.org/efb/downloads.cfm> [December 13, 2010].

107. R. E. D. Clarke, undated, Pollock CICCU Papers, Add. 8545, Cambridge University Library.

108. Goodhew, "The Rise," 67–68; cf. Ian M. Randall, *Evangelical Experiences: A Study in the Spirituality of English Evangelicalism, 1918–1939* (Carlisle: Paternoster, 1999), 37; and Bebbington, *Evangelicalism*, 222–223.

109. Goodhew, "The Rise," 72–74.

110. George Marsden has argued that the IVF was more pietist than fundamentalist: Marsden, "Fundamentalism as an American Phenomenon," 221.

111. "Some Basic Considerations," early 1943, IVF documents, Box 113, held at the offices of the Universities and Colleges Christian Fellowship (UCCF), Leicester. Used with permission.

112. Douglas Johnson to William Greer, October 27, 1948; and Douglas Johnson to Robert Mackie, January 25, 1935, both in IVF documents, Box 113.

113. On the strength of evangelical theology in the interwar period, see, for example, "Evangelical and Protestant Literature," *The Record*, October 9, 1931, 647.

114. For more details on the IVF Biblical Research Committee and Tyndale House, see T. A. Noble, *Research for the Academy and the Church: Tyndale House and Fellowship. The First Sixty Years* (Leicester: Inter-Varsity Press, 2006); and the minutes of the Biblical Research Committee, held at Tyndale House, Cambridge.

115. See Dudley-Smith, *John Stott: The Making*, 131.

116. Stott Papers; quoted in Dudley-Smith, *John Stott: The Making*, 199–200.

117. This would also have been a very natural transition given Nash's involvement in the CICCU; indeed, he spoke at a CICCU meeting within weeks of Stott's arrival at the university; Minutes, July 25, 1940, CICCU Executive Committee Minute Book 3.

118. Weight, *Patriots*, 28–33.

119. Lily Stott to John Stott, January 25, 1941, Stott Papers, quoted in Dudley-Smith, *John Stott: The Making*, 264. On greater openness to ideas of sin and evil, see Bebbington, *Evangelicalism*, 253–254.

120. William Temple, *Christianity and Social Order* (Harmondsworth: Penguin, 1942).

121. *Towards the Conversion of England* (1945). Hugh McLeod, *The Religious Crisis of the 1960s* (Oxford: Oxford University Press, 2007), 32.

122. A. Rendle Short, "The Place of the I.V.F. in the World of Tomorrow," *The Inter-Varsity Magazine*, Lent Term, 1944, 2–3, and B. Godfrey Buxton, "Let Us Prepare Now," *The Inter-Varsity Magazine*, Lent Term, 1944, 7.

123. John Stott to Arnold Stott, draft letter, January 31, 1941, Stott Papers, quoted in Dudley-Smith, *John Stott: The Making*, 166.

124. Dudley-Smith, *John Stott: The Making*, 204.

125. Weight, *Patriots*, 29.

126. 1.7 percent of the relevant age cohort went to university in 1939; McKibbin, *Classes and Cultures*, 248.

CHAPTER 2

1. "What think ye of Christ?" Invitation Card, Pollock CICCU Papers, Add. 8545, Cambridge University Library.

2. "We Congratulate...," *Varsity*, November 15, 1952, 8; "London Rector's Talks in Cambridge," *Cambridge Daily News*, November 15, 1952, 6. On people being turned away on the final night, see Basil Atkinson to John Pollock, undated, in Pollock CICCU Papers. Estimates of the number of converts varied between 180 and 300: see R. H. C. to John Pollock on the 1952 mission, undated, and Basil Atkinson to John Pollock, undated, both in Pollock CICCU Papers. Cf. John Stott, "The Rector's Letter," *All Souls*, December 1952, 7.

3. This is the implication of Stott's comments in John Stott, "The Rector's Letter," *All Souls*, February 1959, 11; and John Stott, "The Rector's Letter," *All Souls*, February 1970, 8–9.

4. John Stott, "The Rector's Letter," *All Souls*, December 1952, 7.

5. John Stott, "The Rector's Letter," *All Souls*, November 1954, 11.

6. John Stott, "All Souls Rectory," *All Souls*, February 1956, 11.

7. John Stott, "African Safari," *All Souls*, September 1959, 16.

8. John Stott, "The Rector's Letter," *All Souls*, May 1963, 11.

9. John Stott, "Evangelism in the Student World," *Christian Graduate*, March 1959, 1.

10. See John Stott, "A Letter from the Rector," *Monthly Notes*, November 1950, 5; John Stott, "The Rector's Letter," *All Souls*, February 1966, 9; and John Stott, "The Rector's Letter," *All Souls*, February 1962, 11. The All Souls parish magazine was known as *Monthly Notes* until the end of 1950, and *All Souls* thereafter.

11. Maurice Wood, "The Mission to Cambridge University," *The Christian*, November 4, 1955, 1. See also "Preface," *Crockford's Clerical Directory, 1948* (Oxford: Oxford University Press, 1948), xvii.

12. John Stott, "The Rector's Letter," *All Souls*, December 1952, 7.

13. John Stott, "The Rector's Letter," *All Souls*, November 1957, 11.

14. John Stott, "The Rector's Letter," *All Souls*, December 1958, 10; John Stott, "The Rector's Letter," *All Souls*, November 1957, 11; and M. A. Green, "Oxford," *All Souls*, January 1958, 16.

15. See Tony Tyndale, "A Brief Report on the Mission at University of British Columbia"; Tony Tyndale, "Report on the Mission in the University of Western Ontario"; Tony Tyndale, "Brief Report on the Lecture Series in the University of Illinois"; Tony and Penny Tyndale, "Report on Lecture Series at University of Michigan," all in Folder 7, Box 355, Collection 300, InterVarsity Christian Fellowship Records, Archives of the Billy Graham Center, Wheaton, Illinois; hereafter IVCF Papers.

16. R. H. C. to John Pollock. See also Richard Harbour to Pollock, undated, Pollock CICCU Papers; "Successful Week of University Mission," *Varsity*, November 15, 1952, 3; and memorandum from Jim Nyquist, December 1956, Folder 7, Box 355, IVCF Papers.

17. Alec Motyer, review of John Stott, *Basic Christianity* (London: Inter-Varsity Fellowship, 1958), in *The Churchman* 72 (1958): 108–113.

18. Stott, *Basic Christianity*, 7. Mark Duane Becton, "An Analysis of John Stott's Preaching as 'Bridge-building' as Compared to the Preaching of David Martyn Lloyd-Jones" (Ph.D. diss., Southwestern Baptist Theological Seminary, 1995), 187.

19. Stott, *Basic Christianity*, 17. Stott later regretted this use of the word "prove" in this context, speaking of it as "a slip." This is, however, more likely evidence of how Stott's thinking had changed by the late-1980s than of any genuine slip in the 1950s. See David L. Edwards with John Stott, *Essentials: A Liberal-Evangelical Dialogue* (London: Hodder and Stoughton, 1988), 231.

20. Stott, *Basic Christianity*, 23.

21. See "Man with a Mission," *Varsity*, November 15, 1958, 4.

22. John Stott, *The Preacher's Portrait* (Grand Rapids, Mich.: Eerdmans, 1961), 55–56.

23. Nicholson did the 1926 CICCU Mission; for comments, see David Goodhew, "The Rise of the Cambridge Inter-Collegiate Christian Union, 1910–1971," *Journal of Ecclesiastical History* 54 (2003): 66–67; an anonymous document, Pollock CICCU Papers; and R. E. D. Clark, undated document, Pollock CICCU Papers. Barnhouse did the CICCU missions in 1946 and 1949; for the above quotation, see Mike Griffiths, "Reflections on the 1949 Mission,"

October 10, 1951, Pollock CICCU Papers; see also Dudley-Smith, *John Stott: The Making*, 337; Goodhew, "The Rise," 77; and the comments of Oliver Barclay, undated, Pollock CICCU Papers.

24. Griffiths, "Reflections on the 1949 Mission."

25. "Man with a Mission"; "Successful Week of University Mission"; Maurice Wood, "The Mission to Cambridge University," 1.

26. On nineteenth-century moderate evangelicals and enthusiasm, see Boyd Hilton, *The Age of Atonement: The Influence of Evangelicalism on Social and Economic Thought, 1785–1863* (Oxford: Clarendon Press, 1988), 20; and David W. Bebbington, *Evangelicalism in Modern Britain: A History from the 1730s to the 1980s* (London: Routledge, 1989), 22–23.

27. Derek Prince to John Stott, November 25, 1952, Pollock CICCU Papers.

28. Callum G. Brown, *The Death of Christian Britain: Understanding Secularisation, 1800–2000* (London: Routledge, 2001), 187, 191; Richard Weight, *Patriots: National Identity in Britain 1940–2000*, corrected edn. (London: Pan Books, 2003), 223–225.

29. Arthur Stretton Reeve, "The Bishop's Letter," *Lichfield Diocesan Magazine*, June 1954, 58 (for similar comments attributed to the Archbishop of Canterbury, Geoffrey Fisher, see Letter from Maurice Wood, *The Times*, August 25, 1955, 14); "Editorial," *The Churchman* 59 (1955): 195; and Maurice A. P. Wood, "The Presidential Address," in *The Church Extends Her Frontiers: The 121st Islington Clerical Conference* (London: Marshall, Morgan & Scott, 1955), 16.

30. Hugh Gough, "Modern Trends in Evangelism," in *The Church Extends Her Frontiers*, 40.

31. See, for example, "Preface," *Crockford's Clerical Directory, 1955–56* (Oxford: Oxford University Press, 1956), xi–xii, xix–xx.

32. See "College Religion," *Varsity*, March 1, 1958, 9.

33. Quoted in Hugh McLeod, *The Religious Crisis of the 1960s* (Oxford: Oxford University Press, 2007), 37.

34. See especially Adrian Hastings, *A History of English Christianity 1920–2000*, 4th edn. (London: SCM Press, 2001), 236–239, 293, 388–389, 444–447; and Alan M. G. Stephenson, *The Rise and Decline of English Modernism* (London: SPCK, 1984), 181.

35. See Stephenson, *The Rise and Decline*, 181, and Bebbington, *Evangelicalism*, 254–255.

36. John Stott, "The Rector's Letter," *All Souls*, April 1958, 10.

37. Keith Robbins, *History, Religion and Identity in Modern Britain* (London: Hambledon Press, 1993), 195–213, provides a fine discussion of the complexities of discussions about Christianity and the war in Britain in 1940. A poem by Timothy Dudley-Smith that related the sacrifices of war, the sacrifice of Christ,

and the nation's duty to remember both, was published in *All Souls*, in 1951. Timothy Dudley-Smith, "November 11," *All Souls*, November 1951, 16.

38. McLeod, *The Religious Crisis*, 31, 45.

39. Hastings, *A History*, 423–424.

40. Bernhard Rieger and Martin Daunton, "Introduction," in *Meanings of Modernity: Britain from the Late-Victorian Era to World War II*, ed. Martin Daunton and Bernhard Rieger (Oxford: Berg, 2001), 11; and Ross McKibbin, *Parties and People: England 1914–1951* (Oxford: Oxford University Press, 2010), 194–195.

41. Peter Clarke, *Hope and Glory: Britain 1900–2000* (London: Penguin, 2004), 232.

42. José Harris, "Tradition and Transformation: Society and Civil Society in Britain, 1945–2001," in *The British Isles Since 1945*, ed. Kathleen Burk (Oxford: Oxford University Press, 2003), 97; Weight, *Patriots*, 201; David Cannadine, *Class in Britain* (London: Penguin, 2000), 157–158.

43. See Ben Pimlott, *The Queen: Elizabeth II and the Monarchy*, 2nd edn. (London: HarperCollins, 2002), 392; and David Cannadine, "The Context, Performance and Meaning of Ritual: The British Monarchy and the 'Invention of Tradition,' c. 1820–1977," in *The Invention of Tradition*, ed. Eric Hobsbawm and Terence Ranger (Cambridge: Cambridge University Press, 1983), 139–155.

44. "And After?" *The Times*, June 3, 1953, 13.

45. On the demise of the Church of England as a national church, see especially David Hempton, *Religion and Political Culture in Britain and Ireland: From the Glorious Revolution to the Decline of Empire* (Cambridge: Cambridge University Press, 1996), 1–24.

46. Quoted in Weight, *Patriots*, 222.

47. Arthur Stretton Reeve, "The Bishop's Letter," *Lichfield Diocesan Magazine*, January 1954, 1.

48. "Preface," *Crockford's Clerical Directory, 1953–54* (Oxford: Oxford University Press, 1954), iv.

49. C. O. Rhodes, "I was Proud of our Church—The Greatest Moment of the Archbishop's Ministry," *Church of England Newspaper*, June 5, 1953, 7.

50. John Stott, "The Rector's Letter," *All Souls*, May 1953, 10.

51. "Parish News," *All Souls*, May 1952, 15.

52. See "The Elizabethan Age," *All Souls*, June 1952, 18; and Dominic Sandbrook, *Never Had it So Good: A History of Britain from Suez to the Beatles* (London: Little, Brown, 2005), 44. Cf. Diarmaid MacCulloch, "The Myth of the English Reformation," *Journal of British Studies* 30 (1991): 9–10.

53. M. A. C. Warren, "The Conference Sermon," in *The Church Extends Her Frontiers*, 59.

54. Hugh McLeod, "Recent Studies in Victorian Religious History," *Victorian Studies* 21 (1977–78): 255.

55. Nicholas Spice, review of David Kynaston, *Family Britain, 1951–57* (London: Bloomsbury, 2009), *London Review of Books*, April 8, 2010, 11. See also Clarke, *Hope and Glory*, 250–251; Robert Hewison, *Culture and Consensus: England, Art and Politics Since 1940*, rev. edn. (London: Methuen, 1997), 50–87; Peter Mandler, "Two Cultures—One—or Many?" in *The British Isles Since 1945*, ed. Burk, 131.

56. On the exaggeration of interwar evangelical weakness and the reasons for it, see especially Martin Wellings, *Evangelicals Embattled: Responses of Evangelicals in the Church of England to Ritualism, Darwinism and Theological Liberalism 1890–1930* (Milton Keynes: Paternoster, 2003), 1–2.

57. See Adrian Hastings, *Church and State: The English Experience* (Exeter: University of Exeter Press, 1991), 61; and Weight, *Patriots*, 223.

58. Letter from H. K. Luce, *The Times*, August 15, 1955, 7. This letter, along with the correspondence that followed in the newspaper and an editorial, were collected and published as *Fundamentalism: A Religious Problem* (London: The Times Publishing Company, 1955).

59. Ian Randall, "Conservative Constructionist: The Early Influence of Billy Graham in Britain," *Evangelical Quarterly* 67 (1995): 328.

60. "College Religion"; Robert H. Thouless, "Billy Graham's Mission in Cambridge," *Cambridge Review*, November 19, 1955, 191; and John Stott, "All Souls Rectory," *All Souls*, December 1955, 10–11.

61. Randall, "Conservative Constructionist," 316–318, 330–331.

62. Alana Harris and Martin Spence, ' "Disturbing the Complacency of Religion?' The Evangelical Crusades of Dr Billy Graham and Father Patrick Peyton in Britain, 1951–54," *Twentieth Century British History* 18 (2007): 481–513. See also McLeod, *The Religious Crisis*, 33–34.

63. "Noises Off at Battersea," *The Times*, July 18, 1955, 5.

64. Mark A. Noll, *American Evangelical Christianity: An Introduction* (Oxford: Blackwell, 2001), 50.

65. Randall, "Conservative Constructionist," 326; William Martin, *A Prophet with Honor: The Billy Graham Story* (New York: W. Morrow and Co., 1991), 174–177; and Frank Colquhoun, *Harringay Story: The Official Record of the Billy Graham Greater London Crusade 1954* (London: Hodder & Stoughton, 1955), 73–75.

66. George M. Marsden, *Understanding Fundamentalism and Evangelicalism* (Grand Rapids, Mich.: Eerdmans, 1991), 1.

67. See "Preface," *Crockford's Clerical Directory, 1953–54*, xx–xxi.

68. Michael Ramsey, "The Menace of Fundamentalism," *The Bishoprick*, February 1956, 24–26.

69. Letter from John Burnaby, *Varsity*, November 19, 1955, 8. Cf. John Burnaby, "What the Bible Says," *Cambridge Review*, November 19, 1955, 191–192.

70. See, for example, Ramsey, "The Menace of Fundamentalism"; Letter from R. C. Marsh, *The Times*, August 22, 1955, 7; Letter from Mervyn Stockwood, *The Times*, August 26, 1955, 9; and Letter from L. John Collins, *The Times*, August 27, 1955, 3.

71. Owen Chadwick, *Michael Ramsey: A Life* (Oxford: Clarendon, 1990), 25–26, 92.

72. Ramsey, "The Menace of Fundamentalism," 25.

73. Letter from R. C. Marsh, *The Times*, August 20, 1955, 7.

74. Letter from Michael Ramsey, *The Times*, August 20, 1955, 7.

75. On the Oxbridge bias amongst clergy, see Robert Towler and A. P. M. Coxon, *The Fate of the Anglican Clergy* (London: Macmillan, 1979), 84.

76. Cf. Michael Saward quoting Geoffrey Fisher as saying that a revivified evangelicalism would be a disaster for the Church, in Michael Saward, *A Faint Streak of Humility: An Autobiography* (Carlisle: Paternoster, 1999), 140.

77. "Misplaced Enthusiasm," *Church Times*, July 22, 1955, 11.

78. "Preface," *Crockford's Clerical Directory, 1953–54*, xxi.

79. For an example of a non-conservative preacher who was experiencing growing congregations during the 1950s, see the comments on Mervyn Stockwood's ministry in Michael De-la-Noy, *Mervyn Stockwood: A Lonely Life* (London: Mowbray, 1996), 86. See also Alister McGrath, *To Know and Serve God: A Biography of James I. Packer* (London: Hodder & Stoughton, 1997), 81.

80. For this latter charge (italics in the original), see Ramsey, "The Menace of Fundamentalism," 25. For background on how he understood and used this term, see Michael Ramsey, "A Threefold Cord," *The Bishoprick*, November 1955, 6–8.

81. "Ordination of a Priest," *Book of Common Prayer*.

82. Letter from Basil Atkinson, *The Times*, August 17, 1955, 9.

83. Text of an address by Philip E. Hughes, "The Archbishop of York's Charge of Heresy," Address to the Annual Meeting of the Fellowship of Evangelical Churchmen, April 24, 1956, Stott Papers.

84. J. I. Packer, *"Fundamentalism" and the Word of God* (London: Inter-Varsity Fellowship, 1958).

85. For Stott on inerrancy, see John Stott, "Evangelical Hypocrisy," *Life of Faith*, January 12, 1949, 1. There was a variety of views on this in the IVF with inerrancy on the more conservative end; see *Evangelical Belief: The Official Interpretation of the Doctrinal Basis of the I.V.F.* (London: Inter-Varsity Fellowship, 1936), 8; T. C. Hammond, *Inspiration and Authority: The Character of Inspiration and the Problems of Authority*, Inter-Varsity Papers No. 3 (London: Inter-Varsity Fellowship, 1936), especially 37; and F. F. Bruce, "The Tyndale Fellowship for Biblical Research" *Evangelical Quarterly* 19 (1947): 56–59.

86. Letter from John Stott, *The Times*, August 25, 1955, 14.

87. John Burnaby, *Is the Bible Inspired?* (London: SPCK, 1959), 113.

88. John Burnaby to John Stott, August 28, 1955, Stott Papers.

89. John Stott to John Burnaby, September 21, 1955, Stott Papers.

90. For the shape of some of these more conservative views, see Bebbington, *Evangelicalism*, 184–191; and George M. Marsden, *Fundamentalism and American Culture: The Shaping of Twentieth-Century Evangelicalism 1870–1925* (New York: Oxford University Press, 1980), 55–62.

91. John Burnaby to John Stott, October 8, 1955, Stott Papers.

92. Douglas Johnson to John Stott, December 1, 1955, Stott Papers.

93. Kathleen Boone describes fundamentalism as evangelicalism's "shirttail relation who for compelling reasons cannot nor will be disowned"; Kathleen C. Boone, *The Bible Tells Them So: The Discourse of Protestant Fundamentalism* (London: SCM, 1990), 11.

94. See, for example, Steve Bruce, *Fundamentalism* (Cambridge: Polity Press, 2000), 13; David W. Bebbington, "Martyrs for Truth: Fundamentalists in Britain," in *Martyrs and Martyrologies*, ed. Diana Wood, Studies in Church History 30 (Oxford: Blackwell, 1993), 419; and David W. Bebbington, "Towards an Evangelical Identity," in *For Such a Time as This: Perspectives on Evangelicalism, Past, Present and Future*, ed. Steve Brady and Harold Rowdon (Bletchley: Scripture Union, 1996), 41.

95. Martin Marty, *A Nation of Behavers* (Chicago: University of Chicago Press, 1976), 95, notes the importance of differences in praxis in distinguishing between fundamentalists and evangelicals.

96. John Stott, "Fundamentalism," *Crusade*, November 1955, 10–11. Stott was to make this last point in a later article written in response to the publication of James Barr, *Fundamentalism* (London: SCM Press, 1977): see John Stott, "Are Evangelicals Fundamentalists?" *Church of England Newspaper*, September 22, 1978, 7. The three extravagances Stott attributed to fundamentalists in the *Crusade* article were the same as those he mentioned in his letter to *The Times*: a total rejection of biblical criticism, excessively literal interpretation, and a "mechanical" view of the inspiration of Scripture; Stott, "Fundamentalism," 10–11.

97. John Stott, "Evangelicals and Evangelism," *Crusade*, May 1956, 4–9.

98. Review of John Stott, *Fundamentalism and Evangelism* (Grand Rapids, Mich.: Eerdmans, 1959), in *Book News Letter*, published by the Augsburg Publishing House, June 1959.

99. "Graham," *Evening Standard*, May 17, 1954, 5.

100. See "Musician's Union?" *Palatinate*, March 7, 1956, 1; and "'Heart Throb' Visits Durham," *Durham County Advertiser*, February 3, 1956, 1. Both McGrath (McGrath, *To Know*, 81), and Dudley-Smith (Dudley-Smith, *John Stott: The*

Making, 366) claim that Ramsey was writing in view of Stott's mission, a contention that seems to find support in the Durham student newspaper (see "Mission Success," *Palatinate*, March 7, 1956, 5).

101. John Stott, "The Rector's Letter," *All Souls*, April 1964. 11; John Stott, "The Rector's Letter," *All Souls*, February 1964, 11.

102. John Stott, "The Rector's Letter," *All Souls*, March 1970, 8.

103. Sandbrook, *Never Had it So Good*, 450.

104. On Malcolm X, see Diary, 1970–71, 19, Stott Papers. On Kenyatta, see Diary, 1973, 11, Stott Papers. For references to Mao Zedong, see Dudley-Smith, *John Stott: A Global Ministry* (Leicester: Inter-Varsity Press, 2001), 179–180.

105. John Stott, "Church and Nation," *All Souls*, July 1968, 12.

106. John Stott, *Basic Christianity*, 2nd edn. (London: Inter-Varsity Press, 1971), 7, 104.

107. "Forward with the Nipple," *Varsity*, February 7, 1970; Avril Groom, "May Week: Freak or Straight?" *Varsity*, April 25, 1970, 5; "Pot Survey in Clare," *Varsity*, January 31, 1970, 4; and "Blueprint," *Varsity*, February 21, 1970, 5.

108. Dudley-Smith, *John Stott: A Global Ministry*, 165–167.

109. "Preacher Rides a Mount," interview of John Stott by Bill Pannifer, *Stop Press with Varsity*, February 19, 1977, 6.

110. See David M. Thompson, *Same Difference? Liberals and Conservatives in the Student Movement* (Birmingham: Student Christian Movement, 1990); Douglas Johnson, *Contending for the Faith: A History of the Evangelical Movement in the Universities and Colleges* (Leicester: Inter-Varsity Press, 1979); Goodhew, "The Rise"; and Oliver R. Barclay and Robert M. Horn, *From Cambridge to the World: 125 Years of Student Witness* (Leicester: Inter-Varsity Press, 2002).

CHAPTER 3

1. *Monthly Notes*, January 1946. *Monthly Notes* was the parish magazine of All Souls. It was renamed All Souls in 1951. Much of the research for and argument of this chapter appeared in Alister Chapman, "Secularisation and the Ministry of John R. W. Stott at All Souls, Langham Place, 1950–70," *Journal of Ecclesiastical History* 56 (2005): 496–513.

2. Harold Earnshaw Smith, "Rector's Letter," *Monthly Notes*, March 1947, 7.

3. Oliver R. Barclay and Robert M. Horn, *From Cambridge to the World: 125 Years of Student Witness* (Leicester: Inter-Varsity Press, 2002), 110–111; Douglas Johnson, Contending for the Faith: A History of the Evangelical Movement in the Universities and Colleges (Leicester: Inter-Varsity Press, 1979), 135; Charles Price and Ian Randall, *Transforming Keswick* (Carlisle: Paternoster, 2000), 30; Harold Earnshaw Smith, "Rector's Letter," *Monthly Notes*, September 1947,

7–8; Harold Earnshaw Smith, "Rector's Letter," *Monthly Notes*, March 1947, 7; Harold Earnshaw Smith, "Rector's Letter," *Monthly Notes*, March 1950, 5.

4. John Stott, "Editorial Letter," *Monthly Notes*, July 1950, 5.

5. John Stott, "A Five-point Manifesto," *Monthly Notes*, July 1950, 7.

6. John Stott, "Editorial Letter," *Monthly Notes*, September 1950, 5.

7. John Stott, "Training School," *Monthly Notes*, October 1950, 8.

8. See Alister C. S. Chapman, "John Stott and English Evangelicalism, 1938–1958" (M.Phil. diss., University of Cambridge, 2001), Appendix 1.

9. Richard Baxter, *The Reformed Pastor* (1656; reprint, Edinburgh: Banner of Truth, 1974), 112.

10. Baxter, *The Reformed Pastor*, 94.

11. See G. W. Bromiley, "Appendix," in G. R. Balleine, *A History of the Evangelical Party in the Church of England*, new edn. (London: Church Book Room Press, 1951), 264; C. A. Martin, "The Pastoral Ministry in the Parish," *The Churchman* 64 (1950): 75–79; and Eric A. Smith, *Another Anglican Angle: Liberal Evangelicalism: The Anglican Evangelical Group Movement 1906–1967* (Oxford: Arnate, 1991), 20.

12. See Stott, *Parochial Evangelism by the Laity* (London: Church Information Office, 1952), 8.

13. "Training the Laity in Evangelism: London Vicar Challenges Islington Conference," *Church of England Newspaper*, January 16, 1953, 3.

14. John Stott, "The Rector's Letter," *All Souls*, February 1953, 8.

15. Both letters are quoted at length in Dudley-Smith, *John Stott: The Making of a Leader* (Leicester: Inter-Varsity Press, 1999), 236–237, 241–242.

16. John Stott, *Christ the Controversialist* (Leicester: Inter-Varsity Press, 1970), 99.

17. John Stott, "The Rector's Letter," *All Souls*, May 1951, 6. See also John Stott to Bernard Gook, November 18, 1958, Stott Papers, and Transcripts of Interviews with John Stott by Dudley-Smith (hereafter Dudley-Smith Transcripts), 16: 1.

18. See, for example, Stott, *Parochial Evangelism*, 3; and John Stott, *One People: Clergy and Laity in God's Church* (London: Falcon Books, 1969), 7.

19. John Stott, "Joy in Jerusalem," *All Souls*, May 1951, 8–9.

20. "We believe that he should now have the opportunity to be the leader of a large and varied team ministry in central London." John Stott, "The Rector's Letter," *All Souls*, June 1970, 9.

21. Report from the Select Committee on the Office of Public Works and Public Buildings, Parliamentary Papers, 1828, Vol. IV, No. 446, 74. See also John Summerson, *The Life and Work of John Nash, Architect* (London: Allen & Unwin, 1980), 76–77, 112, 139.

22. *First Report of the Commissioners of His Majesty's Woods, Forests, and Land Revenues*, Parliamentary Papers, 1812, Vol. XII, No. 357, 88–89.

23. David Hempton, *Religion and Political Culture in Britain and Ireland from the Glorious Revolution to the Decline of Empire* (Cambridge: Cambridge University Press, 1996), 1–24.

24. Some did an excellent job. See, for example, Mark Smith, "The Roots of Resurgence: Evangelical Parish Ministry in the Mid-Twentieth Century," in *Revival and Resurgence in Christian History*, ed. Kate Cooper and Jeremy Gregory, Studies in Church History, 44 (Woodbridge: Boydell & Brewer, 2008), 318–328.

25. See John Stott, "Letter from Mr. Stott," *Monthly Notes*, June 1950, 5; John Stott, "The Rector's Letter," *All Souls*, January 1955, 10; and "The Evangelistic Committee," *All Souls*, January 1960, 19.

26. Scrapbook, "Mobilising the Church for Evangelism," 28, Stott Papers.

27. See especially John Stott, "The Church's Continuing Mission in the Parish," 54–55, in *The Church Extends Her Frontiers: The 121st Islington Clerical Conference* (London: Marshall, Morgan & Scott, 1955). Cf. Adrian Hastings, *A History of English Christianity, 1920–2000*, 4th edn. (London: SCM Press, 2001), 455–456.

28. See Stott, "The Church's Continuing Mission," 54; E. J. H. Nash, *Life at its Best* (n.p., n.d.); and Dudley-Smith Transcripts, 2: 41.

29. John Stott, "Evangelism in the Parish," *All Souls*, May 1955, 15. For evidence that the services at All Souls, including the guest services, were confusing, see Kwang Jeon, "My Impressions of All Souls," *All Souls*, September 1963, 19; and Gill Cooke, "An Australian at All Souls," *All Souls*, July 1964, 19.

30. Stott, "The Church's Continuing Mission," 54.

31. Stott, "A Five-point Manifesto," 7; John Stott, "The Rector's Letter," *Monthly Notes*, July 1950, 6; "Church Services," *All Souls*, January 1954, 11; John Stott, "The Rector's Letter," *All Souls*, February 1952, 7; and Frederick Geoghegan, "Psalm Singing," *All Souls*, February 1951, 15–16.

32. Frederick Geoghegan, "The New Organ," *All Souls*, May 1951, 16–17.

33. "The Passion According to St. John," *All Souls*, April 1954, 19; "Notices," *All Souls*, April 1962, 18; and John Stott, "The Rector's Letter," *All Souls*, November 9, 1966.

34. John Stott, "The Rector's Letter," *All Souls*, August 1970, 8; and Michael Baughen, "The Vicar's Letter," *All Souls*, August 1972, 8.

35. "Parish Notes and News," *Monthly Notes*, October 1946, 10–12. Mark E. Brown, "Anglican Evangelical Approaches to Evangelism: 1800 to the Present Day" (M.Th. diss., Brunel University, 1997), especially 75–78; and "New Team Leaders Week-end," *Monthly Notes*, March 1946, 11–12.

36. "New Team Leaders' Week-end," *Monthly Notes*, March 1946, 11–12.

37. M. A. P. Wood, *Like a Mighty Army* (London: Marshall, Morgan & Scott, 1955), 14, 25–35.

38. Dudley-Smith's claim that under Stott All Souls was a "trail-blazer in parochial evangelism" is therefore potentially misleading; Dudley-Smith, *John Stott: The Making*, 253.

39. Stott, "A Five-point Manifesto," 7–8.

40. John Stott, "Training School," *Monthly Notes*, October 1950, 8; Stott, *Parochial Evangelism*, 4–5; John Stott, *Our Guilty Silence: The Church, the Gospel and the World* (London: Hodder and Stoughton, 1967), 82–85; Stott, *Parochial Evangelism*, 4–7; D. H. Trapnell, "The Evangelistic Committee," All Souls, October 1962, 20; and John Stott, "The Rector's Letter," *All Souls*, May 1967, 9.

41. See, for example, "Parish Notes and News," *Monthly Notes*, January 1950, 7; Sidney Branch, "The Evangelistic Committee," *All Souls*, May 1958, 17; and John Stott, "The Rector's Letter," *All Souls*, October 1964, 11.

42. "Annual Review 1951–1952," *All Souls*, May 1952, 10.

43. Harold Earnshaw Smith, "Rector's Letter", *Monthly Notes*, January 1947, 8; John Stott, "Editorial Letter," *Monthly Notes*, July 1948, 7; Minutes, March 31, 1950, "Annual Church Meeting and Easter Vestry, 1931–1973," P89/ALS/192, London Metropolitan Archives (hereafter LMA); "Letter from Mr. Stott," *Monthly Notes*, June 1950, 5; Dudley-Smith Transcripts, 5: 64; Dudley-Smith, *John Stott: The Making*, 257.

44. John Stott, "All Souls Rectory," *All Souls*, September 1955, 11.

45. See the successive editions of the London Diocese Book.

46. "Confirmation Register, All Souls, Langham Place," P89/ALS/188, LMA.

47. John Stott, "The Rector's Letter," *All Souls*, April 1960, 10.

48. Sidney Branch, "The Evangelistic Committee," *All Souls*, May 1958, 17.

49. For statistics, see "The Parish Church of St Mary Islington, Vestry Minute Book," St. Mary Islington; successive editions of the *London Diocese Book*; "Register of Services, 1961–67," and "St Helen's Church Register of Services, 1968–81," St. Helen's Church, Bishopsgate, London; Smith, "The Roots of Resurgence"; and John Brencher, *Martyn Lloyd-Jones (1899–1981) and Twentieth-century Evangelicalism* (Carlisle: Paternoster, 2002), 237. On overall electoral roll decline, see Hugh McLeod, *The Religious Crisis of the 1960s* (Oxford: Oxford University Press, 2007), 64–65. Electoral roll figures are difficult to interpret, but they serve as useful indicators in the absence of other statistics, particularly as they show a trend in evangelical parishes running counter to the national trend, where there was a 10 percent decrease in electoral roll averages during the 1960s, at a time when the Church of England was seeking to combat inflated roll statistics. For aggregate figures, see Robert Currie, Alan Gilbert, and Lee Horsley, *Churches and Churchgoers: Patterns of Church Growth in the British Isles since 1700* (Oxford: Oxford University Press, 1977), table A1, 128–129.

50. Dominic Sandbrook, *Never Had It So Good: A History of Britain from Suez to the Beatles* (London: Little, Brown, 2005), xxii–xxiv, 726–728.

51. *Marylebone Mercury*, June 1, 1951, 1.

52. John Stott, "The Greater Ministry of the Spirit," *All Souls*, July 1963, 14. See also John Stott, "Be of Good Courage!" *All Souls*, October 1958, 12.

53. Michael Ramsey, *From Gore to Temple: The Development of Anglican Theology Between* Lux Mundi *and the Second World War, 1889–1939* (London: Longmans, 1960), 169; cf. Stott, *Our Guilty Silence*, 46.

54. Cf. the following two volumes which focus on contemporary American evangelicalism and make similar points to the one made here: Christian Smith et al., *American Evangelicalism: Embattled and Thriving* (Chicago: University of Chicago Press, 1998), especially 118–150; and Joseph B. Tamney, *The Resilience of Conservative Religion: The Case of Popular, Conservative Protestant Congregations* (Cambridge: Cambridge University Press, 2002), especially 227–247. See also Paul Chambers, "Factors in Church Growth and Decline (with Reference to the Secularization Thesis)" (Ph.D. diss., University of Wales, 1999), 332.

55. John Stott, "Annual Review," *All Souls*, April 1953, 14–15; John Stott, "Rector at Large: Should We Scrap Confirmation?" *All Souls*, January 1972, 30–31; Hastings, *A History*, 460–465; and David M. Thompson, "The Free Churches in Modern Britain," in *Religion, State, and Society in Modern Britain*, ed. Paul Badham (Lewiston, N.Y.: Edwin Mellen Press, 1989), 106, 115.

56. John Stott, "The Rector's Letter," *All Souls*, September 1954, 10; C. J. E. Lefroy, "University Work," *All Souls*, July 1955, 21; John Stott, "The Rector's Letter," *All Souls*, October 1964, 11; and Raymond Dawes, "All Souls Finances," *All Souls*, November 1967, 25.

57. John Stott, "The Rector's Letter," *All Souls*, September 1966, 8–9; G. E. F. Rawlins, "Spotlight on the Family Service," *All Souls*, February 1964, 17.

58. "Confirmation Register, All Souls, Langham Place"; John Stott, "The Rector's Letter," *All Souls*, July 1952, 7; "Confirmation and Commissioning 1966," *All Souls*, April 1966, 26; and Dawes, "All Souls Finances," 25. In 1957 women accounted for an extraordinary 608 of the 774 who attended the Wednesday Club for twenty-somethings; "The Annual General Meeting," *All Souls*, April 1958, 21. All Souls's experience at this point was representative: see Callum G. Brown, *Religion and Society in Twentieth-century Britain* (Harlow: Pearson, 2006), 30; and Christopher Sinclair, "Le Mouvement Evangélique Anglais de 1942 à 1992" (Thèse de Doctorat Nouveau Régime, Université des Sciences Humaines de Strasbourg, 1994), 81–84. Cf. David W. Bebbington, *Evangelicalism in Modern Britain: A History from the 1730s to the 1980s* (London: Routledge, 1989), 128–129.

59. "Wives Submit," *All Souls*, February 1963, 17; and "Mums at Work," *All Souls*, September 1970, 16–17.

60. "Micro or Mini?" *All Souls*, March 1968, 16–17.

61. On Nash's views, see John Stott, "The Counsellor and Friend," in *A Study in Spiritual Power: An Appreciation of E. J. H. Nash (Bash)*, rev. edn., ed. John Eddison (Crowborough: Highland, 1992), 92–93.

62. John Yates, quoted in John Steer, *Basic Christian: The Inside Story of John Stott* (Downers Grove, Ill.: InterVarsity Press, 2009), 248.

63. Steer, *Basic Christian*, 273.

64. Frances Whitehead, "'I Would not Wish to Have Had Any Other Calling,'" in *John Stott: A Portrait by His Friends*, ed. Christopher J. H. Wright (Leicester: Inter-Varsity Press, 2011), 55.

65. See, for example, John Stott, *I Believe in Preaching* (London: Hodder and Stoughton, 1982), 12.

66. John Stott, *The Incomparable Christ* (Leicester: Inter-Varsity Press, 2001), 13.

67. See *John Stott*, ed. Wright.

68. Matthew Smith, "Watch Out! I Used to be a Boxer!" in *John Stott*, ed. Wright, 206.

69. On Whitehead's respect for Stott, see Steer, *Basic Christian*, 273.

70. John Stott, "Friend of Publican and Sinners," *All Souls*, June 1958, 13.

71. John Stott, "Rekindling the Inner Fire," *All Souls*, January 1960, 12–13.

72. John Stott, "The Rector's Letter," *All Souls*, July 1964, 10.

73. See the statistics in "Confirmation Register, All Souls, Langham Place"; "All Souls, Langham Place Register of Services," P89/ALS/190, LMA; and "All Souls, Langham Place Register of Services," P89/ALS/191, LMA. See also Stott's comments in John Stott, "The Rector's Letter," *All Souls*, March 1959, 10.

74. John Stott, "The Rector's Letter," *All Souls*, March 1951, 6.

75. Stott, *Our Guilty Silence*, 86; quotation from Stott, *One People*, 60–61. Compare the more optimistic assessment by one of Stott's curates in Peter Phenna, "Evangelistic Committee," *All Souls*, November 1964, 21.

76. John Stott, "Genuine Peace," *All Souls*, May 1970, 12.

77. John Stott, "What God Desires," *All Souls*, October 1957, 13.

78. Stott, "A Five-point Manifesto," 7; and John Stott, "Snobbery," *All Souls*, February 1958, 13.

79. Interview with Beryl Ho, parish resident, June 27, 2008.

80. Interview with Beryl Ho; for Cypriots and Spaniards in the parish, see "Register of Parliamentary and Local Government Electors, 1964, London Borough of Camden, Parliamentary Constituency of Holborn and St. Pancras South, Euston Ward (JJ)," in *Register of Electors, 1964, Constituencies of St. Pancras North,*

Holborn & St. Pancras South (London, 1964); and Mike Pentelow and Marsha Rowe, *Characters of Fitzrovia* (London: Chatto & Windus, 2001), 26.

81. For more on this estrangement, see Hempton, *Religion and Political Culture*, 117–142; Peter Mandler, "Two Cultures—One—or Many?" in *The British Isles Since 1945*, ed. Kathleen Burk (Oxford: Oxford University Press, 2003), 128; Richard Weight, *Patriots: National Identity in Britain, 1940–2000*, corrected edn. (London: Pan, 2003), 195–199; and Sarah Williams, *Religious Belief and Popular Culture in Southwark c.1880–1939* (Oxford: Oxford University Press, 1999), 110–112.

82. On proportionately higher upper- and middle-class church attendance in Britain, see Ivan Reid, *Class in Britain* (Cambridge: Polity Press, 1998), 189–197; and Andrew Gimson, "What Think They of Christ?" *The Spectator*, December 13, 1986, 19–20, 24.

83. Grace Davie, *Religion in Britain Since 1945: Believing without Belonging* (Oxford: Blackwell, 1994).

84. For evidence of Stott's practice of not baptizing children of parents whom he did not believe had a solid grasp of the faith, see Quintin Riley to William Wand (Bishop of London), September 23, 1954, and William Wand to John Stott, September 24, 1954, both in Stott Papers. For evidence of contemporary working-class feeling on this issue, see Michael Saward, *A Faint Streak of Humility: An Autobiography* (Carlisle: Paternoster, 1999), 151–154; and William Woodruff, *The Road to Nab End*, new edn. (London: Abacus, 2002), 60.

85. Jeffrey Cox, *The English Churches in a Secular Society: Lambeth, 1870–1930* (New York: Oxford University Press, 1982), 181–202; and Leslie Paul, *The Death and Resurrection of the Church* (London: Hodder & Stoughton, 1968), 14; cf. Hugh McLeod, *Religion and Society in England, 1850–1914* (Basingstoke: Macmillan, 1996), 223–224.

86. Margaret Butterworth, "Social Action Committee," *All Souls*, June 1958, 16.

87. Interview with Nellie Muller, parish resident, June 27, 2008.

88. John Stott, "Editorial Letter," *Monthly Notes*, September 1950, 5.

89. "Parish Notes and News," *Monthly Notes*, November 1946, 9. On the Victorian roots of the mission hall idea, see McLeod, *Religion and Society*, 142–143.

90. John Stott, "All Souls Rectory," *All Souls*, August 1956, 10.

91. John Stott, "All Souls Rectory," *All Souls*, August 1956, 10.

92. Geoffrey Rawlins, "Parish Paper," *All Souls*, August 1957, 17.

93. Peter Phenna, "The Clubhouse Family Outing," *All Souls*, February 1966, 21. For analogous and humorous phoneticization of the Queen's English, see Sue Townsend, *The Queen and I* (London: Methuen, 1992).

94. John Stott, "The Rector's Letter," *All Souls*, April 1966, 9. Graham "seemed to be able to speak with and to Clydeside shipyard workers and university students,

meet the Queen Mother at Clarence House, or take tea with the Queen at Windsor Castle—all with equal facility. He did not have all the social and cultural baggage which would have accompanied a native evangelist operating in such different milieux." Quotation from Keith Robbins, *England, Ireland, Scotland, Wales: The Christian Church 1900–2000* (Oxford: Oxford University Press, 2008), 324.

95. On "old boys" networks and their prevalence in hiring during this period, see David Kynaston, *Austerity Britain, 1945–51* (London: Bloomsbury, 2007), 445–446. On Packer approaching Stott, see Alister McGrath, *To Know and Serve God: A Life of James I. Packer* (London: Hodder and Stoughton, 1997), 59.

96. On Stott giving up his bed, see Dudley-Smith, *John Stott: The Making*, 264.

97. Julian Charley, "The Clubhouse," *All Souls*, July 1964, 21.

98. Interview with Nellie Muller; T. R. Robinson, "The Clubhouse," *All Souls*, September 1962, 20; and Peter Phenna, "The Clubhouse," *All Souls*, February 1967, 25. On Christian youth clubs during this period, see McLeod, *The Religious Crisis*, 104–105.

99. "Anniversary," *Crusade*, March 1959, 5.

100. See "Lessons to Learn," *Crusade*, August 1961, 3, 5.

101. Peregrine Worsthorne, "Class and Conflict in British Foreign Policy," *Foreign Affairs* 37 (1959): 419–431. See also Matthew Grimley, *Citizenship, Community, and the Church of England: Liberal Anglican Theories of the State between the Wars* (Oxford: Clarendon, 2004), 218–219.

102. David Cannadine, *Class in Britain* (London: Penguin, 2000), 160.

103. Peter Clarke, *Hope and Glory: Britain 1900–2000* (London: Penguin, 2004), 293; Callum Brown, *The Death of Christian Britain: Understanding Secularisation, 1800–2000* (London: Routledge, 2001), 178; Roy and Gwen Shaw, "The Cultural and Social Setting," in *The Cambridge Cultural History of Britain*, Vol. 9: *Modern Britain*, ed. Boris Ford (Cambridge: Cambridge University Press, 1988), 18; and David Martin, "The Church of England: From Established Church to Secular Lobby," in *The Kindness that Kills: The Churches' Simplistic Response to Complex Social Issues*, ed. Digby C. Anderson (London: SPCK, 1984), 136.

104. Sandbrook, *Never Had it So Good*, 592, 638–681.

105. Brown, *The Death of Christian Britain*.

106. José Harris, "Tradition and Transformation: Society and Civil Society in Britain, 1945–2001," in *The British Isles*, ed. Burk, 101–102; and David Butler and Gareth Butler, *British Political Facts 1900–1994* (Basingstoke: Macmillan, 1994), 132, 146–147. On the impact of television and cars, see also Richard Sykes, "Popular Religion in Decline: A Study from the Black Country", *Journal of Ecclesiastical History* 56 (April 2005): 303–304.

107. Weight, *Patriots*, 321–323.

108. "Lessons to Learn," 5.

109. McLeod, *The Religious Crisis*, 169–182. See also William Whyte, "The Jackie Generation: Girls' Magazines, Pop Music, and the Discourse Revolution," in *Redefining Christian Britain: Post 1945 Perspectives*, ed. Jane Garnett, Matthew Grimley, Alana Harris, William Whyte, and Sarah Williams (London: SCM Press, 2007), 128–137.

110. Callum G. Brown, "Sex, Religion, and the Single Woman c.1950–75: The Importance of a 'Short' Sexual Revolution to the English Religious Crisis of the Sixties," *Twentieth Century British History* 22 (2011): 189–215. Matthew Grimley has pointed out that some Anglican clergy took the lead in advocating for the decriminalization of homosexual practice. See Matthew Grimley, "Law, Morality and Secularisation: The Church of England and the Wolfenden Report, 1954–1967," *Journal of Ecclesiastical History* 60 (2009): 725–741.

111. "Girls, You Can Earn £100 a week!" *Marylebone Mercury*, May 23, 1969, 17; "Sweet Charity Girls," *Marylebone Mercury*, May 2, 1969, 43; "Abortion Centre of the World? Rubbish!" *Marylebone Mercury*, July 11, 1969, 1; "More Women Choose Birth Pill," *Marylebone Mercury*, June 13, 1969, 1; "Dolly Girls in the Parish Mag," *Marylebone Mercury*, June 6, 1969, 37; and caption of photo of Irenie Horstmann, *Marylebone Mercury*, July 25, 1969, 3.

112. John Stott, "Church and Nation," *All Souls*, July 1968, 10–11.

113. Brown, *The Death of Christian Britain*, 191.

114. Interview with Michael Baughen, June 6, 2008.

115. Stott, "Rekindling the Inner Fire," 13; John Stott, "The Rector's Letter," *All Souls*, March 1960, 11; John Stott, "The Rector's Letter," *All Souls*, June 1960, 10; John Stott, "The Greater Ministry of the Spirit," *All Souls*, July 1963, 14. See also John Stott, "The Rector's Letter," *All Souls*, June 1958, 10; John Stott, "A Study of Revival," *All Souls*, March 1960, 12–14; Stott, "The Promise is to You," 11–14; John Stott, "The Rector's Letter," *All Souls*, February 1962, 10; John Stott, "The Paroxysm of Paul," *All Souls*, November 1962, 12–14; John Stott, "The Rector's Letter," *All Souls*, March 1963, 10; and John Stott, "The Rector's Letter," *All Souls*, May 1963, 10–11.

116. See especially John Stott, "The Rector's Letter," *All Souls*, March 1963, 10.

117. Stott, "Rekindling the Inner Fire," 13–14.

118. See John Stott, *The Baptism and Fullness of the Holy Spirit* (London: Inter-Varsity Fellowship, 1964).

119. See Alister Chapman, "Anglican Evangelicals and Revival, 1945–59," in *Revival and Resurgence in Christian History*, ed. Cooper and Gregory, 307–317.

120. See, for example, John Stott, "The Nature of Man," *All Souls*, November 1954, 14; John Stott, "Honest to God," *All Souls*, August 1963, 13; and John Stott, The

Preacher's Portrait: Some New Testament Word Studies (London: Tyndale, 1961), vii, 25.

121. Ted Schroder, "Thoroughly Modern...," *All Souls*, September 1968, 27.

122. See Niki West, "Outreach Wednesday Club Style: Demos...," *All Souls*, June 1970, 28; Martin Sully, "Outreach Wednesday Club Style: Music...," *All Souls*, June 1970, 28, 30; and Mike O'Neill, "Outreach Wednesday Club Style: Soho and the Drug Scene," *All Souls*, July 1970, 31.

123. "Sex Teach-ins at the Church Wednesday Club," *Marylebone Mercury*, June 6, 1969, 35.

124. For Stott on his debt to Schroder, see Stott, *I Believe in Preaching*, 12; and "We Must Begin with the Glory of God," interview of John Stott by John Capon, *Crusade*, May 1974, 35. On relevance, see John Stott, "Paul's Final Charge," *All Souls*, January 1968, 11; Stott, "Church and Nation," 12; John Stott, "The Rector's Letter," *All Souls*, September 1968, 9; John Stott, "The Rector's Letter," *All Souls*, October 1969, 9; and John Stott, "The Spirit's Message to the Church," *All Souls*, November 1969, 10–11. On "relevance" as a common concern among clergy of the day, see McLeod, *The Religious Crisis*, 89–90. On liturgical innovation, see Timothy Dudley-Smith, *John Stott: A Global Ministry* (Leicester: Inter-Varsity Press, 2001), 53. For treatment of contemporary social issues, see, for example, John Stott, "Jesus Christ and Morality," *All Souls*, April 1968, 10–12, 28; Stott, "Church and Nation," 10–11; and John Stott, "The Biblical Idea of 'Newness,'" *All Souls*, September 1968, 10–12, 25.

125. Stott, "Jesus Christ and Morality," 12.

126. Stott gave up day-to-day responsibility for All Souls in 1970, although he kept the position of rector until 1975.

127. See Timothy Dudley-Smith, *John Stott: A Comprehensive Bibliography* (Leicester: Inter-Varsity Press, 1995), 10–12. Dudley-Smith lists five books for the 1950s and nine for the 1960s, but one of the books in each category—*Fundamentalism and Evangelism* (Grand Rapids, Mich.: Eerdmans, 1959) and *The Baptism and Fullness of the Holy Spirit* (Downers Grove, Ill. InterVarsity Press, 1964)—were published as booklets in the United Kingdom.

128. See, for example, John Stott, "The Rector's Letter," *All Souls*, January 1969, 8–9, 23; John Stott, "The Rector's Letter," *All Souls*, March 1969, 8–9, 25; John Stott, "The Rector's Letter," *All Souls*, September 1969, 8–9, 25; John Stott, "The Rector's Letter," *All Souls*, October 1968, 8–9; John Stott, "The Rector's Letter," *All Souls*, December 1969, 8–9; John Stott, "The Rector's Letter," *All Souls*, March 1970, 9; and John Stott, "The Rector's Letter," *All Souls*, November 1970, 8–9.

129. John Stott, *The Contemporary Christian* (Leicester: Inter-Varsity Press, 1992), 103.

130. On discontent, see John Stott, "The Rector's Letter," *All Souls*, February 1970, 8–9. Michael Baughen mentioned this sermon in an interview, June 6, 2008. He did not reveal the name of the preacher.

131. Minutes, September 20, 1969, "A Proposed Restructuring of the Staff Team," September 1969, stapled at 84 into "All Souls with St Peter and St John, St Marylebone, Minutes of the Proceedings of the Parochial Church Council," P89/ALS/193, LMA.

132. Mary Endersbee, *Hidden Miracles at All Souls* (London: Lakeland, 1977), 9.

133. Dudley-Smith Transcripts 17: 31.

134. On Stott being tired, see "A Proposed Restructuring of the Staff Team."

135. After outlining his plan for parochial evangelism in *Our Guilty Silence* and noting its lack of success, Stott was unable to offer any alternative suggestions. Stott, *Our Guilty Silence*, 79–92.

136. See Michael Baughen, "News from Number Ten," *All Souls*, July 1973, 8–9; "The Vicar's Letter," *All Souls*, March 1972, 8; "The Vicar's Letter," *All Souls*, April 1972, 8–9; "The Vicar's Letter," *All Souls*, July 1972, 8.

137. Michael Baughen, "News from Number Twelve," *All Souls*, January 1973, 8.

138. Pentelow and Rowe, *Characters of Fitzrovia*, 29–30; Mandler, "Two Cultures," 141; and Clarke, *Hope and Glory*, 291–293. Stott was open to Schroder experimenting with new music, but not in church: John Stott, "The Rector's Letter," *All Souls*, November 1968, 9.

CHAPTER 4

1. A prayer Stott composed early in his ministry showed that for him the Church of England and the church in England were pretty much the same thing. Praying for the Church of England, he wrote: "Almighty God, whose mercy reacheth unto the heavens and Thy faithfulness unto the clouds, we bless Thee for Thy gracious providence towards our nation in the creation, perseveration and reformation of Thy church within its borders"; "Church of England," Book of Prayers, Stott Papers.

2. John Stott, "The Rector's Letter," *All Souls*, July 1954, 11.

3. T. S. Eliot, *The Idea of a Christian Society and Other Writings* (London: Faber, 1982), 71.

4. John Stott, "The Rector's Letter," *All Souls*, July 1954, 11.

5. John Stott, "The Rector's Letter," *All Souls*, June 1955, 10.

6. This was a widespread belief at the time. For example, see the anonymous "Preface," *Crockford's Clerical Directory, 1949–50* (Oxford: Oxford University Press, 1950), x: "If England has become or is on the way to becoming a semi-pagan country, it is probably because there are not, and have not been for a generation, nearly

enough clergy to do the Church's work efficiently." Further evidence can be found in the lengthy, annual debates in the Church Assembly on reports by the Central Advisory Council of Training for the Ministry, for example, "'Recruitment for the Ministry': A Report by the Central Advisory Council of Training for the Ministry (C.A. 1101)," *Church Assembly Report of Proceedings* 34 (1954): 55–75; and "Annual Report of the Central Advisory Council for the Ministry (C.A. 1551)," *Church Assembly Report of Proceedings* 45 (1965): 334–338.

7. John Stott, "All Souls Rectory," *All Souls*, September 1956, 10–11. Mary Endersbee, *Hidden Miracles at All Souls* (London, 1977), 57.

8. Stott was on the cusp of a vocational shift among evangelical Anglican clergy here, deciding to stay at home while the two other curates at All Souls in the late 1940s decided to become missionaries. "Mr. Lester Says Good-bye," *Monthly Notes*, September 1948, 11; and "Letter from Mr. Stott," *Monthly Notes*, May 1950, 5.

9. Figures complied from the list of missionaries in S. Farrant Russell, *Full Fifty Years: The BCMS Story* (London: Patmos Press, 1972), 79–89.

10. See, for example, "'As Evangelicals, the Future Belongs to Us,' says President," *Church of England Newspaper*, January 11, 1957, 3, which quoted Maurice Wood saying: "We as evangelicals are now producing more candidates for Ordination than any other group, and the future is ours; so that flexible, continuous revision must favour our position by a growing weight of numbers." See also "Islington 1959," *Church of England Newspaper*, January 16, 1959, 6.

11. See "Christians Becoming Minority—Bishop," *Bristol Evening Post*, January 22, 1955, 11; and "People Turning Back to God, Says Bishop," *Bristol Evening World*, January 22, 1955, 5. The bishop in question was Hugh Gough, Bishop of Barking.

12. John Lefroy suggested the name. See Timothy Dudley-Smith, *John Stott: The Making of a Leader* (Leicester: Inter-Varsity Press, 1999), 304.

13. Dudley-Smith, *John Stott: The Making*, 143.

14. Transcripts of Interviews with John Stott by Timothy Dudley-Smith (hereafter Dudley-Smith Transcripts), 16: 17–18.

15. John Stott, "World-wide Evangelical Anglicanism," in *Evangelicals Today*, ed. John C. King (Guildford and London: Lutterworth, 1973), 180.

16. On the liberal evangelical leaders, see "Preface," *Crockford's Clerical Directory, 1955–56* (Oxford: Oxford University Press, 1956), xi.

17. "How the Keele Congress Came About," *Church of England Newspaper*, February 17, 1967, 16.

18. Adrian Hastings, *A History of English Christianity*, 4th edn. (London: SCM Press, 2001), 449–450; Dudley-Smith, *John Stott: The Making*, 312–314.

19. On Loane's influence, see Dudley-Smith, *John Stott: The Making*, 312–314.

20. "The Evangelical Fellowship in the Anglican Communion," *The Churchman* 76 (1962): 39.

21. T. G. Mohan, "Evangelicalism in the Church of England," EFAC Supplement, *The Churchman* 77 (1963): 263.

22. John Stott, "The Rector's Letter," *All Souls*, November 1961, 11.

23. Talbot Mohan was the person in question.

24. See Timothy Dudley-Smith, *John Stott: A Global Ministry* (Leicester: Inter-Varsity Press, 2001), 55–56.

25. See Minutes, January 27, 1961, and May 26, 1951, "CEEC Minutes March 24, 1960 (the first meeting) – December 1, 1966 with a preamble about the 'C of E Gp'" (hereafter CEEC Minute Book 1), Oak Hill College, London.

26. Minutes, January 27, 1961, CEEC Minute Book 1.

27. Minutes, July 6, 1961, CEEC Minute Book 1.

28. Minutes, October 12, 1961, and August 19, 1964, CEEC Minute Book 1.

29. "Notes and Comments," *The Churchman* 50 (1936): 249; "Notes and Comments," *The Churchman*, 52 (1938): 1–2; and *The Churchman*, 75, no. 2 (1961), passim.

30. Letter from N. L. Dunning, A. L. Kensit, and Donald Hill, *Church of England Newspaper*, September 19, 1958, 10.

31. See evidence of this fear in the letter from Church of England laymen to Michael Ramsey, 1963, Ramsey Papers, Vol. 38, ff. 352–354, Lambeth Palace Library, London. On the 1927–28 debates, see John G. Maiden, *National Religion and the Prayer Book Controversy, 1927–1928* (Woodbridge: Boydell, 2009).

32. Carla Gardina Pestana, *Protestant Empire: Religion and the Making of the British Atlantic World* (Philadelphia: University of Pennsylvania Press, 2009), 63–65.

33. David W. Bebbington, *Evangelicalism in Modern Britain: A History from the 1730s to the 1980s* (London: Routledge, 1989), 205. On Protestantism and English and British national identity, see Linda Colley, *Britons: Forging the Nation 1707–1837* (New Haven, Conn.: Yale University Press, 1986); Gardina Pestana, *Protestant Empire*; and Maiden, *National Religion*.

34. Frank Colquhoun, "The Prayer Book Commentaries," *All Souls*, May 1962, 17.

35. Minutes, June 22, 1962, CEEC Minute Book 1.

36. Frank M. Turner, *John Henry Newman: The Challenge to Evangelical Religion* (New Haven, Conn.: Yale University Press, 2002), 162–206.

37. "Christian Foundations," *The Churchman* 79 (1965): 204–206; and Stott, "World-wide Evangelical Anglicanism," 177.

38. John Stott, "The Rector's Letter," *All Souls*, March 1962, 10.

39. John Stott, "True Heart-worship," *All Souls*, May 1962, 12–14.

40. John Stott, "Authority—Scripture or Tradition?" *All Souls*, July 1962, 12–14.

41. John Stott, *Christ the Controversialist: A Study in Some Essentials of Evangelical Religion* (London: Tyndale, 1970), 196.

42. John Stott, "The Rector's Letter," *All Souls*, March 1962, 11.

43. Stott gave a paper on Calvinism at the 1961 Islington Clerical Conference, which was appreciative yet critical. See "Bishop of Bradford's 'Three Personal Convictions,'" *Church of England Newspaper*, January 13, 1961, 3, 14.

44. John Stott, "The Rector's Letter," *All Souls*, May 1962, 10.

45. Letter from Michael Ramsey and Donald Coggan, July 1962. Ramsey Papers, Vol. 30, f. 230.

46. Letter from John Stott, R. Peter Johnston, the Viscount of Brentford, and Arthur Smith, October 30, 1962, Ramsey Papers, Vol. 30, ff. 283–285.

47. "Challenge to Prayer Book Proposals," *The Times*, October 31, 1962, 7.

48. See especially "Summary of the News," *Church Times*, November 2, 1962, 3.

49. "Church of England," *Hansard*, House of Commons, vol. 669, 1962–63, December 14, 1962, columns 755–847; and "Church Reform Voted Without Division," *The Times*, December 15, 1962, 8.

50. "Church of England," *Hansard*, columns 759–766.

51. Eric Fletcher to John Stott, December 18, 1962, Stott Papers; and John Stott, "Why Evangelicals are So Anxious," *Church Times*, March 22, 1963, 13.

52. For more on the demise of political Protestantism, see John Maiden and Peter Webster, "Parliament, the Church of England and the Last Gasp of Political Protestantism, 1961–4," forthcoming. Maiden and Webster argue that Protestantism continued to stir some MPs during this period, but that it was spent as an effective political force.

53. Richard Weight, *Patriots: National Identity in Britain, 1940–2000*, corrected edn. (London: Pan, 2003), 440–445; Bebbington, *Evangelicalism in Modern Britain*, 256, 272; and Ross McKibbin, *Classes and Cultures: England, 1918–1951* (Oxford: Oxford University Press, 1998), 277–278.

54. Mohan, "Evangelicalism in the Church of England," 259.

55. John Wolffe, *God and Greater Britain: Religion and National Life in Britain and Ireland, 1843–1945* (London: Routledge, 1994), 262; and John Wolffe, "'Religion' and 'Secularization'," in *Twentieth-century Britain: Economic, Social and Cultural Change*, ed. Paul Johnson (London: Longman, 1994), 432; cf. Peter Clarke, *Hope and Glory: Britain 1900–2000* (London: Penguin, 2004), 320, on the mid-1960s as the proper start of post-imperial reckoning in Britain.

56. O. R. Johnston, *Nationhood: Towards a Christian Perspective* (Oxford: Latimer House, 1980), 26. On the importance of imperial decline for British identity, see A. G. Hopkins, "Back to the Future: From National History to Imperial History," *Past & Present* 164 (1999): 240; and David Cannadine, *Ornamentalism: How the British Saw Their Empire* (London: Penguin, 2001), 172.

57. For Stott's views here, see especially the articles that the *Church Times* invited him to write after the October 1962 letter to MPs: John Stott, "Why Evangelicals Are So Anxious"; and John Stott, "Amending the Prayer Book," *Church Times*, March 29, 1963, 10.

58. "Facing the Future," March 2, 1966, Stott Papers.

59. Dudley-Smith, *John Stott: A Global Ministry*, 40–46, especially 44. The reference to this probability on 44 comes from a document in Stott's hand where he tabulated the pros and cons of accepting an invitation to become principal of Wycliffe Hall, a theological college in Oxford; Undated Thoughts on Position at Wycliffe Hall [1969], Stott Papers.

60. Dudley-Smith Transcripts, 9: 18, quoted in Dudley-Smith, *John Stott: The Making*, 310–311. More generally, see Dudley-Smith Transcripts, 18: 7, where Stott talked about the perception of him on the part of the bishops of London and Willesden. Michael Saward quoted Michael Ramsey saying that Stott was intransigent; see Saward, *A Faint Streak of Humility* (Carlisle, Paternoster, 1999), 291–292.

61. Attached in the minute book after Minutes, January 15, 1965; CEEC Minute Book 1.

62. See Dudley-Smith, *John Stott: A Global Ministry*, 79–80.

63. I am grateful to David Bebbington for his insights on the relationship between the Keele Congress and the Islington Clerical Conference.

64. See Douglas Webster to John Stott, May 10, 1966, Stott Papers; quoted in Dudley-Smith, *John Stott: A Global Ministry*, 84.

65. See Roger Beckwith, "Time for Secession?" *Church of England Newspaper*, July 24, 1964, 12; Letter from R. J. B. Eddison, *Church of England Newspaper*, July 31, 1964, 5; Letter from H. M. Carson et al., *Church of England Newspaper*, September 4, 1964, 6; J. I. Packer, "The Clergyman's Wardrobe," *Church of England Newspaper*, September 4, 1964, 13; "Cambridge Vicar Resigns," *Church of England Newspaper*, November 27, 1964, 3; "'Tongues' Vicar Resigns," *Church of England Newspaper*, December 11, 1964, 40; and "Infant Baptism," *Church of England Newspaper*, January 1, 1965, 5.

66. "Islington 1965," *Church of England Newspaper*, January 15, 1965, 16. See also the account of the "Facing the Future" conference at Swanwick, February–March 1966, in Dudley-Smith, *John Stott: A Global Ministry*, 81–82. For more on the secession crisis, see Andrew Atherstone, "Lloyd-Jones and the Anglican Secession Crisis." *Engaging with Martyn Lloyd-Jones: The Life and Legacy of 'The Doctor'*, ed. Andrew Atherstone and David Ceri Jones (Nottingham: Apollos, 2011), 261–292.

67. John Wenham, *The Renewal and Unity of the Church in England: Some Thoughts of an Evangelical* (London: SPCK, 1972), 10–12; Michael Saward, "I Went to Nottingham," *Church of England Newspaper*, September 25, 1964, 6.

68. See the comment by Jim Packer, quoted in Randle Manwaring, *From Controversy to Co-existence: Evangelicals in the Church of England, 1914–1980* (Cambridge:

Cambridge University Press, 1985), 209. See also the comments of Michael Walker quoted in Dudley-Smith, *John Stott: A Global Ministry*, 81–82.

69. See letter from Paul Betts, *Church of England Newspaper*, March 22, 1963, 7. Michael Saward and Colin Craston were other prominent members of this group.

70. Martyn Lloyd-Jones, "Evangelical Unity: An Appeal," in D. M. Lloyd-Jones, *Knowing the Times: Addresses Delivered on Various Occasions, 1942–1977* (Edinburgh: Banner of Truth, 1989), 246–257.

71. See Dudley-Smith, *John Stott: A Global Ministry*, 67–68.

72. See Iain H. Murray, *David Martyn Lloyd-Jones: The Fight of Faith 1939–1981* (Edinburgh: Banner of Truth, 1990), 495–567; Iain H. Murray, *Evangelicalism Divided: A Record of Crucial Change in the Years 1950–2000* (Edinburgh: Banner of Truth, 2000), 79–111; and Alister McGrath, *To Know and Serve God: A Life of James I. Packer* (London: Hodder & Stoughton, 1997), 116–128.

73. See John Brencher, *Martyn Lloyd-Jones (1899–1981) and Twentieth-century Evangelicalism* (Carlisle: Paternoster, 2002), 116–117.

74. See Brencher, *Martyn Lloyd-Jones*, 193–195, and 142–173.

75. For evidence of Stott's continuing strong commitment to the doctrines of the Protestant Reformation and opposition to unity with the Roman Catholic Church as it stood, see John Stott, "The Rector's Letter," *All Souls*, June 1966, 8–9.

76. For Anglican evangelical responses to Lloyd-Jones's address, see letter from Edward Atkinson, *Church of England Newspaper*, October 28, 1966, 6; and Julian Charley, "Come out from Among Them?" *Church of England Newspaper*, November 11, 1966, 7. Cf. letter from Trevor Marzetti, *Church of England Newspaper*, November 4, 1966, 6, which included the following words: "May I also say that I am not quite sure what Evangelical Nonconformity has to offer Anglicans who leave their fold, whereas we surely have so much to offer them: the fine nation-wide parochial system which they could strengthen and which at the moment they only duplicate in many different denominations and sects, wasting money, time, manpower and brick and mortar; more freedom for evangelistic thrust within each parish set-up than they have in their own local churches; a magnificent Scriptural liturgy, which we are seeking to improve and which they could help in; a sound doctrinal basis they as a whole seem to lack and which they could help to re-emphasise within our Church; definite Conservative Evangelical theological colleges for training, that they do not possess; untold opportunities to reach people in many and varied spheres that they have no influence over at the moment, and so on, and so on."

77. John Stott to Bryan Green, August 5, 1965, Stott Papers.

78. "Statement by Stott, to be given to 133rd Islington Clerical Conference on January 10, 1967," Stott Papers; and "Statement Made at a Press Conference," March 14, 1967, Stott Papers; John Stott, "Attempt to Face To-day's Crucial Questions," *Church Times*, March 31, 1967, 11; and "Evangelicals at Keele Next Week," *Church Times*, March 31, 1967, 1.

79. "Evangelicals at Keele Next Week," 1. Cf. "John Stott's Lament—No Irish Accent," *Church of England Newspaper*, May 6, 1966, 3, for an earlier use. See also Baden Hickman, "Evangelicals 'Coming Out of their Ghettos' to Speak," *The Guardian*, April 5, 1967, 3.

80. Dudley-Smith, *John Stott: A Global Ministry*, 90–91.

81. "The Congress Statement," in *Keele'67: The National Evangelical Anglican Congress Statement*, ed. Philip Crowe (London: Falcon, 1967), 38.

82. "The Congress Statement," 34.

83. See "Statement from Keele," *Church Times*, April 14, 1967, 10; and "Preface," *Crockford's Clerical Directory*, 1967–68 (Oxford: Oxford University Press, 1968), xi.

84. John Stott, "The Rector's Letter," *All Souls*, June 1967, 8.

85. Ramsey to Mervyn Stockwood, April 4, 1967, Ramsey Papers, Vol. 118, f. 226; John Stott to Michael Ramsey, April 8, 1967, Ramsey Papers, Vol. 118, f. 241.

86. John Stott to Michael Ramsey, April 8, 1967.

87. See "Count-down to Keele—Will there be a 'Minor Explosion'?" *Church of England Newspaper*, February 10, 1967, 1, 16; and John King, "Impatient Young Men," *Church of England Newspaper*, March 10, 1967, 8.

88. John King, "Warm, Friendly Animal," *Church of England Newspaper*, April 14, 1967, 6.

89. On penitence, see John Stott, "Introduction to the Statement," in *Keele'67*, ed. Crowe, 18.

90. Letter from John Rosser, *Church of England Newspaper*, May 12, 1967, 6.

91. Letter from A. G. Pouncy, *Church of England Newspaper*, August 4, 1967, 4.

92. See "The Congress Statement," 37.

93. John Stott, "An Evangelical at Uppsala," *Church of England Newspaper*, August 16, 1968, 6.

94. John Stott to Carson Blake, March 22, 1968, Stott Papers, quoting from "The Congress Statement," 37.

95. Stott, "An Evangelical at Uppsala," 6.

96. John Stott, "Evangelicals in a Changing World," *Church of England Newspaper*, November 1, 1968, 12.

97. Minutes, December 4, 1970, and March 4, 1971, "Church of England Evangelical Council Minutes January 5, 1967—3 May 1973" (hereafter CEEC Minute Book 2), Oak Hill College, London. Dudley-Smith, *John Stott: A Global Ministry*, 153.

98. John Stott, "John Stott Reviews," *All Souls*, October 1973, 18.

99. The intercommunion debate eventually went their way, but it is unlikely that their stance on the matter was the decisive factor in an increasingly ecumenical climate where a whole variety of historic ecclesiastical barriers were falling; see Hastings, *A History*, 628–629; cf. Gervase Duffield, "What Happened to B 15?" *Church of England Newspaper*, February 25, 1966, 9. As for liturgical revision, there were several points at which evangelical opinion was heard and heeded, but never often enough nor definitely enough for those who were suspicious of the whole process in the first place; for a thorough discussion of the evangelical element of one part of these discussions, see Christopher J. Cocksworth, *Evangelical Eucharistic Thought in the Church of England* (Cambridge: Cambridge University Press, 1993).

100. Michael De-la-Noy has summed up the differences neatly: "The high church party saying the Service of Reconciliation was not ordination and ought to be, the low church party saying it was ordination (and a slur on the Methodists) and ought not to be." Michael De-la-Noy, *Michael Ramsey: A Portrait* (London: Collins, 1990), 199.

101. The classic case here was evangelical involvement in *Subscription and Assent to the Thirty-nine Articles* (London: SPCK, 1968). This retained the requirement for Anglican clergy to subscribe to the Articles, but modified the form of this subscription to make the declaration easier on those who did not agree with all the doctrinal details. The perceived watering-down of the form of subscription was all the more galling given that one of their most prominent leaders, Jim Packer, had been a non-dissenting member of the commission. See "Clergy Oppose Change in Assent to Articles," *Church of England Newspaper*, March 14, 1969, 3.

102. Maiden, *National Religion*, 6–10.

103. Another example comes from the proposed union of the Anglican and Methodist churches, where the core of the service of reconciliation to which the evangelicals objected was based on the Lambeth Quadrilateral of 1888, a document in which Anglicans committed themselves to seeking church unity on the fundamentals of the Bible, the Creeds, the sacraments of baptism and the Lord's supper, and, crucially, the historic episcopate. Since that time, influential books such as Michael Ramsey's *The Gospel and the Catholic Church* (London: Longmans Green, 1936) had argued persuasively for the importance of episcopacy as an essential part of the nature of the church, arguments that could gain an even more ready hearing in an age where Protestant sentiment was on the decline. It was hardly surprising, then, when such was enshrined in the Anglican-Methodist proposals. Nor was it surprising that when evangelicals argued for an approach to union modeled on the ecumenical union of the Church of South India (which had not insisted on

episcopal ordination for the Methodist, Presbyterian, and Congregationalist ministers who had joined the Anglicans in its ranks, and had consequently been held at arm's length by the Church of England), their suggestions were not taken very seriously.

104. Cf. John Stott to Michael Ramsey, October 18, 1968, Stott Papers, which gives evidence that this was how Ramsey saw the evangelicals' advocacy of the Church of South India scheme.

105. See the arguments of John Pocock on how involvement in a debate demands the appropriation of the terms being used in ways that will shape the person concerned. See J. G. A. Pocock, "The Concept of a Language and the *Metier d'Historien*: Some Considerations on Practice," in *The Languages of Political Theory in Early-modern Europe*, ed. Anthony Pagden (Cambridge: Cambridge University Press, 1987), 34–35 (I am grateful to Mark A. Noll for drawing my attention to this article). Cf. Stott's more optimistic comments in "Interview," interview of John Stott by Brian Harris, *Evangelical Magazine of Wales*, August–September 1975, 9.

106. Minutes, April 17, 1969, CEEC Minute Book 2.

107. Minutes, December 4, 1969, CEEC Minute Book 2.

108. Letter from Alan Stibbs, *Church of England Newspaper*, February 7, 1969, 10; cf. John Stott, "Series II: More Intelligible, Biblical, Congregational But…," *Church of England Newspaper*, January 24, 1969, 12.

109. Letter from Reg Burrows, *Church of England Newspaper*, February 9, 1972, 11.

110. See John Rosser and David Gregg, "Evangelicals in the Church of England: Compromise of Whole Truth?" *Church of England Newspaper*, January 19, 1973, 13. Another critic of Stott's position was John Eddison, an old friend from their days together at Nash's camps. Eddison, however, had stuck more closely to Nash's very conservative evangelicalism and joined the camp staff. He was dismayed by what he saw as the evangelicals' dalliance with the dangers of Catholicism and made his opinion plain in sarcastic verse published in the *Church of England Newspaper*, to be sung to the tune of "Onward Christian Soldiers." Letter from R. J. B. Eddison, *Church of England Newspaper*, February 9, 1972, 118.

111. John King, *The Evangelicals* (London: Hodder & Stoughton, 1969), 150–151.

112. Colin O. Buchanan, *Evangelical Structures for the Seventies* (Northwood: Northwood Christian Book Centre, 1969), 6.

113. McGrath, *To Know and Serve God*, 132; R. R. Osborn, "Keele and the Liberal Evangelicals," *Church of England Newspaper*, July 7, 1967, 7; and Robin Nixon, "Evangelical Identity," *Churchman* 92 (1978): 99–100.

114. John Stott, "The Rector's Letter," *All Souls*, April 1967, 8.

115. See the reference to Stott in David Coomes, "NEAC'77 Not to Offer Slick Answers to Complex Questions," *Church of England Newspaper*, September 24,

1976, 2. "Cohesion" returned in an article Stott wrote in the mid-1980s; see John Stott, "I Believe in the Church of England," in *Hope for the Church of England?* ed. Gavin Reid (Eastbourne: Kingsway, 1986), 21.

116. John King, "Dedicated, Energetic but Slightly Puzzled...," *Church of England Newspaper*, February 11, 1977, 10–11; Roger Beckwith, "Still Not Too Late if...," *Church of England Newspaper*, February 25, 1977, 12; and Hugh Craig, "A Feeling of Profound Unease," *Church of England Newspaper*, March 25, 1977, 6.

117. John King, "Stresses, Strains Out in Open," *Church of England Newspaper*, February 4, 1977, 3; cf. Dudley-Smith, *John Stott: A Global Ministry*, 160.

118. For more discussion of changes in British evangelicalism during this period from a sociologist's perspective, see Rob Warner, *Reinventing English Evangelicalism, 1966–2001: A Theological and Sociological Study* (Milton Keynes: Paternoster, 2007).

119. John Capon, *Evangelicals Tomorrow: A Popular Report of Nottingham 77, the National Evangelical Anglican Congress* (Glasgow: Fount, 1977), 30.

120. See Eddie Neale, "Nottingham '77," in *77 Notts Untied*, by Eddie Neale, Michael Smout, Colin Bedford, and Dick Williams (London: Lakeland, 1977), 16.

121. John Stott, "The Rector's Letter," *All Souls*, January 1969, 8–9, 32; and John Stott, "The Rector's Letter," *All Souls*, September 1969, 8–9, 25. On the lack of lay interest in detailed ecclesiastical discussions, see John King, "The Dizzy Heights of Sixteenth Century Theology," *Church of England Newspaper*, March 13, 1970, 4. See also John Stott, to members of the Congress Planning Committee and Research Groups, July 1975, Stott Papers, where Stott said that one of the aims of the congress was "to bring the 'centre' and the 'constituency' together, so as to increase mutual understanding and trust."

122. "Question of Prophecy," *Church of England Newspaper*, April 22, 1977, 7. Compare Stott's more optimistic assessment of this aspect of Nottingham, in John Stott, "Anglican Evangelicals speak out," *Christianity Today*, July 8, 1977, 30, where he wrote: "The participants [at Nottingham]...threw themselves with evident relish into three and a half days of intellectual work."

123. See John Stott, *What is an Evangelical?* (London: Church Pastoral Aid Society, 1977), 3–4. For comparable debates in the United States, see Jon R. Stone, *On the Boundaries of American Evangelicalism: The Postwar Evangelical Coalition* (Basingstoke: Macmillan, 1997), 21.

124. Buchanan, "The Shifts at Gut Level," *Church of England Newspaper*, May 6, 1977, 11; and O. R. Johnston, "So, What is an Evangelical?" *Church of England Newspaper*, June 10, 1977, 4.

125. See Capon, *Evangelicals Tomorrow*, 34.

126. J. I. Packer, *The Evangelical Identity Problem: An Analysis* (Oxford: Latimer House, 1978).

127. See Gordon Fyles, "'Don't Drop the Evangelical Label,'" *Church of England Newspaper*, January 27, 1978, 1, 4; and Gordon Fyles, "Evangelicals in 'Identity Crisis,'" *Church of England Newspaper*, December 22, 1978, 1, 4.

128. "Evangelicals in Perspective," *Church of England Newspaper*, January 26, 1979, 3.

129. "Evangelicals Now 'A Major Force,'" *Church of England Newspaper*, May 11, 1979, 1, 4.

130. N. T. Wright, *Evangelical Anglican Identity: The Connection Between Bible, Gospel and Church* (Oxford: Latimer House, 1980).

131. Packer, *The Evangelical Identity Problem*, 33–39; and "Evangelicals in Perspective."

132. "'C of E has Drifted from its Moorings,'" *Church of England Newspaper*, February 15, 1980, 1; Stott, "I Believe in the Church of England," 21; and John Stott to J. D. Rushton, October 30, 1978, Stott Papers.

133. "Preface," *Crockford's Clerical Directory, 1977–79* (Oxford: Oxford University Press, 1979), xvi.

134. John Stott, "Enormous Contribution to the Cause of Christ," *Church of England Newspaper*, July 28, 1978.

135. McGrath, *To Know and Serve God*, 217–222, 232–237, especially 220. For more on Packer as an outsider to the upper-class world of Anglican evangelicalism, see Carl R. Trueman, "J. I. Packer: An English Nonconformist Perspective," in *J. I. Packer and the Evangelical Future: The Impact of His Life and Thought*, ed. Timothy George (Grand Rapids: Mich.: Baker Academic, 2009), 118.

136. Cf. David M. Thompson, *Same Difference? Liberals and Conservatives in the Student Movement* (Birmingham: SCM, 1990), 16.

137. Stott, "The Anglican Evangelical Identity Problem," 8, Stott Papers.

138. John Stott, Diary, Australia May–June 1981, 5, Stott Papers.

139. John Hick, ed., *The Myth of God Incarnate* (London: SCM Press, 1977); and the response, Michael Green, ed., *The Truth of God Incarnate* (London: Hodder & Stoughton, 1977).

140. It was indicative of the nature of evangelicalism that the three former groups continued to exist; CEEC was pleased to secure a role for itself as the standing committee for the assembly.

141. "Battle Cry of Church Society," *Church of England Newspaper*, October 14, 1983, 1. See also Donald Allister, "Surprise Man for Society," *Church of England Newspaper*, December 3, 1982, 1.

142. D. N. Samuel, ed., *The Evangelical Succession in the Church of England* (Cambridge: J. Clarke, 1979).

143. The friend in question was Harold Hoehner, who related the story to Peter J. Williams, Warden of Tyndale House, Cambridge.

144. James D. G. Dunn, "The Authority of Scripture According to Scripture (Part 1)," *Churchman* 96 (1982): 104–122, quotation at 118; and James D. G. Dunn, "The Authority of Scripture According to Scripture (Part 2)," *Churchman* 96 (1982): 201–225.

145. George Marchant, "Why Launch ANVIL when We've CHURCHMAN?" *Church of England Newspaper*, December 9, 1983, 13.

146. "Anglican Evangelical Theological Journals," October 20, 1983, Stott Papers. For more detail on the arguments over *Churchman* and the founding of *Anvil*, see Andrew Atherstone, *An Anglican Evangelical Identity Crisis: The Churchman—Anvil Affair of 1981–84* (London: Latimer Trust, 2008). Atherstone points out that in the end both journals welcomed contributors from the whole range of the evangelical Anglican spectrum; Atherstone, *An Anglican Evangelical Identity Crisis*, 66–67.

147. Cf. Weight, *Patriots*, 544, 562–566.

148. See "The Editorial Board," *Churchman* 98 (1984): 4–5; see also Grant Wacker's comments on the use of such language in Wacker, *Heaven Below: Early Pentecostals and American Culture* (Cambridge, Mass.: Harvard University Press, 2001), 86.

149. Minutes, December 6, 1984, CEEC Minutes 1983–1986, hereafter CEEC Minute Book 5, Oak Hill College, London.

150. Cf. Minutes, April 12, 1984, CEEC Minute Book 5; and Dudley-Smith Transcripts, 18: 38–39.

151. For information on Lucas's growing influence from the 1980s, see Chris Green, "Preaching that Shapes a Ministry: Dick Lucas and St Helen's, Bishopsgate," in *When God's Voice is Heard: Essays on Preaching Presented to Dick Lucas*, ed. David Jackman and Chris Green (Leicester: Inter-Varsity Press, 1995), 11–23. Cf. Trevor Beeson, *The Church of England in Crisis* (London: Davis-Pointer, 1973), 178.

152. Letter from L. A. Rawlinson, *Church of England Newspaper*, January 26, 1968, 5.

153. On the decline of Anglo-Catholicism, see W. S. F. Pickering, *Anglo-Catholicism: A Study in Religious Ambiguity* (Routledge: London, 1989).

154. "Looking Ahead—A Statement of 'The Record's' Policy," *The Record*, March 21, 1947, 152.

155. Mark A. Noll, *America's God from Jonathan Edwards to Abraham Lincoln* (New York: Oxford University Press, 2002), 174.

156. Cf. Hastings, *A History*, 618.

157. For "bishop," see David Winter, "Keele Calling," *Crusade*, April 1967, 14; for "archbishop," see Michael Smout, "What is an Evangelical Anglican?" in *77 Notts Untied*, Neale et al., 34; for "cardinal," see Douglas Johnson to Dick France, in DJ—D. Broughton Knox File, Tyndale House, Cambridge; for "patriarch,"

see John King, "Only Nibbling at Life-style Problem," *Church of England Newspaper*, February 6, 1976, 4; and for "Pope," see David L. Edwards, "Evangelicals All," review of Manwaring, *From Controversy to Co-existence*, in *Church Times*, November 29, 1985, 6.

158. Eamon Duffy, *Saints and Sinners: A History of the Popes* (New Haven, Conn.: Yale University Press, 1997), 368–370.

159. Roger Steer, *Inside Story: The Life of John Stott* (Leicester: Inter-Varsity Press, 2010), 241–242.

160. McGrath, *To Know and Serve God*, 218–219.

161. The committee was "unhappy at any suggestion of losing Mr. Stott as chairman." Minutes, June 4, 1970, and January 7, 1971, CEEC Minute Book 2; Minutes, February 3, 1977, "CEEC Minutes June 7, 1973 – June 11, 1981," CEEC Minute Book 3, Oak Hill College, London.

162. Peter Johnston to John Stott, June 20, 1975, Stott Papers; Fyles, "Evangelicals 'in Identity Crisis,'" 4.

163. Saward, *A Faint Streak*, 291–292.

164. Quoted in Dudley-Smith, *John Stott: A Global Ministry*, 45. Dudley-Smith provides further discussion of this question, 41–46.

CHAPTER 5

1. "Struggling with Contemporary Issues," interview of John Stott by Alex Mitchell, *Third Way*, February 1982, 12.

2. Timothy Dudley-Smith, *John Stott: The Making of a Leader* (Leicester: Inter-Varsity Press, 1999), 75–78.

3. This is not to say that Keswick had nothing to say about social issues. See Charles Price and Ian M. Randall, *Transforming Keswick: The Keswick Convention Past Present & Future* (Carlisle: OM Publishing, 2000), 127–143.

4. Timothy Dudley-Smith, *John Stott: A Global Ministry* (Leicester: Inter-Varsity Press, 2001), 34.

5. See David W. Bebbington, *Evangelicalism in Modern Britain: A History from the 1730s to the 1980s* (London: Routledge, 1989), 211–217; Ian M. Randall, "The Social Gospel: A Case Study," in *Evangelical Faith and Public Zeal: Evangelicals and Society in Britain 1780–1980,* ed. John Wolffe (London: SPCK, 1995), 155–174, and David W. Bebbington, "The Decline and Resurgence of Evangelical Social Concern 1918–80," in *Evangelical Faith,* ed. Wolffe, 175–197.

6. Dudley-Smith, *John Stott: The Making*, 132–133.

7. Bebbington emphasizes the importance of encounter with urban poverty for the development of Christian social concern; Bebbington, *Evangelicalism*, 212.

8. "Camp 1946," *Monthly Notes*, September 1946, 10.

9. "Summer Camps, 1947," *Monthly Notes*, September 1947, 12.

10. On the home for elderly residents of the parish, see Roy Calvocoressi, "Loneliness in Old Age: An All Souls House for Old People," *All Souls*, October 1959, 21; and John Stott, "The Rector's Letter," *All Souls*, November 1960, 10–11. On the school, see especially "Annual Review 1952–53," *All Souls*, April 1953, 14.

11. Margaret Butterworth, "Social Action Committee," *All Souls*, June 1958, 16.

12. John Stott, "The Rector's Letter," *All Souls*, August 1961, 10–11; John Stott, "The Rector's Letter," *All Souls*, December 1960, 10.

13. John Stott, "Snobbery," *All Souls*, February 1958, 12–14.

14. This is not to say that consensus was absolute. See Harriet Jones and Michael Kandiah, eds., *The Myth of Consensus: New Views on British History, 1945–64* (Basingstoke: Macmillan, 1996).

15. Matthew Grimley, *Citizenship, Community, and the Church of England: Liberal Anglican Theories of the State Between the Wars* (Oxford: Clarendon Press, 2004), 22, 24, 206–207, 209–210.

16. John Stott, "Church and Nation," *All Souls*, July 1968, 11. Here Stott called England a "professing Christian country," while elsewhere he said it was a becoming a pagan country and was a mission field (see John Stott, *Motives and Methods in Evangelism* (London: Inter-Varsity Fellowship, 1962), 4; and John Stott, "The Rector's Letter," *All Souls*, September 1962, 10). See also Stott's hope that all would go to church on the Sunday of coronation week ("The Rector's Letter," *All Souls*, May 1953, 10) and his support for a national day of prayer in 1968 (John Stott, "The Rector's Letter," *All Souls*, May 1968, 9). For more widespread belief in this idea, see Grimley, *Citizenship*, 209.

17. John Stott, "The Rector's Letter," *All Souls*, May 1955, 10.

18. See "Old People's Welfare," *All Souls*, March 1954, 19, which makes it clear that it was the Commissioned Workers who performed this function.

19. Stott, "Church and Nation," 11–12.

20. John Stott, "The Great Commission," in *One Race, One Gospel, One Task: World Congress on Evangelism, Berlin 1966*, Vol. 1, ed. Carl F. H. Henry and W. Stanley Mooneyham (Minneapolis, Minn.: World Wide Publications, 1967), 37–56.

21. John Stott, "Evangelicals at Keele Next Week," *Church Times*, March 31, 1967, 1. See also John Stott, "Attempt to Face Today's Crucial Questions," *Church Times*, March 31, 1967, 11; John Stott, "That Word 'Radical'," *Church of England Newspaper*, February 24, 1967, 7; "'No Platitudes from Keele'—John Stott Makes Declaration of Intent," *Church of England Newspaper*, January 13, 1967, 1, 16.

22. Norman Anderson, "Christian Worldliness: The Need and Limits of Christian Involvement," in *Guidelines: Anglican Evangelicals Face the Future*, ed. J. I. Packer (London: Church Pastoral Aid Society, 1967), 211–232; quotation at 214.

23. John Stott, "Evangelicals in a Changing World," *Church of England Newspaper*, November 1, 1968, 12, italics mine. See also John Stott, "Evangelicals in the Church of England: A Historical and Contemporary Survey," in *Die Kommende Ökumene*, ed. Hans-Friedemann Richter (Wuppertal: Rolf Brockhaus, 1972), 173–174; and "Struggling with Contemporary Issues," interview of Stott by Alex Mitchell, 9. For later corroboration of the influence of Anderson's paper, see transcript of interview of John Stott by Timothy Chester, November 26, 1992, 2.

24. John Stott, "An Evangelical at Uppsala," *Church of England Newspaper*, August 16, 1968, 6; see also John Stott, "The Rector's Letter," *All Souls*, October 1968, 8. On John Stott in the developing world, see John Stott Diaries, 1959, 12–13; 1960, 12; 1962, 3, Stott Papers.

25. John Stott Diaries, 1973, 11; and 1977, 1–3, Stott Papers.

26. John Stott, *Basic Christianity*, 2nd edn. (London: Inter-Varsity Press, 1971), 140. Compare John Stott, *Basic Christianity* (London: Inter-Varsity Fellowship, 1958), 142, where the emphasis is exclusively on evangelism.

27. On evangelicals paying attention to social issues before Keele, see Bebbington, "The Decline and Resurgence," 184–185. On the Church of England Evangelical Council discussing homosexuality and abortion prior to 1967, see Minutes, February 3, 1966, and March 3, 1966, in "CEEC Minutes March 24, 1960 (the first meeting)—December 1, 1966, with a Preamble about the Church of England Group," Oak Hill College, London.

28. See Julian Charley, "Christians and Politics," *All Souls*, March 1962, 7; Letter from John Stride, *Church of England Newspaper*, March 17, 1967, 7; "Countdown to Keele—Will there be a 'Minor Explosion'?" *Church of England Newspaper*, February 10, 1967, 1, 16; "One Clear Duty," *Church of England Newspaper*, February 10, 1967, 1; "Do-it-Yourself Keele Statement," *Church of England Newspaper*, March 10, 1967, 7; and "Evangelicals in a Strong Position," *Church of England Newspaper*, Keele Supplement, March 30, 1967, ii.

29. Quoted in Timothy Chester, *Awakening to a World of Need: The Recovery of Evangelical Social Concern* (Leicester: Inter-Varsity Press, 1993), 85.

30. See *Church Assembly Report of Proceedings*, passim.

31. "The problem facing an agent who wishes to legitimate what he is doing at the same time as gaining what he wants cannot simply be the instrumental problem of tailoring his normative language in order to fit his projects. It must in part be the problem of tailoring his projects in order to fit the available normative language." Quentin Skinner, *The Foundations of Modern Political Thought*, Vol. 1: *The Renaissance* (Cambridge: Cambridge University Press, 1978), xii–xiii.

32. For Stott on involvement, see Stott, "Evangelicals in a Changing World," 12; John Stott, *Christ the Controversialist: A Study in Some Essentials of Evangelical*

Religion (London: Tyndale, 1970), 173–191; Stott, "Evangelicals in the Church of England," 176–177; John Stott, "The Significance of Lausanne," *International Review of Mission* 64 (1975): 290; John Stott, "Obeying Christ in a Changing World," *Church of England Newspaper*, October 1, 1976, 7; John Stott, "The Anglican Evangelical Identity Problem," Stott Papers; "Struggling with Contemporary Issues," interview of Stott by Alex Mitchell, 9; John Stott, "Seeking Theological Agreement: The Consultation on the Relationship between Evangelism and Social Responsibility," *Transformation* 1 (1984): 21; and John Stott, *Issues Facing Christians Today* (Basingstoke: Marshalls, 1984), 2–28 (all subsequent references to this book are to this first edition, unless otherwise specified). On involvement more generally, see A. Michael Ramsey, *Canterbury Essays and Addresses* (London: SPCK, 1964), 24.

33. John Stott, "The Rector's Letter," *All Souls*, April 1970, 8–9, 25.

34. John Stott, "A Visit to Latin America," *Christianity Today*, September 9, 1977, 50.

35. John Stott to Ulrich Mennen, March 25, 1974, Stott Papers.

36. Dudley-Smith, *John Stott: A Global Ministry*, 179–180.

37. John Stott, "Transcendence: Now a Secular Quest," *Christianity Today*, March 23, 1979, 37. See also John Stott Diaries, 1970–71, 44–45; 1973, 23–24; and "Calcutta (January 27–28)," 1981, 23, Stott Papers. See also "Struggling with Contemporary Issues," interview of Stott by Alex Mitchell, 9; and Stott, "An Evangelical at Uppsala," 6. For Stott's most careful comments on this subject, where he accepts capitalism per se, but rejects exploitative forms of it, see Stott, "A Visit to Latin America," 50. For links between left-wing politics in Britain and questioning of levels of consumption, see Jim Tomlinson, "Inventing 'Decline': The Falling Behind of the British Economy in the Postwar Years," *Economic History Review* 49 (1996): 745–752; and Nick Tiratsoo, "Popular Politics, Affluence and the Labour Party in the 1950's," in *Contemporary British History 1931–61: Politics and the Limits of Policy*, ed. Anthony Gorst, Lewis Johnman, and W. Scott Lucas (London: Pinter, 1991), 53–54.

38. William Martin, *A Prophet with Honor: The Billy Graham Story* (New York: W. Morrow and Co., 1991), 449–450; the words are Martin's. Leighton Ford to John Stott, May 22, 1980, Folder 16, Box 5, Collection 46, Lausanne Committee for World Evangelization, Archives of the Billy Graham Center, Wheaton, Illinois.

39. John Stott, "Script for Radio Merseyside (to be recorded November 28, 1973)," 1–2, Stott Papers.

40. John Stott, *Our Guilty Silence: The Church, the Gospel and the World* (London: Hodder and Stoughton, 1967), 69–73; Stott, *Christ the Controversialist*, 191; and Stott, *Issues*, 24. The debt to Vidler is mentioned in the first and third of

these. Alec R. Vidler, *Essays in Liberality* (London: SCM Press, 1957), 95–112; and Alec R. Vidler, ed., *Soundings: Essays Concerning Christian Understanding* (Cambridge: Cambridge University Press, 1962).

41. Stott, "Evangelicals in the Church of England," 176. Joseph Fletcher, *Situation Ethics: The New Morality*, 1st British edn. (London: SCM, 1966), 160–161.

42. See Letter from R. J. French, *Church of England Newspaper*, May 13, 1977, 13.

43. E. R. Norman, *Church and Society in England 1770–1970: A Historical Study* (Oxford: Oxford University Press, 1976), especially 469–474.

44. Michael Frayn, "Festival," in *Age of Austerity*, ed. Michael Sissons and Philip French (London: Hodder and Stoughton, 1963), 319–320.

45. On Norman's conservatism, see Norman, "Christianity and Politics," in *Conservative Essays*, ed. Maurice Cowling (London: Cassell, 1978), 69–81; and Peter Catterall, "The Party and Religion," in *Conservative Century: The Conservative Party Since 1900*, ed. Anthony Seldon and Stuart Ball (Oxford: Oxford University Press, 1994), 659–660. For critiques of Norman, see Haddon Willmer, ed., *Christian Faith and Political Hopes: A Reply to E. R. Norman* (London: Epworth, 1979); Robin Gill, *Prophecy and Praxis: The Social Function of the Churches* (London: Marshall Morgan & Scott, 1981), especially ch. 2; and Raymond Plant, "The Anglican Church and the Secular State," in *Church and Politics Today: The Role of the Church of England in Contemporary Politics*, ed. George Moyser (Edinburgh: T & T Clark, 1985), 330–335.

46. This is also a problem with the standard survey of Christian social action in twentieth-century Britain, G. I. T. Machin, *Churches and Social Issues in Twentieth-century Britain* (Oxford: Clarendon Press, 1998).

47. Stott, *Issues*, 302.

48. Matthew Grimley, "Law, Morality and Secularisation: The Church of England and the Wolfenden Report, 1954–1967," *Journal of Ecclesiastical History* 60 (2009): 732–740.

49. David Brooks, "Who is John Stott?" *New York Times*, November 30, 2004, 23.

50. Christian Smith et al., *American Evangelicalism: Embattled and Thriving* (Chicago: University of Chicago Press, 1998), 89. For an application of Smith's argument to British evangelicalism, see Derek Tidball, "What's Right with Evangelicalism?" in *British Evangelical Identities Past and Present*, Vol. 1, ed. Mark Smith (Milton Keynes: Paternoster, 2008), 266–269.

51. John Stott, "Church Worship—1 Corinthians 11," *Life of Faith*, November 21, 1963, 1197.

52. Stott, *Issues*, 258–279.

53. John Stott, *Issues Facing Christians Today*, 4th edn., fully revised and updated by Roy McCloughry with a new chapter by John Wyatt (Grand Rapids, Mich.: Zondervan, 2006), 351. It is possible that McCloughry made the change here, but

McCloughry stated that he did not allow his own opinions to shape the book. In addition, Stott approved all the revisions. See Stott, *Issues*, 4th edn., 16.

54. John Stott to Timothy Dudley-Smith, September 10, 1995; quoted in Dudley-Smith, *John Stott: A Global Ministry*, 408.

55. John Stott, "Abortion, Deformity and 'Vegetables,'" *Church of England Newspaper*, November 5, 1971, 5.

56. Psalm 139:13, New Revised Standard Version.

57. John Stott, "Does Life Begin Before Birth?" *Christianity Today*, September 5, 1980, 50–51. See also Stott, *Issues*, 280–298.

58. Stott, *Issues*, 286.

59. Stott referenced one of the key books from the American perspective in his article, namely Francis A. Schaeffer and C. Everett Koop, *Whatever Happened to the Human Race?* (Old Tappan, N.J.: F. H. Revell Co., 1979): see Stott, "Does Life Begin Before Birth?" 51. For an example a conservative view on the subject from an English evangelical, see O. R. Johnston, *Christianity in a Collapsing Culture* (Exeter: Paternoster, 1976), 26.

60. Catterall, "The Party and Religion," 654–655.

61. Jenny Diski, "Short Cuts," *London Review of Books*, November 4, 2010, 24.

62. Dudley-Smith, *John Stott: A Global Ministry*, 319.

63. Stott, *Issues*, 109–121; quotation at 119–120.

64. John Stott Diaries, 1979, 19, Stott Papers.

65 Adrian Hastings, *Robert Runcie* (London: Mowbray, 1991), 90.

66. Francis Bridger, "Mrs Thatcher's Policies," *Third Way*, September 1982, 17.

67. David Hempton, *Religion and Political Culture in Britain and Ireland: From the Glorious Revolution to the Decline of Empire* (Cambridge: Cambridge University Press, 1996), 167–172.

68. Boyd Hilton, *The Age of Atonement: The Influence of Evangelicalism on Social and Economic Thought* (Oxford: Clarendon Press, 1988), 26; Peter Brierley, *Christian England: What the 1989 English Church Census Reveals* (London: MARC Europe, 1991), 162–163.

69. Hugo Young, *One of Us: A Biography of Margaret Thatcher*, 2nd edn. (London: Macmillan, 1991), 425.

70. See Hugh McLeod, *Religion and Society in England, 1850–1914* (Basingstoke: Macmillan, 1996), 220.

71. See Alan Storkey, "Inadequate Christian Politics," *Third Way*, May 4, 1978, 3–4.

72. John Stott to Dennis Healey, May 25, 1977; John Stott to David Owen, May 25, 1977; and John Stott to Judith Hart, May 25, 1977, all in Stott Papers.

73. Edmund Dell to John Stott, June 3, 1977; I. R. Callan to John Stott, July 4, 1977; K. Howe to John Stott, July 20, 1977; and A. Humm to John Stott, June 16, 1977, all in Stott Papers.

74. See Sir Geoffrey Howe to John Stott, June 1, 1977, Stott Papers.

75. On the Festival of Light rallies, see Dudley-Smith interview with John Stott, Transcripts, 20: 11; and "Sinner Saving, not Sinner Bashing," *Church of England Newspaper*, October 14, 1977, 1. On the SPUC rally, see John Stott, "Address for SPUC rally in Hyde Park," June 25, 1983, Stott Papers; and Stott, *Issues*, 285. On fair trade, see picture of Stott with article, "Help the Poor in the West End," *Church of England Newspaper*, November 29, 1985, 16. Stott was also involved with the World Development Movement, an organization that lobbied the government on issues of world debt, trade, and hunger. See Chester, *Awakening to a World of Need*, 104–105.

76. Conversation with Michael Schluter, former director of the Jubilee Centre, June 3, 2008.

77. "Bishops...still have a lot of influence, and I would have loved the opportunity to use that influence to serve the people of God and to defend and preach the Gospel." Quoted in Timothy Dudley-Smith, *John Stott: A Global Ministry*, 45.

78. Margaret Thatcher, "The Spirit of the Nation," *Third Way*, May 1981, 4–6.

79. Digby Anderson, ed., *The Kindness that Kills: The Churches' Simplistic Response to Complex Social Issues* (London: SPCK, 1984).

80. For more detailed comments on the founding and progress of the London Institute for Contemporary Christianity, see Dudley-Smith, *John Stott: A Global Ministry*, 285–295 and 368–369.

81. See John Stott, "A Tentative Proposal for St. Paul's Institute," December 13, 1979, 2–3, Stott Papers; "Counterblast to Secularism: New London Institute Seeks to Reverse Secular Drift," press release, January 11, 1982, Stott Papers; *The London Institute for Contemporary Christianity Bulletin*, no. 1, passim; and "Struggling with Contemporary Issues," interview of Stott by Alex Mitchell, 12.

82. See John Stott, "A Community of Christian Concern," memo, March 30, 1977, 3–4, Stott Papers; Michael Alison, "World Poverty and Christian Responsibility," *Christian Graduate*, December 1979, 13–17; and Michael Alison, "The Feeding of the Billions," in *Christianity and Conservatism: Are Christianity and Conservatism Compatible?* ed. Michael Alison and David L. Edwards (London: Hodder and Stoughton, 1990), 197–216.

83. Brian Griffiths, *The Creation of Wealth* (London: Hodder and Stoughton, 1984), especially 14; Brian Griffiths, *Morality and the Market Place: Christian Alternatives to Capitalism and Socialism* (London: Hodder and Stoughton, 1982) (the published version of the London Lectures in Contemporary Christianity, 1980); Brian Griffiths, *Monetarism and Morality: A Response to the Bishops* (London: Centre for Policy Studies, 1985); "Christian Economist at No 10 Downing Street," interview of Brian Griffiths by Roy McCloughry, *Church of England Newspaper*,

October 25, 1985, 5, 8; and John Stott, "The London Institute for Contemporary Christianity: The Need and the Vision," February 1981, Stott Papers.

84. See "View from the Bridge," Clare Catford interviewing Roy Clements, *Christian Impact*, no. 6, undated (1988?), 7–10; and Michael Schluter and Roy Clements, *Reactivating the Extended Family: From Biblical Norms to Public Policy in Britain* (Cambridge: Jubilee Centre Publications, 1986).

85. "Struggling with Contemporary Issues," interview of Stott by Alex Mitchell, 12.

86. Stott, *Issues*, 330–331.

87. Stott, *Issues*, 67. See also 66, where Stott speaks of "capturing positions of influence for Christ."

88. Stott, *Issues*, 75–76. See also John Stott, *Christian Counter-culture* (Leicester: Inter-Varsity Press, 1978), especially 15–21; and John Stott, *God's New Society: The Message of Ephesians* (Leicester: Inter-Varsity Press, 1979), especially 9–10. For the idea of a counterculture, see especially Theodore Roszak, *The Making of a Counter Culture: Reflections on the Technocratic Society and Its Youthful Opposition* (Garden City, N.Y.: Doubleday, 1969).

89. Quoted in Brian Harrison, "Mrs Thatcher and the Intellectuals," *Twentieth Century British History* 5 (1994): 218.

90. See especially John Capon, *...And there was Light: Story of the Nationwide Festival of Light* (London: Lutterworth, 1972); David W. Bebbington, "Evangelicals and Reform: An Analysis of Social and Political Action," *Third Way*, May 1983, 10–13; and David W. Bebbington, "Baptists and Politics since 1914," in *Baptists in the Twentieth Century*, ed. Keith Clements (London: Baptist Historical Society, 1983), 87.

91. Raymond Johnston, "The Christian Counter-attack has Begun," *Crusade*, April 1975, 29–32.

92. Stott, "A Community of Christian Concern," 3. For an outline of these two distinct approaches, see Bebbington, "Evangelicals and Reform," 10–13.

93. John Gladwin was Bishop of Guildford 1994–2003, and Bishop of Chelmsford, 2003–2009; Michael Baughen was Bishop of Chester, 1982–1996. On Gladwin working with Stott, see John Stott, "A Tentative Proposal for St. Paul's Institute," 5. On evangelical Conservative MPs, see Catterall, "The Party and Religion," 655, 663. See the editions of *Christian Impact* for more information on the influence of the London Institute, and email from Martyn Eden, former Director of the London Institute for Contemporary Christianity, December 3, 2008. For anecdotal testimony, see Dudley-Smith, *John Stott: A Global Ministry*, 292–295.

94. Grimley, *Citizenship*, 221–222. This contradicts Callum Brown's focus on the increased militancy of British Christianity at the end of the twentieth century; Callum Brown, *Religion and Society in Twentieth-century Britain* (Harlow: Pearson Education, 2006), 297–301. On evangelical organizations, see Chester, *Awakening to a World of Need*, 145–174.

95. Both these organizations have published collections of articles (Christopher Bryant, ed., *Reclaiming the Ground* (Sevenoaks: Spire, 1993), and Alison and Edwards, eds., *Christianity and Conservatism*), and both have active and detailed websites: see <http://www.christiansocialist.org.uk> and <http://www.ccf-website.com>. On the religious beliefs of Tony Blair and Ann Widdecombe, see John Rentoul, *Tony Blair: Prime Minister* (London: Warner Books, 2001), 350–357; Blair's foreword to Bryant, ed., *Reclaiming the Ground*, 9–12; and Nick Kochan, *Ann Widdecombe: Right from the Beginning* (London: Politico's, 2000), 35–36, 100–107.

96. Brian Mawhinney, *In the Firing Line: Politics, Faith, Power and Forgiveness* (London: HarperCollins, 1999), 212, 214.

97. Peter Clarke, *Hope and Glory: Britain 1900–2000* (London: Penguin, 2004), 160.

98. Conversation with Michael Schluter, June 3, 2008.

99. Conversation with Stephen Timms, June 27, 2008.

100. Stott, *Issues*, 69.

CHAPTER 6

1. John Stott, "European Countries—Occupied, Liberated, and Neutral," November 3, 1944, Stott Papers. Much of the research for and argument of this chapter appeared in Alister Chapman, "Evangelical International Relations in the Post-Colonial World: The Lausanne Movement and the Challenge of Diversity, 1974–89," *Missiology* 37 (2009): 355–368.

2. Wesley Mei, "Missionaries Still Needed," *Monthly Notes*, February 1946, 12–13. See also "Mrs. Yü's Generosity," *Monthly Notes*, December 1945, 8; and Ralph E. Toliver, "Going Home from School," *Monthly Notes*, May 1946, 13–14.

3. John Stott, "All One in Christ Jesus," *Monthly Notes*, September 1946, 11–12; John Stott, "News from France," *Monthly Notes*, January 1948, 8–10.

4. Timothy Dudley-Smith, *John Stott: A Global Ministry* (Leicester: Inter-Varsity Press, 2001), 105.

5. David Kynaston, *Family Britain: 1951–1957* (London: Bloomsbury, 2009), 387.

6. John Stott, Diary, 1958, 33, Stott Papers.

7. John Stott Diary, 1961, Stott Papers; quoted in Dudley-Smith, *John Stott: A Global Ministry*, 117–118; 400.

8. Billy Graham to Hugh Gough, July 5, 1952, Papers of the Rt. Rev. Hugh R. Gough, Small Collection 9, Archives of the Billy Graham Center, Wheaton, Illinois (hereafter BGC Archives).

9. C. J. E. Lefroy, "A Letter from Mr Lefroy," *All Souls*, June 1962, 10.

10. See John Stott, Diaries, Stott Papers; and Dudley-Smith, *John Stott: A Global Ministry*, 297–298, 312; see also 373.

11. Peter Clarke, *Hope and Glory: Britain 1900–2000* (London: Penguin, 2004), 320.

12. "Parish Notes and News," *All Souls*, May 1952, 15. Cf. "Parish Notes and News," *Monthly Notes*, May 1950, 9.

13. John Stott, "The Rector's Letter," *All Souls*, June 1950, 10.

14. John Stott, "More Labourers," Book of Prayers, Stott Papers.

15. Dudley-Smith, *John Stott: A Global Ministry*, 152.

16. For more on Lausanne movement; the best starting points are Brian Stanley, *The Global Diffusion of Evangelicalism* (Leicester: Inter-Varsity Press, forthcoming), ch. 6; Timothy Yates, *Christian Mission in the Twentieth Century* (Cambridge: Cambridge University Press, 1994); Charles E. Van Engen, "A Broadening Vision: Forty Years of Evangelical Theology of Mission, 1945–1986," in *Earthen Vessels: American Evangelicals and Foreign Missions, 1880–1980*, ed. Joel A. Carpenter and Wilbert R. Shenk (Grand Rapids, Mich.: Eerdmans, 1990), 203–232; and Valdir R. Steuernagel, "The Theology of Mission in its Relation to Social Responsibility within the Lausanne Movement" (Ph.D. diss., Lutheran School of Theology at Chicago, 1988).

17. See, for example, John Stott to Jack Dain, June 15, 1973, Folder 35, Box 35, Collection 46, Lausanne Committee for World Evangelization, BGC Archives (hereafter LCWE Papers). For an introduction to the WCC at this time, see Yates, *Christian Mission*, 199–200.

18. J. D. Douglas, ed., *Let the Earth Hear His Voice: International Congress on World Evangelization, Lausanne, Switzerland, Official Reference Volume* (Minneapolis, Minn.: World Wide Publications, 1975).

19. See especially George M. Marsden, *Fundamentalism and American Culture: The Shaping of Twentieth-century Evangelicalism, 1870–1925* (New York: Oxford University Press, 1980), 91–93; and Joel A. Carpenter, *Revive Us Again: The Reawakening of American Fundamentalism* (New York: Oxford University Press, 1997), 78, 118.

20. Clyde Taylor to Richard Sturz, March 28, 1969, Folder 3, Box 2, Collection 324, Records of Premier Congreso Latinamericano de Evangelización (CLADE), BGC Archives.

21. Samuel Escobar to Paul Little, June 13, 1974; and Paul Little to Samuel Escobar, June 18, 1974, both in Folder 4, Box 1, LCWE Papers. The names were removed before the paper appeared in the published version of the papers, Douglas, ed., *Let the Earth Hear*.

22. Samuel Escobar, "Evangelism and Man's Search for Freedom, Justice and Fulfilment," in *Let the Earth Hear*, ed. Douglas, 303–319, quotation at 304.

23. René Padilla, "Evangelism and the World," in *Let the Earth Hear*, ed. Douglas, 116–133, especially 125–132.

24. John Stott, "The Biblical Basis for Evangelism," in *Let the Earth Hear*, ed. Douglas, 65–78.

25. See the entry for McGavran in *Twentieth-century Dictionary of Christian Biography*, ed. J. D. Douglas (Grand Rapids, Mich.: Baker, 1995), 246.

26. Donald A. McGavran, "The Dimensions of World Evangelization," in *Let the Earth Hear*, ed. Douglas, 94–107, quotations from 96.

27. See, for example, Donald A. McGavran, *Understanding Church Growth* (Grand Rapids, Mich.: Eerdmans, 1970), 257–258, where McGavran wrote: "There should be no tension between mission and the advocates of social action. There is the most urgent need for *both* extension of the benefits of the Gospel to all communities and countrysides where there are no Evangelical Christians at all, *and*, where Christians are found, the application of Christian principles to all of life." The qualification "where Christians are found" is revealing.

28. Ralph D. Winter, "The Highest Priority: Cross-cultural Evangelism," in *Let the Earth Hear*, ed. Douglas, 213–225, especially 215–216.

29. Donald A. McGavran, "The Dimensions of World Evangelization," 113. On the importance of a scientific, statistical approach, see McGavran, *Understanding*, 67–82.

30. "The Lausanne Covenant," in *Making Christ Known: Historic Mission Documents from the Lausanne Movement 1974–1989*, ed. John Stott (Carlisle: Paternoster, 1996), 24.

31. John Capon, quoted in Dudley-Smith, *John Stott: A Global Ministry*, 215.

32. See "Report on Questionnaire on Follow-up Organization," Folder 16, Box 18, Collection 426, Papers of Paul E. Little (hereafter Little Papers), BGC Archives. On plans for the ongoing work of Lausanne before the congress, see, for example, Jack Dain to John Stott, January 22, 1973, Folder 35, Box 35, LCWE Papers.

33. John Stott to Jack Dain, December 2, 1974, Folder 7, Box 34, LCWE Papers.

34. "Continuation Committee by Continents," Folder 2, Box 19, Little Papers.

35. His address was published as Billy Graham, "Our Mandate from Lausanne '74," *Christianity Today*, July 4, 1975, 5.

36. See John Stott, Diary, "India, Nepal, Mexico and U.S.A., 26 December 74 to 3 February 75," 26, Stott Papers; referred to in Dudley-Smith, *John Stott: A Global Ministry*, 221–222.

37. See John Stott to Jack Dain, March 21, 1975, Folder 7, Box 34, LCWE Papers; and Timothy Chester, *Awakening to a World of Need: The Recovery of Evangelical Social Concern* (Leicester: Inter-Varsity Press, 1993), 85.

38. Chester, *Awakening to a World of Need*, 85–86.

39. Billy Graham to John Stott, April 1, 1975, Stott Papers.

40. John Stott, Diary, "India, Nepal, Mexico and U.S.A.," 29, Stott Papers.

41. Dudley-Smith, *John Stott: A Global Ministry*, 221.

42. John Stott to Jack Dain, March 21, 1975, Folder 7, Box 34, LCWE Papers.

43. See Richard Weight, *Patriots: National Identity in Britain 1940–2000*, corrected edn. (London: Pan Books, 2003), 165.

44. John Stott, *The Message of Galatians* (London: Inter-Varsity Press, 1968); and John Stott, *The Message of Romans: God's Good News for the World* (Leicester: Inter-Varsity Press, 1994), especially 25–31.

45. John Stott, "The Battle for World Evangelization: An Open Response to Arthur Johnston," *Christianity Today*, January 5, 1979, 34–35.

46. John Stott, Diary, "Bermuda and U.S.A. – January 1978," 4, Stott Papers.

47. John Stott, "Our Challenge for Today," *World Evangelization*, November–December 1988, 32.

48. John Stott, "That Day," *All Souls*, January 1956, 13.

49. David L. Edwards, with John Stott, *Evangelical Essentials: A Liberal-Evangelical Dialogue* (Downers Grove, Ill.: InterVarsity Press, 1988), 312–320.

50. Dudley-Smith, *John Stott: A Global Ministry*, 352–355.

51. William Martin, *A Prophet with Honor: The Billy Graham Story* (New York: W. Morrow and Co., 1991), 448.

52. Adrian Hastings, *A History of English Christianity, 1920–2000*, 4th edn. (London: SCM Press, 2001), 615–616. There is an interesting parallel here between the roles of Graham and Stott, and those of the American John Mott and the British J. H. Oldham in the missionary movement of the early twentieth century.

53. "John Stott Urges Sensitivity in Evangelism," *World Evangelization*, April 1980, 1.

54. John Stott, "Jesus is Lord! Has Wide Ramifications," *Christianity Today*, June 12, 1981, 55.

55. John Stott, *Evangelical Truth: A Personal Plea for Unity* (Leicester: Inter-Varsity Press, 1999), 141.

56. The three conferences referred to were the Colloquium on the Homogeneous Unit Principle, Pasadena, Calif., 1977; an International Consultation on "Gospel and Culture," Willowbank, Bermuda, 1978; and the International Consultation on the Relationship between Evangelism and Social Responsibility, Grand Rapids, Mich., 1982. For a short historical account of these events and others, as well as the statements that came out of them, see *Making Christ Known*, ed. Stott, xvii–xx, 57–72, 73–113, 165–213.

57. John Stott to Leighton Ford, April 18, 1979, Folder 16, Box 5, LCWE Papers.

58. "With John Stott," interview of John Stott by Thomas Wang, *World Evangelization*, November–December 1987, 1.

59. The committee planning the Lausanne congress considered inviting Kissinger as a high-profile speaker, but decided not to, partly because of this point. See

Leighton Ford to Jack Dain, Donald Hoke, and Paul Little, January 18, 1974, Folder 4, Box 1, LCWE Papers.

60. Cf. Grant Wacker, "Second Thoughts on the Great Commission: Liberal Protestants and Foreign Missions, 1890–1940," in *Earthen Vessels*, ed. Carpenter and Shenk, 297–298.

61. John Stott, "The Maturity of Love," *Church of England Newspaper*, December 13, 1974, 7. For pentecostalism as part of evangelicalism, see Paul Freston, *Evangelicals and Politics in Asia, Africa and Latin America* (Cambridge: Cambridge University Press, 2001), 288. On the essentially non-pentecostal nature of Lausanne, see Jacques Matthey, "Milestones in Ecumenical Missionary Thinking from the 1970s to the 1990s," *International Review of Mission* 88 (1999): 293.

62. Cf. Robert T. Coote, "Lausanne II and World Evangelization," *International Bulletin of Missionary Research* 14 (1990): 13.

63. On the education of influential American evangelicals, see Pierard, "*Pax Americana* and the Evangelical Missionary Advance," in *Earthen Vessels*, ed. Carpenter and Shenk, 170.

64. Jack Dain to John Stott, December 15, 1975, Folder 7, Box 34, LCWE Papers. See also Stanley, *The Global Diffusion of Evangelicalism*. Cf. William R. Hutchison, "Innocence Abroad: The 'American Religion' in Europe," *Church History* 51 (1982): 83–84.

65. See the evidence of this in Jack Dain to John Stott, September 11, 1972, Folder 35, Box 35, LCWE Papers. On anti-Americanism among the middle and upper classes in Britain, see Weight, *Patriots*, 176, 303, 496.

66. Joel A. Carpenter, "Propagating the Faith Once Delivered: The Fundamentalist Missionary Enterprise, 1920–1945," in *Earthen Vessels*, ed. Carpenter and Shenk, 130. See René Padilla patiently explaining to Harold Lindsell that he was not a Marxist: Padilla to Lindsell, June 28, 1976, Folder 9, Box 1, Collection 192, Harold Lindsell Papers, BGC Archives.

67. C. Peter Wagner, *Church Growth and the Whole Gospel: A Biblical Mandate* (London, 1981), 62–63.

68. John Stott to Leighton Ford, April 18, 1979; and Leighton Ford to John Stott, May 30, 1979, both in Folder 16, Box 5, LCWE Papers.

69. InterVarsity Press has sold more than 6,000,000 titles by John Stott, including 700,000 of his *Basic Christianity*; email from Greg Vigne of InterVarsity Press, Downers Grove, Ill., July 28, 2010. On his frequent visits there, see especially Dudley-Smith, *John Stott: A Global Ministry*, 312.

70. Peter Beyerhaus, "Evangelicals, Evangelism and Theology: An Assessment of the Lausanne Movement," *World Evangelization*, March 1987, 8.

71. John Stott, "Comments on a New World Evangelical Organization," May 1973, Folder 17, Box 35, LCWE Records; and John Stott to Jack Dain, December 2,

1974. See also "The Lausanne Covenant Today," interview of John Stott by Thomas Wang, *World Evangelization*, January 1989, 38.

72. Billy Graham, *Just as I Am: The Autobiography of Billy Graham* (San Francisco, Calif.: Harper San Francisco, 1997), 574; cf. Graham's comments in "Billy Graham Challenges Lausanne Movement," *World Evangelization*, December 1986, 3. It was certainly not a case of financial problems for the Billy Graham Evangelistic Association, which poured millions of dollars into large-scale events for evangelists; see "Graham Announces 1986 Evangelists' Conference," *World Evangelization*, June 1985, 16.

73. See Thomas Wang, "By the Year 2000—Is God Telling us Something?" *World Evangelization*, June 1987, 8–9, and evidence on the response to Wang's article in David B. Barrett and James W. Reapsome, *Seven Hundred Plans to Evangelize the World: The Rise of a Global Evangelization Movement* (Birmingham, Ala.: New Hope, 1988), iii. Wang was one of the five members of the working committee for the new movement: see Thomas Wang, "Keep Spawning," *World Evangelization*, November–December 1988, 2.

74. For the names of the five members of the committee, see Wang, "Keep Spawning," 2. For their participation at Lausanne II, see J. D. Douglas ed., *Proclaim Christ Until He Comes: Calling the Whole Church to Take the Whole Gospel to the Whole World* (Minneapolis, Minn.: World Wide Publications, 1990).

75. See, for example, Coote, "Lausanne II," 13.

76. See "There is a Lot to be Done," *World Evangelization*, January 1993, 30; and the order form for the magazine in *World Evangelization*, January 1993, 31.

77. See Martin, *A Prophet with Honor*, 455.

78. Leighton Ford to Walter D. Shepard, December 28, 1989, Folder 1, Box 97, LCWE Papers; Thomas Wang to Billy Graham, March 23, 1989, Folder 7, Box 223, LCWE Papers; and "Finance Conf [*sic*] Call," April 28 [1989], Folder 7, Box 223, LCWE Papers.

79. "Graham Announces 1986 Evangelists' Conference," 16.

80. Three out of the four top donor-nations for the Cape Town congress were Asian (China, South Korea, and India; the fourth was the United States), a sign of how much had changed in global Christianity and the world economy since the initial Lausanne congress in 1974. Email from Julia Cameron, January 10, 2011.

81. Ford, *A Vision Pursued*, 28, 32, 53–56.

82. I am grateful to Rick W. Ifland and Philip J. Stone for conversations relating to this point.

83. See Stott's response to questions sent out by Paul Little to delegates to Lausanne's continuation committee in November 1974, Folder 4, Box 18, Little Papers (see also Little to the continuation committee members, November 17, 1974, Folder 15,

Box 3, Little Papers). "The Lausanne Covenant today," interview of Stott by Thomas Wang, 38.

84. For more on this theme as it relates both to evangelicalism in particular and Christianity in general, see Freston, *Evangelicals and Politics*, passim, especially 286–287, 313–316; Stephen Kaplan, "The Africanization of Missionary Christianity: History and Typology," in *Indigenous Responses to Western Christianity*, ed. Steven Kaplan (New York: New York University Press, 1995), 9–28; and Lamin Sanneh, *Translating the Message: The Missionary Impact on Culture* (Maryknoll, N.Y.: Orbis, 1989).

85. John Stott, "Paralyzed Speakers and Hearers," *Christianity Today*, March 13, 1981, 44.

86. "Evangelism Plus," Interview of John Stott by Tim Stafford, *Christianity Today*, October 2006, 96.

87. Dudley-Smith, *John Stott: A Global Ministry*, 233.

88. Dudley-Smith, *John Stott: A Global Ministry*, 371.

89. See Laurenti Magessa, "From Privatized to Popular Biblical Hermeneutics in Africa," in *The Bible in African Christianity: Essays in Biblical Theology*, ed. H. W. Kinoti and J. M. Waliggo (Nairobi: Acton, 1997), 25–26.

90. John Stott, *I Believe in Preaching* (London: Hodder and Stoughton, 1982), 125–133. On expository preaching as Western, see Grant LeMarqaund, "New Testament Exegesis in (Modern) Africa," in *The Bible in Africa: Transactions, Trajectories, and Trends*, ed. Gerald O. West and Musa W. Dube (Leiden: Brill, 2000), 72–102; and Justin S. Ukpong, "Popular Readings of the Bible in Africa and Implications for Academic Readings," in *The Bible in Africa*, ed. West and Dube, 582.

91. Paul Gifford, *African Christianity: Its Public Role* (London: Hurst & Co., 1998), 45, 308–322.

92. On the influence of Stott in eastern Europe, see Peter Kuzmic, "A Modern-day Church Father," in *John Stott: A Portrait by His Friends*, ed. Christopher J. H. Wright (Leicester: Inter-Varsity Press, 2011) 130, 133.

93. See, for example, the chapters on Richard Wurmbrand and Festo Kivengere in John Stott, *People My Teachers: Around the World in Eighty Years* ([London]: Candle Books, 2002), 24–31, and 48–53. Philip Jenkins, *The New Faces of Christianity: Believing the Bible in the Global South* (New York: Oxford University Press, 2006), 186–187.

94. Conversation with Joel Carpenter, March 4, 2009.

95. In one sermon in 1960, Stott lamented that many church people were "content…with a juvenile smattering of religious knowledge which would not get them through Common Entrance." John Stott, "The Promise is to You," *All Souls*, July 1960, 12–13. Common Entrance was the exam taken by

people wishing to attend one of Britain's prestigious private schools, and the fact that Stott could refer to this in a sermon says a lot about his congregation.

CONCLUSION

1. John Stott, *Christian Counter-culture* (Leicester: Inter-Varsity Press, 1978), 172–173.
2. John Stott, *People My Teachers: Around the World in Eighty Years* ([London]: Candle Books, 2002), 49.
3. John Stott, *Calling Christian Leaders: Biblical Models of Church, Gospel and Ministry* (Leicester: Inter-Varsity Press, 2002), 129–130.
4. Chris Sugden, "Where is the Next John Stott?" *EFAC Bulletin* 41 (Advent 1990): 3.
5. On this point, see Jeffrey Cox, *The English Churches in a Secular Society: Lambeth 1870–1930* (Oxford: Oxford University Press, 1982), 265.
6. John Stott, *Issues Facing Christians Today* (Basingstoke: Marshalls, 1984), 338.
7. See photo, *Church of England Newspaper*, May 20, 1949, 5.
8. I discuss the impact of secularization theory on church leaders like Stott in more depth in Alister Chapman, "Secularisation and the Ministry of John R. W. Stott at All Souls, Langham Place, 1950–70," *Journal of Ecclesiastical History* 56 (2005): 496–513.
9. John 15:5.
10. On the danger of overemphasizing the moribund nature of evangelicalism in interwar England, see especially Martin Wellings, *Evangelicals Embattled: Responses of Evangelicals in the Church of England to Ritualism, Darwinism and Theological Liberalism 1890–1930* (Milton Keynes: Paternoster, 2003), 1–2.
11. See, for example, Chris Sugden, "The Way Forward," presentation at the National Evangelical Anglican Congress, November 15, 2008, available: <http://www.anglican-mainstream.net/?p=5609> [January 13, 2009]; and Graham Kings, "Splitters United or Patient Pressure?," Fulcrum Newsletter, November 2006, available: <http://www.fulcrum-anglican.org.uk/?168> [January 13, 2009]. Graham Kings was right to picture Stott as someone who bridged different streams within Anglican evangelicalism: Graham Kings, "Canal, River and Rapids: Contemporary Evangelicalism in the Church of England," *Anvil* 20 (2003): 167–184, available: <http://www.fulcrum-anglican.org.uk/?2>. On the influence of preachers among evangelicals, see David W. Bebbington, "Evangelicalism and Cultural Diffusion," in *British Evangelical Identities Past and Present*, Vol. 1: *Aspects of the History and Sociology of Evangelicalism in Britain and Ireland*, ed. Mark Smith (Milton Keynes: Paternoster, 2008), 24.

12. John Stott, *Your Mind Matters: The Place of the Mind in the Christian Life* (Downers Grove, Ill.: InterVarsity Press, 1974).

13. Mark Noll, who was a student at Wheaton College and had few immediate contacts with IFES, has commented on how often he has met evangelical academics who attribute their intellectual curiosity to this movement. Personal conversation, July 2001.

14. For further discussion of this as it relates to North America, where the factors in the evangelical intellectual renaissance have sometimes been different, see especially Mark A. Noll, *The Scandal of the Evangelical Mind* (Grand Rapids, Mich.: Eerdmans, 1994), especially 211–239. Noll mentions the importance of the British Inter-Varsity Fellowship for greater intellectual engagement among American evangelicals.

15. Joel Carpenter, "Now What? Revivalist Christianity and Global South Politics," *Books & Culture*, March/April 2009, 36.

16. David B. Barrett, George T. Kurian, and Todd M. Johnson, *World Christian Encyclopedia*, 2nd edn. (New York: Oxford University Press, 2001), 14.

Index

Lightning Source UK Ltd.
Milton Keynes UK
UKHW011505140920
369883UK00005B/1313